DATE DUE

PRINTED IN U.S.A.

First Get Mad, Then Get Justice

First Get Mad,
Then Get Justice

The Handbook for Crime Victims

Charles G. Brown

A Birch Lane Press Book

Published by Carol Publishing Group

To my brother Robert Clarke Brown...
always there when I need him.

A Birch Lane Press Book
Published by Carol Publishing Group
Birch Lane Press is a registered trademark of Carol Communications, Inc.
Editorial Offices: 600 Madison Avenue, New York, N.Y. 10022
Sales and Distribution Offices: 120 Enterprise Avenue, Secaucus, N.J. 07094
In Canada: Canadian Manda Group, P.O. Box 920, Station U, Toronto, Ontario M8Z 5P9
Queries regarding rights and permissions should be addressed to Carol Publishing Group, 600 Madison Avenue, New York, N.Y. 10022

Carol Publishing Group books are available at special discounts for bulk purchases, for sales promotion, fund-raising, or educational purposes. Special editions can be created to specifications. For details, contact: Special Sales Department, Carol Publishing Group, 120 Enterprise Avenue, Secaucus, N.J. 07094

Manufactured in the United States of America
10 9 8 7 6 5 4 3 2 1

Library of Congress Cataloging-in-Publication Data

Brown, Charles G.
    First get mad, then get justice : the handbook for crime victims / by Charles G. Brown.
        p.   cm.
    "A Birch Lane Press book."
    ISBN 1–55972–170–7
    1. Victims of crimes—United States.   2. Reparation—United States.   3. Victims of crimes—Legal status, laws, etc.—United States.   I. Title.
HV6250.3.U5B74   1993
362.88—dc20   92–39829
                                                        CIP

Contents

PART V
Crime Prevention: Don't Be Victimized Again

PART VI
Justice

DIRECTORIES

Acknowledgments

This four-year project has had the support of so many fine people. Their faith in my work has reminded me that none of us are alone on this planet, either spiritually or emotionally. Thank you to:

My parents, my daughter Tara, and my brothers Sherrod and Bob.

Karen Kalergis, my research assistant, who pulled so much of this book together.

Peggy Re, the talented graphic designer of the charts contained in this book; Mike McClory, writing instructor *par excellence*; and Jean Gibson, the therapist advisor for this book.

My dedicated and visionary editor Gail Kinn.

My indefatigable agent Faith Hamlin.

My mentor Ray Marvin.

My cocounsel Alan Thiemann.

My associate Geroge Shmelhammer.

Rob Abbot, Alexandra Aherns, Linda Braswell, Melissa Burkolder, Howard Conklin, Marc Dann, Dan Eddy, Robin Hurst, Alice Hypes, Parrish McKittrick, Brian Morris, Anne Seymour, John Stein, Thomas "Doc" Sweitzer, Jim Turner, J.D. Underwood, Bill and Ellie Wegener, Steve White, Ron Ziegler.

The thousands of wonderful Americans who work or volunteer to provide services to victims of crime.

Preface

An act of violence is committed every twenty-six seconds in America today. Every six minutes a woman is raped, and every twenty-eight minutes an American is murdered. Child-abuse incidents have more than tripled in the past decade. The United States Department of Justice estimates that one out of every three American families is affected by violent crime. For Americans aged fifteen to twenty-four, violence is the leading cause of death.

These numbers are indeed horrifying, made more so because victims of such crimes often come up against a brick wall when they try to be informed of and to participate in the critical stages of a criminal case or to receive just compensation for the damages resulting from the crime.

What kind of society is ours in which a child molester—who lives in the same home as the child—posts bail and returns to the home to await trial? A district attorney secretly negotiates a deal with the lawyer for an accused rapist, reducing the charges without the victim even knowing about it? A state paroles a prisoner without it telling the victim, even though the inmate had vowed to get even after release?

It is a society that needs to ask itself many questions. How will it protect its own citizens? What are its priorities?

The fact that the above situations have become a common experience may not provide much comfort to those of you who are suffering. But the numbers have created an advantage for the individual victim: a breakthrough in the opportunities for participating in and receiving some form of justice. In recent years, a ground swell of activism on a grass-roots level by new movements and organizations has had a direct impact on state laws, court procedures, and individual attention to the victim. Crime victims can now find a host of support groups and counseling, a system of justice that, with prodding, pays some attention to their problems and has created new opportunities for financial recovery.

Up until recently, crime victims in America have been routinely excluded from participating in the criminal-justice system and denied the financial recovery they are entitled to. But through victims' efforts, the law is being forced to catch up.

Like many lawyers, I have been so engulfed in the criminal justice system that, often, I haven't seen the forest for the trees—victims' rights didn't concern me. But when I became attorney general of West Virginia in 1985, I found myself in constant contact with people whose problems were ignored by the system of justice, just at the time they most needed help. That experience awakened me to just how outrageously these problems have been neglected.

In 1987 I created a Victims' Rights Commission, and held hearings in six West Virginia cities. What I learned astonished me. Families of murder victims, parents of abused children, counselors at rape crisis centers, and others who had experienced first-hand the capricious methods of our criminal courts came to the hearings. This mobilized us to call for changes in our laws and court procedures.

Everyone who sat through these hearings came away convinced that there are fundamental deficiencies in our system of justice. How could they not, when they heard that a mother, whose eighteen-year-old daughter was killed by a drunk driver, appeared late because she was told the wrong time for the sentencing hearing, and her testimony was not allowed? Or that the lawyer for a brutal defendant is allowed to ask for and obtain the victim's home address at a pretrial hearing? Or that the murderer of a young woman is released from prison in less than two years? When victims get treated this way by the very system that is supposed to protect them, a second crime is committed.

By pursuing your case, you can not only have an impact on your own situation, but make it easier for future victims to get help and support. Politicians, bureaucrats, and the media will pay attention to victims only if victims stand up and assert their rights.

Fortunately, things are changing. Today victims are gaining a voice at critical stages of the criminal case: bail, plea bargains, sentencing, and parole. Further, every state has a crime-victim compensation board that will pay all or part of victims' unpaid medical bills and lost wages. Increasingly, judges are ordering criminals to pay damages to their victims, and victims are suing third parties ultimately responsible for their injuries. There is also much help available in the form of rehabilitation, self-help groups, temporary shelter, and government assistance.

Some people say that the campaign for victims' rights is an effort to roll back the clock on the rights of defendants. Not so. These people—usually lawyers or special-interest groups who profit from the status quo—act as if the court system is built for their benefit rather than for the benefit of all. But America must defend the rights of both defendants *and victims*.

For the first 170 years after the adoption of the Bill of Rights, poor people accused of a major crime had to defend themselves if they could not afford a lawyer. Shocking differences existed between rich and poor, and between whites and blacks, in the sentences imposed for identical crimes. Truant children were corralled into adult prisons. Gradually the system underwent fundamental changes to protect the rights of the accused.

In the years after World War II, the courts took many steps to protect the rights of defendants—and it was the right thing to do. The Supreme Court required that a lawyer be appointed for a defendant who cannot afford one, and that poor people have the same right of appeal as everyone else. Criminal laws aimed at racial or religious minorities, vagrants, or any particular group, were ruled unconstitutional. The courts have given teeth to the ideal that every American deserves due process of law before being convicted and sentenced.

Now it's time to work on another problem: rights for the victims of crime.

How do we do it?

First, we need to make sure our public officials respond to the needs of victims. Our legal system must provide justice for all, including victims. Last year, I started the Victims' Rights Political Action Committee. Its goal is to give victims more clout in the political process.

Second, victims need to empower themselves. Victims must step forward and assert their rights—both to work toward their own emotional, physical, and financial recovery, and to play a constructive role in our system of justice by helping to see that criminals are punished.

As a victim, you must remember that you are not alone—you can find help. This book provides a road map for what you need at each stage of the process, helping you to secure justice in the fairest, quickest, and least costly way.

Part I

Help: Benefits and Services for Victims

CHAPTER 1

Programs That Help Victims

Let's say you are out driving one evening and suddenly your car is smashed by a drunk driver. Hardly injured, he—or she—leaves the scene of the accident immediately. You, on the other hand, are badly hurt. By your second night's stay in the hospital, you realize you will recover, but perhaps with permanent injuries. Your predicament begins to dawn on you—you are facing a painful recovery period, a large gap in earnings, huge medical bills, and that drunk driver is still out there, ready to maim or kill the next unsuspecting driver or pedestrian.

Here, then, is your situation as a victim: you may be in physical pain, you are probably incurring major financial losses, you might well have to change your career path, and you are suffering emotionally.

Where do you turn? What can you do? Fortunately, in recent years, many benefits and services have become available to meet the needs of crime victims. Faced with manifold problems—physical, emotional, and financial—victims may need to turn to a variety of providers in the government, nonprofit, and private sectors for assistance.

1. The Victim-Assistance Program

The victim-assistance program is your link to the criminal justice system. The program has one or more trained specialists whose sole duty is to help meet the needs of victims of crime. It is the *first* place you should look for help and guidance.

The victim-assistance representative should navigate you

through the criminal process, steering you to counseling, emergency assistance, and financial recovery programs.

A victim-assistance program exists in all larger America counties, in most medium-sized ones, and in some small counties as well. In some places, it is associated with a program to assist witnesses to crimes (which include the victim as well). Thus many of them are called victim/witness-assistance programs.

There is no standard rule for *where* to find such a program in your county. In some counties, they are part of the district attorney's office; in others, they can be found within the sheriff's office or the police department; or, they are located within a government agency entirely separate from any other part of the criminal-justice system, e.g., the New York City Victim Assistance Agency, the nation's largest program for victims. Finally, the victim-assistance program can be housed within a private non-profit group, such as a rape-crisis or domestic-violence center. (The federal system is the same everywhere: if the investigation is being handled by federal officials, contact the office of the local United States Attorney.)

It is possible that the program in the county where the crime occurred may be so good that you can get help from start to finish. Or it may be so overworked and underfunded that you may only get some help in orienting you to the criminal-justice system, but not the hands-on attention you deserve. Or your local criminal justice system may have no such program at all. But all is not lost. Keep in mind that many police officers and assistant district attorneys have been functioning informally as "victim advocates" for years, long before the term even existed. Ask for help from the police, the sheriff's office, or the assistant prosecutor, or go to an outside group that focuses on your area of victimization (sexual assault, drunk driving, etc.). Be creative in your search. For example, reporters assigned to the courthouse beat may be able to explain the process better than anyone else.

A warning is needed here. It's almost certain that you will be disappointed with the criminal-justice system at some point, or at all points. Still, you must keep pushing—I cannot emphasize this enough. Even though you can't see it happening, cream does ultimately rise to the top; there are good people out there, and they will work for you.

Let's assume that you do have a victim-assistance representative for your case. This person is paid by the taxpayers to be your representative in the criminal justice process from start to finish. He or she can provide these services to you:

The criminal-justice process:
- Teach you how the criminal justice process works, from investigation through trial.
- Orient you to court operations.
- Inform you, in advance, of the date of court hearings.
- Help you work with the district attorney's office, both to make the case go smoothly and to ensure that your views are known and considered.
- Escort you to and from court, and perhaps stay in court with you.
- Prepare you to be a witness.

Financial needs:
- Help you apply to your state's victim-compensation program for coverage for medical bills, counseling, and lost wages.
- Advise you on whether you need your own lawyer for a private lawsuit, or for dealing with your financial needs. Provide information about the local legal aid society and/or the private bar.
- Provide transportation to court, or child care while you are there.
- Talk to your employer about the need for you to attend upcoming court procedures.
- Help you with hospital bills and other expenses resulting from the crime.
- Advise you on local procedures for the return of your property, if it is in the court's possession.

Access to services:
- Provide information on women's shelters, elder-abuse programs, child-abuse services, sexual-assault centers, and similar programs.
- Advise you on the right kind of personal counselor for your needs.
- Give you information about support groups.

Dealing with the accused:
- Inform you of the ways the state protects its victims and witnesses from danger or harassment. *Note:* If you feel you

are in danger, say it, and keep saying it until law-
enforcement personnel and the district attorney's office
listen, and do something about it.

- Advise you of your choice to sit in a different waiting room
from the accused when waiting for court sessions to begin.
(Such a right exists only in some states, but local courts can
always make such separate accommodations available. One
of the first things that prosecutor and victims'-rights
advocate Bill Schenk did a decade ago was separate victims
from defendants in the courthouse waiting rooms in Xenia,
Ohio.)

- Advise you of your right not to talk to the accused, or the
accused's lawyers or investigators, unless so ordered by a
court.

- Discuss alternatives to incarceration if the accused is a
family member; for example: alcohol and drug treatment,
therapy programs to help spouse or child abusers, or
mediation instead of a trial.

Remember: if you are afraid of the accused, ask the district
attorney's office to ask the judge to deny bail because of the threat
to public safety; or, failing that, to make the accused's staying out
of your neighborhood and away from where you work a *condition*
of bail. (Also, if the defendant does not know where you live, the
district attorney should fight like mad to make sure that neither
the defendant nor his lawyer find out this information.) If bail is
granted and you have reason to be in bodily fear, demand police
protection. The state must act to protect the safety of its witnesses
and victims.

2. Counseling

As a victim or the family member of a victim, you must take care of
your emotional needs. Violent crime is probably the most traumatic event of anyone's life, so please look to community resources
for help.

Many people find spiritual guidance an essential part of their
recovery. The Bible quotes the Lord as saying that His strength is
made perfect in weakness, and many people experience intense
spiritual growth in a tragedy. Talk to your minister, priest, rabbi,
or mullah. Increasingly, the clergy are receiving training in

counseling crime victims. The chart on pages 8–9 gives advice from Father Ken Czillinger in Cincinnati on the stages of emotional recovery.

A wide variety of counselors in your community may be available to assist you. Psychiatrists, psychologists, social workers, or licensed counselors are among those trained to provide help for victims of crime. Jean Gibson, a topflight therapist in Raleigh, North Carolina, gives advice on finding the right counselor in a special section located at the end of this chapter.

Do not assume that you cannot afford counseling. First, your own health insurance may cover the visits. Or the victim-compensation fund of your state (see the next section) may pay for counseling. You may be able to find a counselor who will wait to be paid by the fund, instead of asking you to advance the money and wait for the fund to pay you back.

Seek out support groups in your community. Across the nation, people with common experiences, such as victims, meet regularly to share their grief and plan the next phase of their lives. Some of these groups are modeled after the self-help system of Alcoholics Anonymous. Others have been created by skilled therapists. Still others are not based on a predesigned system, but are developed and run quite informally. Your victim/witness coordinator, religious leader, or local counseling agency may know of good volunteer organizations or therapy sessions you can join or attend.

If you cannot find a good local group, contact the national victims' rights organizations that pertain to your specific needs— Directory B lists national victims'-rights organizations. For example, if you are a drunk-driving victim, look to the local chapter of Mothers Against Drunk Driving, or call the national office (800/GET-MADD). If you are unsure of which group to contact, call one of the two national umbrella victims'-rights groups: the National Organization for Victim Assistance (800/879-NOVA), or the National Victims Center (800/FYI-CALL).

Remember: *The crime is not your fault! It's not your family member's fault!* The blame lies with the person who *committed* the crime.

3. Help in Paying Bills

Besides the physical and emotional pain that crime brings, it exacts a major financial burden. An entire section of this book is devoted to financial recovery (see Part III). Here are some initial tips in dealing with the problem of large bills and your reduced ability to pay them.

State victim compensation boards

With Maine signing up in 1992, all fifty states now have a program to pay for the medical bills, lost wages, death benefits, and incidental costs of victims of violent crime, if they are not already covered by insurance. Chapter 4 provides specific details—suffice it to say here that you should get in touch with the compensation board in your state. Directory A lists the address and telephone number of each board.

Employee benefits

Check the health insurance, disability, and leave policies of the family breadwinner(s) to learn of benefits available to you. Make

---

Father Ken Czillinger's Advice for Survivors

❶ Generally, it takes 18 to 24 months just to stabilize after the death of a family member. (For other crimes a substantial recovery period can also be expected.)...Beware of developing unrealistic expectations of yourself.

❷ Your worst times usually are not at the moment a tragic event takes place. Then, you're in a state of shock or numbness. Often, you slide "into the pits" four or seven months after the event. Strangely, when you're in the pits and tempted to despair, this may be the time when most people expect you to be over your loss.

❸ When people ask you how you're doing, don't always say "fine." Let people know how terrible you feel.

❹ Talking with a true friend or with others who have been there and survived can be very helpful. Those who have been there speak your language. Only they can really say, "I know, I understand." You are not alone.

❺ Often, depression is a cover for anger. What you're going through seems so unfair and unjust. Learn to uncork your bottle and find appropriate ways to release your bottled-up anger.

❻ Take time to lament, to experience being a victim. It may be necessary to spend some time feeling sorry for yourself.

❼ It's all right to cry, to question, to be weak. Beware of allowing yourself to be "put on a pedestal" by others who tell you what an inspiration you are because of your strength and your ability to cope so well. If only they knew!

❽ Remember, you may be a rookie at the experience you're going through. . . . You need help!

❾ Reach out and try to help others, at least in some small ways. This little step forward may help prevent you from dwelling on yourself.

❿ Many times of crisis ultimately can become times of opportunity. Mysteriously, your faith in yourself, in others, in God can be deepened through crisis. Seek out persons who can serve as symbols of hope to you.

Remember: It's not your fault! It's not your family member's fault! The blame lies with the one who committed the crime.

---

*Father Czillinger is personnel director for the Catholic Diocese of Cincinnati and a co-founder of Parents of Murdered Children.

sure you understand your eligibility for each. Specific details on this area can also be found in chapter 4.

Physical rehabilitation

All states have a vocational rehabilitation program to help seriously injured people (whether by crime or otherwise) recover and become employable again. Contact your victim-assistance representative, county government, or state department of human services. The state also has programs for children in need of rehabilitation; it may be located in a separate department of government specifically for children or be part of the state department of human services.

Not everyone can recover from a physical injury. Crime can leave permanent debility. A beating or a bullet can confine someone to a wheelchair. Head trauma from a drunk driver's recklessness can bring a lifetime of major impairment. For many, crime means months or years of rehabilitation. It takes hard work and enormous energy to undergo rehabilitation, and often a complete rethinking of how to meet life's challenges. Dreams must be postponed, redirected, or even abandoned. Rehabilitation is itself a full-time challenge for the individual, and often for the family as well.

Government programs
Federal benefits available to victims and their families are based on eligibility depending upon income, age, and previous military status. Fully disabled people may draw Supplemental Security Income (SSI) even if they are not eligible for other benefits. A death in the family can make widows, widowers, and minor children immediately eligibile for Social Security. For information on these two programs, contact the Social Security Administration.

Veterans are entitled to health care and funeral benefits. Contact your local Veterans Administration office. Senior citizens are entitled to have the bulk of their hospital costs and doctors' bills covered by Medicare.

For the permanently disabled, the federal government offers Supplementary Security Income (SSI), run by the Social Security Administration.

State or local governments offer a wide array of social services, such as Aid to Families with Dependent Children (AFDC), food stamps, Medicaid, and emergency shelter.

If the bottom drops out on your income, you may be eligible for food stamps a federal program that is administered locally. Aid to Families with Dependent Children helps those below the poverty level in income and assets. Applying for such assistance is an honorable action if your children are in need. Despite the stories about welfare chiselers, most recipients use public assistance for a temporary, difficult period of their lives, then return to the work force. Medicaid pays health-care bills and has a slightly higher income threshold. For more information, call the local office of your state department of human services or similar county program.

Medicaid, which is available in forty-nine states, pays health-care bills for needy citizens. (The fiftieth, Arizona, has a similar program, which focuses on health-care cost containment and also meets the needs of the uninsured.) Due to recent changes in the law, more people are now eligible for Medicaid benefits. If you do not have health insurance and your income is below average, check whether or not you qualify for Medicaid.

Emergency shelter is based on immediate need. For example, most large and medium-sized communities now have shelters for battered women and their children.

Legal protection
If your bills significantly exceed your assets and your ability to pay them, consider bankruptcy. You can probably keep your home and car. But there are some problems to keep in mind. Your credit availability will be hampered substantially for at least the next seven years. Talk to a lawyer who specializes in consumer bankruptcy to review your options.

Disability can trigger various benefits. For example, some contracts provide that car or life insurance payments are waived. Individual Retirement Accounts are normally accessible, without a tax penalty, if you are completely disabled.

Creditors and bill collectors may not harass you to pay. All states have strict requirements to prevent creditors from making your life miserable. For example, they are not permitted to contact your employer, or to call you late at night, or to tell your neighbors or any family members who don't live with you, about your debt. If you feel harassed, contact you state attorney general's office of consumer protection.

Creditor intervention
This statement will surprise you: Many creditors are sympathetic to people faced with hardships beyond their control. Why? I guess it's partly because creditors don't want the bad public relations of foreclosing on a crime victim, and partly because they figure you will ultimately pay up (you catch more flies with sugar than with vinegar) if they wait long enough. Besides, they get so many cock-and-bull stories from debtors that hearing the truth—"I can't pay now, but let's work it out"—is probably quite refreshing.

Call your creditors and explain your situation; they often agree to a less burdensome payment schedule. An excellent book for debtors is *Conquer Your Debt* by William Kent Brunette (Prentice Hall Press, 1990). Brunette suggests that you call your creditors and tell them (1) what happened (in your situation, it was an unforeseen crime that debilitated you or a member of your family), (2) you are making a conscientious effort to develop a reasonable repayment plan, and (3) under such a plan, you will save the creditor the costs of fighting to collect your account.

Don't offer to pay someone else's debts. Unless your name is already on the bill or loan when it happens, you are not required to pay—it is not your debt. A favorite trick of some hospitals—and a dastardly one, I might add—is to send the hospital bill to the next of kin when someone dies and tell him or her to pay it. The hospital is entitled to be paid out of the dead person's estate, but is not entitled to the relative's own money. If the estate's debts are greater than its assets, it is the hospital that is out of luck, not you.

Dealing with health-care bills

Many hospitals in this country began with a charitable mission, and most *say* they'll take patients regardless of ability to pay. With the stakes so high for your family, ask, demand, or plead that the hospital put its money where its public relations mouth is. Call the state or county medical association and ask about programs in which doctors provide free care for indigents. Call the closest university medical school and ask about its free clinic—many have one.

Even Americans who think they are totally insured are finding a big gap between what the insurance company covers and the size of the hospital or doctor bill. To deal with this gap, I worked with West Virgina consumers to help them make their demands to the insurance companies and the health providers. I suggest that you do the same for yourself.

Remember, three things can happen to bridge this gap: (1) the insurance company can increase its coverage, or (2) the health provider can reduce the bill, or (3) you can pay it. Try options 1 and 2 first. See if the other guy, not you, will make up the difference! Even if you succeed only partially with the insurer or the provider, your financial burden is at least reduced.

First, check your bill. Hospitals are notorious for including charges for services not actually rendered. Talk to the hospital and get those charges removed. Get clarification for items you do not understand. Then contact your insurance company and ask why it didn't pay the entire bill. Did it feel that the provider charged too much? If so, go to the doctor or hospital and ask that the bill be reduced to reflect the "usual and customary" rates in that community. The insurance company pays a standard fee, but in your case the doctor may have had to do something more difficult than usual. If so, ask the doctor to inform the insurance company, so that it may increase its coverage on the bill. Your goal is to see that the insurance company pays more if it is shortchanging you on your coverage, and to see that the doctor or hospital charges less if they are overbilling.

Will these strategies work? I've seen them work for consumers in West Virginia—both in increasing the coverage by insurance companies, and in reducing the size of the medical bill. They might work for you, if you try!

Victims often face serious difficulties in recovering from the crime. Many avenues are available to provide financial assistance. Federal, state, and local agencies, as well as the private sector, have programs available to meet the needs of victims of crime. If you have been a victim, don't hesitate to ask for financial assistance. By law, you are entitled to it!

4. The Media

Why, you may ask, are the media listed as a community resource for victims? It's easy to count off the *disservice* of the press to victims of crime: glorifying the criminal life-style, sensationalizing a crime, or invading the privacy of the victim. Too often, it seems that the press thrives on the misery of others.

But the media, like so many other double-edged swords, can be a force for good as well. They convey information to the public. If you want or need to get a message to the public, they are your primary means to do so.

In American today, the media are the primary force setting the agenda for politicians. Though such a statement, which no political scientist (or candid politician) would seriously dispute, is troubling, consider this. Most politicians are timid about innovation and generally wait for others' suggestions. So perhaps it's just as well that they respond to the media's agenda as to the agenda of other special-interest groups.

If you have lots of money or political power yourself, then don't worry about working with the media. But if you are like the 90 percent of us who don't, then you must work through the media to get the attention of your elected officials.

Think of dealing with the media in two ways: reactive and proactive. The "reactive" approach involves your response to ongoing news that concerns your case. Chances are that by the time you read this book, the media coverage of your crime has

---

Reactive Media Strategies

1. Remember K.I.S.S.—Keep It Short and Simple.

2. Have a theme—repetitiveness is a virtue with the media.

3. Have one consistent spokesperson.

4. Decide in advance the point or points you want to make, then make them, regardless of what questions you are asked.

5. Dress neatly and conservatively.

Proactive Media Strategies

• Write a letter to the editor of the local newspaper.

• Have a news conference.

• Arrange to be on a radio talk show.

• Sit down one-on-one with a reporter.

• Do something creative and ask the press to cover it.

• Ask the radio to put on a public service announcement.

---

already broken. But your media relations will still be important to future news events, such as the trial, and because of the potential for a "proactive response."

Using the proactive media approach means *you* generate the news event. You can call attention to a rapist about to be released on parole and put the parole board on the public hot seat. You can start a community awareness program about preventing certain crimes. Or you can write a letter to the editor calling attention to the lack of sufficient law enforcement in your neighborhood.

Work on proactive media with a goal: to persuade a public official to do something, to alert the community about a problem, to correct a community's perception about a crime, or to build a victims'-rights network in your community.

5. Victims'-Rights Groups

Today politicians and the media pay more attention and respect to victims' rights because of the actions of national and local victims' rights organizations.* Although most were started on a shoestring, they have shown that enthusiasm and organization can still bring results in America.

The two national umbrella victims'-rights organizations are the National Organization for Victim Assistance (NOVA), based in Washington, D.C., and the National Victim Center (NVC), based in Fort Worth, Texas, and Arlington, Virginia. Both groups are engaged in a broad range of actions and services; they assist victims and other victims'-rights groups, provide information to federal and state officials on victims' issues, lobby the Congress for victims' rights, host national conferences, organize public education programs, organize crisis-response teams, run excellent research libraries, and much, much more.

NOVA, the older of the two groups, sponsors the North American Victims Conference, the major annual event for victim advocates, which brings together 2000 people to work on a 50-state strategy to help victims.

In 1993, NVC created a national service to provide general information on over 70 topics covering the full range of crime-victim and criminal-justice concerns. Just as important, the service will refer victims to services and organizations in their local communities. This new program, operating out of Fort Worth, Texas, can be reached at 800-FYI-CALL from Monday to Friday, from 10:00 a.m. to 8:00 p.m. Eastern Standard Time.

Another excellent national victim-assistance resource is the American Bar Association's Victim/Witness Project in Washington.

---

*Directory B is a list of the addresses and telephone numbers of the victims groups discussed here. Many have local chapters or can tell a victim about organizations in his or her community responsive to a particular need. Keep in mind that there may be excellent local organizations and centers in your community that are not mentioned here.

The other national organizations focus specifically on one area of crime or one group of victims.

Children:
The National Committee for the Prevention of Child Abuse in Chicago (with chapters in all fifty states);
The National Center for Missing and Exploited Children in Arlington, Virginia, and its affiliate, the Adam Walsh Foundation in West Palm Beach, Florida;
Parents of Murdered Children in Cincinnati;
The National Resource Center on Child Sexual Abuse in Huntsville, Alabama;
The National Assault Prevention Center in Columbus, Ohio;
The Children's Defense Fund in Washington, D.C.;
The American Bar Association's Center on Children and the Law in Washington.

Senior citizens:
The American Association of Retired Persons in Washington;
The National Committee for the Prevention of Elder Abuse in Worcester, Massachusetts.

Crimes at colleges and universities:
Security on Campus, Gulph Mills, Pennsylvania.

Drunk driving:
Mothers Against Drunk Driving, in Dallas (telephone 1-800-GET-MADD), has local chapters in most American cities;
Remove Intoxicated Drivers, based in Schenectady, New York.

Consumer fraud:
White-Collar Crime 101, in Vienna, Virginia.

The clergy and religious needs:
Spiritual Dimensions in Victim Services in Sacramento.

Victim compensation:
The National Association of Crime Victim Compensation Boards in Washington.

Strong statewide victim advocacy and support groups exist in a number of states:

For example, Maryland (the Stephanie Roper Committee, based in Upper Marlboro), Oregon (Citizens for Justice/Crime Victims United, based in Portland), and Washington (Families and Friends of Missing Persons and Violent Crime Victims, based in Seattle).

Complete listings are available in Directory B, which covers national organizations, and Directory C, which lists local groups, but even those lists are far from complete. Many of the strongest victims' organizations are entirely local, drawing their strength from the grass-roots concerns of that community.

Postscript—From Victim to Survivor

I did not write this book to say that you *can be* or even that you *should be* a survivor. I have a different message—you *must be a survivor.* I wish I could tell you how to work through your grief. Family, friends, and trained therapists can help you with that. This book can, however, provide you with the information you need on community resources, on the criminal process, and on financial recovery. After that, my friend, it's up to you. "I, the victim" will become "I, the survivor."

Choosing a Therapist

by Jean P. Gibson, M.S.W., A.C.S.W., C.C.S.W.
Psychotherapist, Raleigh, North Carolina

When to Seek Therapy
As a crime victim, you may need therapy to help you deal with the event and its aftereffects. The crime, it is likely, was a major trauma that has disrupted your life. You may be in crisis and have difficulty returning to your usual way of living. You may be in shock, unable to accept what has happened. If you have suffered tremendous losses, you may feel irreparably damaged, demoralized and helpless. Perhaps you are experiencing over-whelming rage and a need for revenge. Be assured that all of

these reactions are very human responses to crime. If you are experiencing a high degree of distress and/or having difficulty returning to your usual pattern of living, therapy may be an empowering tool for you.

Consider therapy if you have any of the following symptoms:

1. You are preoccupied with or having painful flashback memories of the crime.
2. You have any of the following feelings that persist and are, at times, overwhelming: sad, blue, nervous, tense, helpless, hopeless, angry, grief-stricken, mistrustful.
3. You are having difficulty carrying out your daily activities.
4. You are confused about your life and the direction you are headed in. Perhaps you have lost your sense of meaning and purpose. You may have feelings of helplessness and hopelessness about your future.

Finding the Right Therapy

Choose the right kind of therapy. There are two basic types. *Brief psychotherapy* is crisis intervention, focusing on resolving specific problems and helping a person to stabilize (that is, to regain the ability to cope with problems and to feel more in control). Such brief therapy, which usually takes six months or less, is useful for someone who generally functions well, but runs into a situation or a problem that is so overwhelming that he/she lacks the resources to solve it.

The other type of therapy, *long-term therapy,* helps people to change by understanding patterns from childhood that contribute to difficulties in how they think, feel, and act as adults. Lasting one to three years, this type of therapy is appropriate for a person who has more difficulty managing his or her life and relationships, or who has problems that are more deep-rooted, or who seeks greater fulfillment of his potential.

For you as a crime victim, brief therapy/crisis intervention should be your first step, particularly if your life was relatively satisfactory before the crime. The therapy should help you cope with the impact of the crime itself and find ways to deal with the often far-reaching aftereffects. For example, parents of a murdered child not only have to deal with the overwhelming loss, but also the changes in their daily life. Friends may feel awkward and not know how to react, causing the parents to feel even more estranged and isolated from those they need the most. A rape victim not only must deal with the sense of violation, but may feel depressed and perform poorly at work or school, and be too embarrassed to explain the reason. The therapy should help you find ways of coping with the many issues, such as these, that result. At the end of therapy, you should have a sense of empowerment—that although your life may never be the same again, you can cope with what has happened and can face what may lie ahead. Therapy may need to be continued beyond six months if the crime and its aftereffects were particularly devastating and far-reaching. You may, for example, be distressed due to long and continuing involvement with the police and the legal system.

In some cases, a person may need long-term therapy. Brief therapy may not be adequate for someone who was already having life difficulties prior to the crime. Even if the person was managing well, the trauma of the crime may unearth unresolved or forgotten events from childhood that interfere with recovery. For example, a rape victim might have greater difficulty recovering if she had been abused or molested in childhood. A victim of a childhood crime such as physical or sexual abuse would need long-term therapy to deal adequately with the trauma. The decision to undertake long-term therapy is best made with your therapist. If long-term therapy is recommended, you should feel that you fully understand the reasons.

Finding the Right Therapist

Psychotherapists are generally psychiatrists, psychologists, clinical social workers, psychiatric nurses, or marriage and family therapists. All of these disciplines provide therapy. In addition, psychiatrists can prescribe medication and hospitalization when needed. Psychologists can administer tests when they are needed for diagnosis. A therapist from one of these disciplines who works specifically with victims of adult (or, for children, childhood) trauma would be your best bet. Other good choices include therapists who are trained in crisis intervention or posttraumatic stress disorder, and therapists with skill and experience with Vietnam veterans, victims of natural disasters, emergency service workers, or grief and bereavement.

Finding a competent therapist is often done by word-of-mouth. Your primary physician, friends, family members, minister, or attorney are often familiar with therapists. Some companies have Employee Assistance Programs (EAPs) which offer information and referral and sometimes crisis intervention and short-term counseling. Local mental-health agencies, such as the Mental Health Association, often keep referral information. You might check with local chapters of the following professional organizations for referrals: the American Psychiatric Association, American Psychological Association, National Association for Social Workers, Clinical Society for Social Work, American Nursing Association, American Association for Marital and Family Therapists. Most are based in Washington, D.C. These sources would most likely know if there are therapists in your area who work with crime victims, or who could best treat your situation. If you are a member of an HMO or PPO, you will be referred to one of their designated therapists.

Evaluating your Therapist

The first two or three sessions with a therapist is a chance for both of you to assess whether you can work together effectively. Feel free to ask the therapist about training and experience that is pertinent to your situation. A therapist may have a wonderful reputation with the right skills and experience, but might not be the right person for you. Therapy is an art as well as a science. You need to have a rapport with your therapist, that is, a feeling of comfort and safety and a belief that you are understood. You should have a sense that your problems are important and that your feelings are respected and accepted. Your therapist should be able to specify to you the problems and issues that you need to work on. After a few sessions, you should feel that you are beginning to progress, although you may not feel you have solutions to your difficulties.

Paying for Therapy

Your medical insurance or Medicaid or Medicare will likely cover part of the cost of therapy. Check your coverage to determine which disciplines your plan covers. If you do not have insurance coverage, as a crime victim you are entitled to apply to your state's crime-victim compensation board to cover such costs. (See Directory A for its address.) Otherwise, you will need to pay out of pocket. If private therapy is too expensive, there are other good public agencies that provide therapy on a sliding-scale fee basis. Check with your local mental-health center or family-service agency. There may be other local agencies that offer reduced-fee services as well.

Part II

Participation: Making the Justice System Work for Victims

CHAPTER 2

From the Crime to the Plea Bargain

Most victims have an idealistic conception of how the criminal-justice system is supposed to work. But when you are forced to participate in the system, very few of those expectations will be fulfilled. Instead, you will find a criminal-justice system plagued by the following problems:

• It is slow—and humiliatingly so—because the calendar of everyone (the judge, the district attorney, the defendant, the defense lawyer), *except* the victim, is cause for continual delays.

• Plea bargains are rampant, disposing of well over 80 percent of cases which reach that stage, an event that often means that the *victims'* opportunity for their day in court goes down the drain.

• Victims are usually ignored or politely tolerated at crucial points in the trial, *even though the effective administration of justice is usually improved by their participation.*

While the above criticisms characterize many courts, most assuredly it does not describe *all* courts. We know of examples in all parts of the country where victims' rights exist, and where the system of justice works better because of them. And if victims' rights are implemented in some American counties, they can be everywhere.

It is true, and it should always be true, that accused people have a presumption of innocence, that their guilt needs to be proved beyond a reasonable doubt in a court of law.

But what is equally true is that victims of crime have suffered real and traumatic losses. They, or a member of their family, may have been killed, raped, assaulted, or robbed. In meting out justice, courts must recognize this injustice and take steps to provide a fair remedy.

Unfortunately, most states lack an *enforcement mechanism*. On the one hand, if *defendants'* rights are ignored, they can get an immediate hearing or even a dismissal of their case. But if *victims* are ignored, most states give them no procedure to go before the judge to demand that their rights be enforced. If the bottom line is the ability to enforce your rights in a court of law, in most places you, the victim, have no rights at all!

Fortunately, changes are coming. In the past few years, eight states amended their constitutions to give victims the right to participate in the criminal process and to have those rights enforced: Arizona, California, Florida, Michigan, New Jersey, Rhode Island, Texas, and Washington. Then, in 1992, five more states signed on: Colorado, Illinois, Kansas, Missouri, and New Mexico. While the rules in each of those states vary, in general their constitutions now state that judges and district attorneys must listen to victims at the critical stages of the criminal proceeding. So, if you live in one of those states, go in and demand your rights!

What do you do if you don't live in one of the thirteen states with a constitutional amendment for victims? Two options exist. You may be lucky enough to live in a county where the district attorney and/or judge are adamant that victims' rights be respected, or where state laws strongly encourage the participation of victims. If not, you must follow the pioneers' adage that the squeaky wheel gets the grease. Victims must come forward and assert themselves, asking that their views be heard. They need to talk to—and if necessary write to—the officials handling the case at that stage, i.e., the police officer, the assistant district attorney, the probation officer, or whoever. They need to let it be known that the system of justice does not exist just for the benefit of the defendants, the lawyers, the courthouse employees. It's time to put justice into the criminal-justice system!

Many of the politicians, lawyers, and courthouse officials who run the system of justice have missed a point that every good cop on the beat knows—*victims can play a key role in fighting and reducing crime.* Instead of public officials trying to protect their turf, let's see them welcoming victims into the process because of the assistance they can render.

Victim participation leads to a better system of justice. Involvement of victims leads to more arrests and more certainty in ensuring that the accused is the perpetrator. Victims can and do provide needed input at bail hearings, at plea bargains, at sentencing, and at parole. In short, when victims participate, the system of justice is more fair and more effective.

But the forces of the status quo—those who like the criminal justice system as it is—continue to run things in most American counties. They include elected officials who do not want their public decisions scrutinized, courthouse employees who are clock watchers rather than workers, and lawyers who like to wheel and deal on behalf of their clients instead of try cases. Fortunately, such people are now being challenged by elected officials, public employees, and lawyers who will not hesitate to make sure that victims' rights become a reality.

When this revolution in victims' rights succeeds, as it will, the system of justice will finally take the same responsibility for ensuring victims' rights as it now does in protecting criminal defendants' rights.

There is a useful precedent on the side of the victims' movement and, oddly, it comes from the movement to protect those accused of crimes. Until the 1950s, poor people accused of a crime rarely had a chance in court. They could not afford a lawyer and, being unrepresented, were generally unable to assert their defense in a court of law. Frequently, they would go through an entire proceeding without ever having their constitutional rights explained to them. Fortunately, the Supreme Court, led by Chief Justice Earl Warren, stepped in and decided that the same Constitution that applied to the rich would apply to the poor. Regardless of their ability to pay for it, criminal defendants were granted the right to counsel *(Gideon* v. *Wainwright)* and the right to appeal *(Escobedo* v. *Illinois)*. All suspects must be advised of their rights before being questioned *(Miranda* v. *Arizona)*.

Rather than condemn this development of a generation ago, the victims' movement would be best served by imitating it. Just as well-meaning people stepped in to help protect *defendants'* rights in the 1950s and 1960s, it is now time for well-meaning people to step in and protect *victims'* rights. The pendulum has swung far enough in one direction and now needs to return to a balance.

Only a few states give victims the *right* to participate in all of these stages. But, in almost all states, victims have the *opportunity* to participate in most or all stages. Because opportunities ex-

Stages of the Criminal Process

Investigation: Law enforcement authorities gather evidence on the crime and the perpetrator.

Filing of Charges: In most states, for major crimes, a grand jury must decide to indict after secret hearing on the evidence. The defendant is notified or arrested.

Bail: The defendant moves to be set free until the trial and the judge sets bail. It can be high, low or zero; at rare times, bail can be denied.

Plea Bargain Negotiations and Other Pretrial Activity: Motions are made on legal issues. Usually the defendant's lawyer and the district attorney's office will discuss a plea bargain.

Trial: The jury (or the judge) will decide if the accused is innocent or guilty. A unanimous decision by the jury is required in most states.

Sentencing: This is not done at the end of the trial anymore. The judge gets a report and may hear evidence, then decides the sentence. In some states the jury decides, or plays a role in, the sentencing.

Appeal: The conviction can be reversed if the judge misinterpreted the law. Defendants who win on appeal usually must stand trial again; rarely are charges dismissed outright.

Parole: The parole board holds hearings on each prisoner. If the board releases the inmate, he or she is monitored by a parole officer for an extended period.

ercised often enough can become rights, I suggest that you try to participate regardless of the way things are done now in your state or county.

Criminal cases have eight stages. A case must pass through each stage before it can go on to the next one, and at each stage important decisions are made. The case can end at any stage. The chart (above) lists these stages. Following the chart is a list of what you, as a victim, need to do or may do at each of these stages.

This chapter covers the first four stages of the criminal process: the investigation, the filing of charges, the bail hearing, and pretrial activity.

Stage 1: Investigation

Without help from the victim, many investigations don't get very far. The police and other law-enforcement officials need your help. Most of them are courteous and sympathetic in working with victims.

It is hard to give general rules about how victims should be treated. It can be safely said, however, that in recent years police sensitivity toward victims of sexual assault and of domestic violence has grown substantially. New York, for example, requires that victims of such crimes be interviewed by law-enforcement officials in a private setting. Many jurisdictions have set up what they call "multidisciplinary teams"—law enforcement officials, social workers, and district attorneys—for sex offenses. And although improvements are still needed, law-enforcement officials in most areas are also giving greater attention to minority victims than a generation ago.

Victims should start by contacting the victim/witness-assistance program. It can be part of the police, sheriff's, or district attorney's office. Or it may be a separate agency, as it is in New York City. As explained in Chapter 2, the victim/witness program will direct you to the appropriate people, including the detective assigned to your case.

If the county where the crime against you occurred does not have a victim/witness program, go to the law-enforcement agency where the crime occurred and see the investigator handling your case. Or call the National Victim Center at (800) FYI-CALL for help in getting connected to the victim assistance program or support group.

Victims may be able to help the police in lots of ways. Two of the most important are preserving evidence and making an identification.

Preserving evidence
In the case of violent crime, even preserving the evidence can be traumatic. But the police need to gather evidence as the starting point for all investigations. Sexual-assault victims must be examined by a physician before they have bathed. Tattered or blood-stained clothing of a murdered or injured family member must be preserved intact.

Some victims complain that it takes far too long to get their property returned to them. Often they are right. Although the district attorney needs to preserve the important evidence until the trial, for other items a photograph would be sufficient evidence in many states. Victims won't always get their property back before a trial, but they should ask. It's the responsibility of the victim/witness coordinator to advocate for you and explain the legal reasons if your property must still be held.

Sometimes the behavior of local courthouse officials is insensitive to the point of being ridiculous. In one West Virginia county, a young man was murdered in his own van. The van was kept as evidence, and the murderer tried and convicted. The man's mother was then notified that she could pick up the van but that she must pay the county for eighteen months of storage! As attorney general, I was able to step in and had the fee waived.

Making an identification

Identification of the accused, if possible, is of obvious importance. The police may want to show pictures to the victim or have a lineup of potential suspects. Sometimes a police artist will draw a sketch of the assailant, based on the victim's memory. Identification of other matters could also be very helpful. Every detail about the place, the time, the people, and surroundings should be told to the police, even those details the victim thinks are not important. Stories of detectives finding the perpetrator based on the slightest nuances of evidence are legendary and are not confined to Sherlock Holmes's feats.

In addition, great advances have been made in the science of forensics. Not only fingerprints, but hair and blood are becoming increasingly reliable means of identification. National computer banks track the whereabouts of people who meet the physical profile, or the *modus operandi* profile. DNA testing of blood or body fluids is accepted increasingly by courts as evidence of guilt or innocence.

The victim should get the name and telephone number of the detective, police officer, or sheriff's deputy assigned to the case. Future conversations should be held with that person, unless the agency delegates that role to the victim/witness advocate.

The investigation process can be a difficult and painful emotional experience for the victim. Most law-enforcement officers or victim/witness advocates will be as helpful and courteous as possible, but may be quite overworked with other assignments. If you feel you are being ignored, talk to the officer's superior about it. Get first in line, and stay there.

Law-enforcement officers must be cautious. They can make an arrest only if there is "probable cause"; that is, a likelihood that strong evidence of guilt exists.

When the victim is a child, an incomprehensible new process unfolds for the youngster, right after an inexplicable crime has occurred. Law-enforcement departments have stepped up their attention, training, and resource commitment in this area in the past five years. Teams of police officers, assistant district attorneys, and counselors are working hard to reduce the trauma on the child, although the competence and time availability of such teams continue to vary greatly. Indeed, experts disagree on the right approach to take with children after a crime, and courts continue to be uncertain how much they can protect a child from testifying without violating the defendant's constitutional rights. Chapter 7, "Crimes Against Children," discusses the criminal process for the child victim.

Stage 2: Filing of Charges

The decision to arrest is made by the law-enforcement agency. The decision to proceed to a filing of formal charges is made by the district attorney.

If there is an arrest, the state must show immediately why the individual was arrested. A preliminary or "show cause" hearing before a judge or magistrate establishes that the state had sufficient evidence to make the arrest—if the state fails to show cause, the accused is immediately released. The United States Supreme Court has held that the "show cause" hearing must be held within forty-eight hours after a person is arrested.

In addition to staying in touch with the detective making the investigation, it is essential that the victim and the victim's family talk with the assistant district attorney assigned to the matter. Do not assume that the district attorney will file charges! You, the victim, need to do two things: explain the facts of the case as you know them to be, and communicate your request about the filing of charges.

I repeat—and this is something many victims do not understand—the decision to move forward against an accused is in the discretion of the district attorney. If the district attorney believes that the evidence is not sufficient, he or she can drop the entire matter, even if there has been an arrest.

Victims must also be prepared for the filing of lesser charges. For crimes like murder and rape, the district attorney may choose from a wide variety of charges. In a homicide, the charges can be first-degree murder, second-degree murder, voluntary manslaughter, and involuntary manslaughter (see Chapter 12, "Murder"). For sexual assault, the names of the charges are less standardized, but they are based on whether bodily injury occurred, whether the victim was in danger of her or his life, and the specific type of behavior the defendant engaged in (see Chapter 10, "Sexual Assault").

The method used by the district attorney to file charges depends on the state and sometimes on local procedures as well. The first question is whether the act in question constitutes a *misdemeanor* or a *felony*. A misdemeanor is a minor crime. People who commit misdemeanors can be sent to the county jail for a short time, but not state prison. Quite often, violators are fined rather than jailed. However, one misdemeanor that used to result in fines, now often results in jail time: drunk driving. In some states, the victim, as well as the district attorney, may file misdemeanor charges.

A *felony* is a serious crime, punishable by time in state (or federal) prison. The decision to proceed on felony charges cannot be made by the victim; it must be initiated by the district attorney. Because felonies are serious crimes, the procedures in those cases are addressed here.

The most serious felony is a *capital* crime, one where the death penalty is an option, in those thirty-six states where it exists. But victims who believe the death penalty is the appropriate punishment need to be realistic; it is carried out in only the rarest of circumstances, and then only after seemingly interminable appeals. A more attainable goal for victims who seek the maximum punishment is life in prison—without parole.

In felony cases, the most common procedure used in this country by district attorneys is presentation of the case to the *grand jury* to obtain an indictment.

1. Grand jury indictment

In all but some western states (such as California), indictment by a grand jury is the most common way in which formal charges are filed. The indictment is the formal bringing of criminal charges against someone. It announces that "probable cause" exists to try that person for the crime or crimes spelled out in the written charges. It is not, repeat not, a pronouncement of guilt.

The jury system began in England as a way for the citizenry to protect themselves from arbitrary action by the king. No person could be formally charged with a crime until a yes vote by the "grand" (French for "large") jury, and no one could be convicted until after a trial and a guilty vote by the "petit" (French for "small") jury. The grand jury had twenty-three members, and a vote of the majority was required for an indictment. The petit jury had twelve members, and needed a unanimous vote for a conviction. In time, the petit jury became known as today's "jury," while the grand jury retained its original name.

To obtain an indictment today, the district attorney's office presents the case in secret to the grand jury. It is likely to have about sixteen members, but many states still require a yes vote from twelve of them. Illinois requires a yes vote of nine of its grand jurors.

The grand jury hears only the evidence presented by the district attorney. In that sense, the grand jurors hear only one side of the story. For that reason, when the trial starts and the defendant gets his or her day in court, the full evidence may show that he or she is innocent.

The accused may appear before the grand jury, but in cases of violent crime rarely does. Most lawyers advise the accused not to appear before the grand jury. The defendant's case at trial could be made much more difficult because the district attorney may use that testimony against him or her. In his 1992 rape trial in Indianapolis, heavyweight boxing king Mike Tyson started with two strikes against him because he had testified before the grand jury. At the trial, the district attorney pointed out contradictions between Tyson's testimony to the grand jury and his testimony at trial. In contrast, William Kennedy Smith did not testify at the grand jury, so at his rape trial in West Palm Beach he had no previous statements that could be contradicted. Tyson was convicted; Smith was acquitted.

Hearsay is permitted in a grand jury. Hearsay is a repetition by a witness of what someone else told him or her, and is therefore often unreliable. With some well-defined exceptions, hearsay is *not* permitted at the actual trial. Instead, judges usually tell lawyers to bring in whoever actually said the words, so that person can be cross-examined to determine what the words actually meant.

On the other hand, courts usually permit nearly anything said by a *party,* including the defendant, to be admitted as evidence in the trial.

The news media often seem to trumpet an indictment in a way that indicates that the accused is guilty of a crime. In reality, an indictment is no such thing. After all, the grand jury hears only one side of the story, and it listens to potentially unreliable information, such as hearsay.

Often the district attorney does not call the victim to testify before the grand jury. Instead, the state may bring in the police officer, who will recite what the victim said to the police (which, as stated above, is hearsay, but which is permitted in *grand jury* proceedings).

On other occasions, the victim may be called to appear. In such a circumstance, you will be given a subpoena, which means that your attendance is required.

The grand jury meets in a much less formal setting than a courtroom. Usually the grand jurors will sit around a long table, along with the district attorney, the court stenographer, and perhaps a police officer. Everyone in the room, except the witness, is sworn to secrecy, with penalties for disclosing anything. As a witness, you will sit and answer questions, first from the district attorney, then from the grand jurors themselves.

Witnesses may repeat what they said to the grand jury, but of course may also keep silent. If a TV reporter sticks a microphone in your face after you leave the grand jury room, you don't need to say a thing. It's your decision whether or not to talk.

If the grand jury does not indict (the term is "no true bill"), the case is over, although the case can be re-presented to another grand jury in its next term, which usually commences a few months later. If the grand jury indicts, the case proceeds toward—but not necessarily to—trial.

Although grand juries were created as independent bodies and are theoretically under the control of the court, they have become virtual playthings of the district attorneys. District attorneys invariably can convince the grand jury to go their way. It has become a truism that if district attorneys want an indictment, they get it; if they don't, it doesn't happen. So if the grand jury does not indict in a case where you are the victim, it is likely the district attorney didn't want it, no matter what protestations you may hear later from his or her staff.

The prosecutor's virtual absolute control over the process extends both to getting an indictment—and to stopping one. A New York judge once said a particular district attorney could "get a ham sandwich indicted" after a politically motivated grand-jury indictment. On the other side is the prosecutor who doesn't want an indictment, a situation starkly illustrated in the 1992 Rocky Flats, Colorado, plea bargain.

A federal investigation of the Rocky Flats nuclear-weapon plant turned up evidence of serious environmental crimes. After a two-year investigation, the grand jury, according to press reports, decided to indict five employees of Rockwell International and three federal officials from the United States Department of Energy. The grand jury even drew up its own indictment. The United States Department of Justice ignored it, agreeing instead to a plea bargain with Rockwell itself and no charges against individuals. The grand jury then wrote a report of wrongdoing, but the report was squelched by the judge, who then asked for an investigation of *the grand jurors* for violating their secrecy oath.

In some states, if there is no indictment, you—the victim—may get a second chance. Some states, such as my state of West Virginia, permit the victim or other "credible person" to go directly before the grand jury, and the district attorney is not allowed to block their access.

2. Other methods of filing charges

Sometimes, in the federal courts and in the grand-jury states, the district attorney can bypass the grand jury. This technique is called an *information:* a filing of charges by the district attorney. In the federal system and in many states, an information is filed only with the consent of the accused, usually after he or she has agreed to a plea bargain. In other states, such as Illinois, the information may be used instead of an indictment. There, the state's attorney must then convene a probable-cause hearing and convince the judge that he or she had sufficient reason to file the information.

In states that do not rely on a grand jury, generally in the West, the filing of charges by the district attorney triggers a preliminary hearing, sometimes known as a coroner's jury. At that point, the judge or coroner's jury must decide whether, based on the evidence, the defendant must stand trial.

"Show cause" hearings can turn into a mini-trial. Usually the district attorney will try to reveal as little as possible, but enough to convince the judge that probable cause exists. If the victim testifies, he or she will then be cross-examined by the lawyer for the accused, who will seek to gather as much information as possible for the trial. In such settings, defense lawyers tend to be more unpleasant than at trial—at trial, they risk alienating the petit jury, but here no such roadblock exists. As at trial, victims need to state the truth, stay calm and relaxed, and give short answers. The next chapter gives tips for testifying at a trial, advice that can also be helpful at a preliminary hearing.

Statute of limitations

The statute of limitations is defined as the period after a crime by which time charges must be filed. All crimes except murder have a statute of limitations—killers have to live with the knowledge that they can be arrested at any time for the rest of their natural lives.

If the perpetrator is not identified soon after the crime, the statute of limitations can become important. For most federal crimes, the period is five years. Each state has its own statute of limitations.

In child-sexual-abuse cases, the statute can be a big problem. Generally, charges can be filed up to a short period after the child reaches eighteen, regardless of the age when the violation took place; that is, the statute does not expire until after the victim becomes an adult. Even then, because the child may have blocked out that childhood event into postadolescence, this most heinous of crimes could go unpunished.

A better rule is to permit child-sexual-abuse victims to be allowed to present their evidence even after they are well into adulthood, when they rediscover the crime and realize it for what it was. A good example occurred in Wyoming, where a woman abused by her father from the age of seven was so traumatized in her young-adult years that she was thirty-eight when she returned to the state and pressed charges. Fortunately, she had the courage to act—her father pleaded guilty to sexually abusing her and two nieces, and probably would have kept on abusing children.

Stage 3: Bail

Most people who are arrested or indicted are allowed to post bail. The amount of bail is set high enough to ensure that the defendant shows up for trial.

Bail follows the filing of charges, whether resulting from arrest or an indictment. So bail can be posted before or after a grand-jury indictment, depending on whether the accused had been arrested.

Why are defendants let out on bail before trial? Because every person is innocent until proven guilty. First, people must have their day in court, the trial by jury (unless they waive that right by pleading guilty). Therefore, presence at trial was the historical rationale for bail and remains its chief reason today.

But what about defendants who are an imminent threat to the community, or to the victim, or to witnesses who will testify against them? While judges certainly have kept such people in jail by denying bail or setting bail at an enormous amount, it was not until recently that federal legislation recognized these factors as legitimate reasons to deny bail. Increasingly, courts are recognizing that some people in our society are such repeat offenders that the chances of their committing a violation while on bail are quite great.

In one case, two teenage boys in Maryland decided that they needed money to go to a concert, and phoned for a pizza. They gave the address of a vacant house. The pizza was delivered by the manager of the local outlet, a young man in his twenties. The teenagers shot and killed him, took his money, and went to the concert. The boys were arrested and, astoundingly, the local judge immediately granted the younger boy, aged fifteen, bail in the custody of his father (who was a police officer). The community was outraged that such a callous killer could be immediately returned to the streets, so the prosecutor got a second bail hearing before a different judge. This time, the bail was revoked and the boy rearrested—and he remained in jail throughout his trial. A few months later, the boy was tried as an adult, convicted, and sent directly to prison.

Victims'-rights groups have brought several issues regarding bail to the forefront. One of those controversies is bail after conviction. It used to be quite common for a person to be convicted of a major crime by a jury of his peers, then continue to be free for another year while the case was appealed. Studies show that people out on bail, awaiting their appeal of a violent-crime conviction, are quite likely to commit another crime. In the federal system, Congress has now severely limited the right to be free pending appeal. Some states—but by no means all—have done the same. In Texas, for example, those who could be sentenced to more than fifteen years in prison are not allowed bail while they appeal. Your state may still be doing things the old way and letting such violent criminals go home for a year. If so, you should lobby your state legislator.

A concern we addressed in West Virginia is in the area of child sexual offenses. Adults could be accused of sex crimes against children in their household, then released on bail to return to that very house. We succeeded in passing a law that makes a condition of bail in such cases that the defendant reside elsewhere until the trial is over and his or her guilt or innocence has been determined legally.

In bail hearings, victims can:

1. Give information to the district attorney about any contacts from the defendant or his/her friends since the crime. The potential that an accused would tamper with or harm witnesses is in itself a reason for bail to be denied.

2. Tell the district attorney what you want. Realize that only rarely is bail denied, but if you believe it is the right course of action, ask for it. The district attorney should listen to the victim and the victim's family and present supportive evidence to the judge.

3. Try to obtain conditions for bail. Conditions of bail are rarely opposed by the accused, whose main goal is to get out! Reasonable conditions include (1) no contact whatsoever with the victim and the witnesses, (2) staying out of the victim's neighborhood and work place (if the defendant already knows where the victim lives and works), and (3) continual drug testing.

Stage 4: Plea bargaining negotiations and other pretrial activity

Plea bargains dominate the criminal-justice system. Perhaps nine out of ten indictments that reach the pretrial stage end with a plea bargain, rather than a trial on the merits of the case.

A plea bargain is an agreement in which a defendant pleads guilty to a lesser charge or a smaller number of charges, and the district attorney, in return, drops the other charges. In most states, the district attorney also makes a recommendation on the sentence, although a sentencing recommendation is not customary procedure in some counties.

Three questions emerge when discussing plea bargains. First, why is there plea bargaining? The simple answer is that there is too much crime and too few resources—prosecutors, courts, judges—to try all the cases. Such is the case in every state but one: Alaska does not allow plea bargains. In some counties elsewhere, too, plea bargains, as a matter of policy by the district attorney, are not made.

The second question—one more to the point—is why is there a plea bargain in a particular case? The answer could be one among these:

- the evidence against the defendant is not strong enough to win the case;
- the problem can be resolved by a plea to a lesser crime (for example, the sentence could be about the same);
- the crime is less important than other pending cases;
- the district attorney's office is too lazy to try the case;
- the district attorney sees no political gain or media coverage in this case, as opposed to a case against a high-profile defendant or a crime sensationalized by the media;
- the district attorney and the defense lawyer agree to a deal because of their political or social relationship;
- a trial may be too traumatizing for the victim, such as a child rape victim.

Obviously, then, there are both good and bad reasons for plea bargains.

But the crucial question is this: why is there a plea bargain in *your* case? That is the question that you, the victim, should get an answer to, and get it well before a plea bargain is sprung on you.

It's wrong for a district attorney to agree to a plea bargain on a major case without talking to the victim. The behavior of district attorneys varies. Some consult the victim scrupulously, while others ignore the victim totally.

Victims need to tell the district attorney's office whether they want to be consulted about a plea bargain. If the response from the government is negative or vague, then write the district attorney (not the assistant) and outline your views about any upcoming plea-bargain negotiations. Letters are harder to ignore than telephone conversations: they could cause political embarrassment to the district attorney in a future election.

In a prime example of such embarrassment, in rural New Hampshire, a seventy-five-year-old woman was brutally raped on Easter morning, just before she was going to go to church. The man, who had committed other rapes, was arrested. The district attorney accepted a plea bargain, one that sent the rapist to prison for twelve years. The woman, desiring a longer sentence out of fear for her granddaughters' safety at the end of this period, went public with her name and her outrage. Virtually every resident of her hamlet packed the courthouse at the plea bargain hearing, and the woman's story was page-one news all over New England.

I wouldn't want to be that district attorney's campaign manager in the next election.

Victims should not expect the district attorney always to follow their wishes on a plea bargain. After all, trained lawyers can assess the chances of winning a case better than a layperson can.

The key is *input* by victims, not control of the process by victims. The final decision on all matters of criminal justice rests not with victims, defendants, or prosecutors—but with our judiciary.

What if the district attorney's office strikes a plea bargain without consulting the victim? There still remains an opportunity: write the judge or go to court on plea-bargaining day. Ask the judge (it's better to ask the clerk or probation officer in advance) to speak on the issue and give your views in open court or, if you prefer, in a letter to the judge. It is entirely appropriate for others in the community to write the judge as well.

Remember: No plea bargain can be finalized without the approval of the judge. If the judge rejects the plea bargain, there is no deal, and the trial must go forward.

In southern West Virginia a few years ago, three deputy sheriffs went to visit a woman whose husband was in jail. They had sex with her, which she claimed was against her will. A prosecuting attorney from another county came in to try the case and plea-bargained it instead. The plea bargain was objected to vociferously by women's organizations, and the state supreme court stepped in and undid it. Judges, like the rest of us, are affected by the events around us and are in a unique position to undo a social injustice.

Not all plea bargains are wrong. But, given the number of cases that are disposed of this way, if victims' rights are ever to mean anything at all, it is essential that victims have a voice at this stage.

Other pretrial proceedings:
Many other things can happen before a trial. Here are some examples:

• Motions to dismiss. The defense lawyer will usually make motions to throw out the case. Sometimes those motions succeed and the case is dismissed. The most common such motion is to exclude evidence by charging that it was wrongly obtained by law-enforcement authorities. Because these issues frequently involve legal issues only, there usually is no role for the victim here. But because the outcome of such rulings can have a major effect on the case, you may want to attend such a hearing.

• Interviews. The defense lawyer of defendant's investigator may want to interview you. You may talk to them if you want to, or you may refuse. I recommend that you refuse, because when you testify, the defense lawyer will try to use what you said earlier against you. At the very least, talk to the district attorney's office before you talk to the defense lawyer. You may request that the assistant district attorney attend the interview.

• Scheduling of a hearing. Tell the victim/witness coordinator or the assistant district attorney to notify you about any upcoming hearing and to tell you in advance when a hearing is postponed. If a hearing causes a severe disruption in your schedule, say so. Calendars are adjusted for the convenience of everyone else—why not for the victim, too?

• Court delays. For many victims, a bigger concern than schedule conflicts is delay by the defendant's lawyer. You should object to continual delays of your case. Do so in writing to both the district attorney and the judge. For judges and district attorneys that haven't gotten the message, defendants *and victims* deserve swift and fair justice.

Your case may be over by now—because the criminal wasn't caught, or because he or she was not indicted, or because the case was thrown out on a motion, or because of a guilty plea or plea bargain. Or your case may be headed to trial, the subject of the next chapter.

CHAPTER 3

The Trial, Sentencing, and Parole

The trial is the defendant's day in court, but it is the state that must prove guilt beyond a reasonable doubt.

The trial should be the victim's day in court, too.

Defendants' rights—but not victims' rights—are enshrined in the Constitution. A brief history lesson may explain why. The Founding Fathers of the Constitution inherited a pretty good system of justice from England, but knew they could improve it. The Bill of Rights, crafted by James Madison and based on earlier work by Virginian George Mason, was written to make sure that the arbitrary power of the state could not be used against individuals.

Madison, Mason, and friends had good reason to be concerned. Tyranny by rulers on every continent had existed all through human history. Judges received all their authority from the throne and were rarely independent. Judges' failure to follow the royal line lost them their jobs and sometimes their lives. New Haven, Connecticut, the home of Yale University, was so named because it was founded by three judges who sentenced King Charles I of England to beheading in 1649. When the king's brother James returned from France to reclaim the throne, the judges didn't need to wait to see their picture on wanted posters to know they'd better leave England. The three judges found their new home to be a safe haven, hence the name New Haven, and the three main streets in town are named for them.

Before 1776, there had been isolated examples of republican government, but they were in small areas, like Switzerland, the

Greek city-states, and the Roman republic. Never had a large country maintained a democratic government.

Fortunately, the framers of the Constitution were perhaps the most farsighted group ever to assemble. They accepted the advice from their intellectual mentor, Thomas Jefferson, then serving as ambassador to France, that America become an "empire of liberty." Individual rights were not included in the original 1787 document, but were immediately called for the next year by Madison, Alexander Hamilton, and John Jay in *The Federalist Papers*.

Having written the Constitution and played a major role in securing its passage in the states, Madison decided to stand for Congress in 1788 from his home base in western Virginia. He didn't have time to go home and campaign, but was notified that he must do something fast, or a young upstart named James Monroe would beat him. He made a last-minute campaign promise, to submit amendments to the Constitution that created a Bill of Rights. He subsequently won the only race ever where two future presidents squared off for Congress. His Bill of Rights was approved by the first session of Congress in 1789, and was quickly ratified by the states.

The guarantees in the Bill of Rights, which state courts as well as federal courts must adhere to, include the right to a lawyer, the right to be tried by a jury, protection from unreasonable searches, protection from testifying against yourself, protection from excessive bail, and protection from cruel and unusual punishments. And the Bill of Rights came on top of the inherited common-law system from England, which had already evolved to one far better than what their neighbors on the European continent offered. The English system, enshrined since the Glorious Revolution of 1688, required that guilt be proved by the king's representative, under rules of evidence, before a jury of one's peers.

But why is there nothing in the Constitution about victims? The history is less documented. Some scholars believe that victims' rights were so well taken care of by the legal system in 1789 that no victim's-rights language was needed. Others feel that the framers, as men of property, were concerned with the types of crimes that *they* could be accused of committing, such as what we would today call white-collar crime, and thus were not focusing on victims of violent crime.

In any case, as we enter the third century of the Bill of Rights, it is time to add a provision on victims' rights. The movement has started—by putting such language into *state* constitutions.

Stage 5: The Trial

It is hard to compete with the drama of an American trial. The press, the lawyers, the judges, the spectators—all see the event as a time of excitement, pressure, and professional opportunity. As a lawyer, I have experienced the same reactions.

But hold it—something much more fundamental transcends all this. In Scott Turow's novel, *Presumed Innocent,* the protagonist, Rusty Sabich, is about to go on trial for a murder he did not commit. At the start of the trial, he looks around and thinks about the thrilling event about to unfold. Then he checks himself, realizing that his freedom and his reputation are at stake.

This is what a trial should be about: fairness to the accused, justice for the victim, and security for the community.

Who are the participants? First, the judge, of course, assisted by the bailiff, and the court reporter or stenographer. Second, the defendant, and the lawyer(s) for the defendant. Third, the lawyer(s) prosecuting the case, who go by many names, depending on the state: district attorney (as in California, New York, and Texas); prosecutor or prosecuting attorney (as in Ohio and West Virginia); commonwealth's attorney (as in Kentucky and Virginia); state's attorney (Illinois); state attorney (Florida); and the United States Attorney in the federal system.

The case is called "The State v. (the name of the defendant)." The "v." stands for versus (against). In the four states that are commonwealths—Kentucky, Massachusetts, Pennsylvania, and Virginia—the case is "The Commonwealth v. _____." California and New York use the term "The People vs. _____." And of course the federal government's criminal cases are titled "The United States v. _____."

At Al Capone's trial for tax evasion, the bailiff announced the start of the case of "The United States of America versus Al Capone." The gangster turned to his lawyer and said, "How can we ever beat odds like that?" He didn't.

And the fourth key participant: the jury. The jury is the factfinder, which decides guilt or innocence. The judge is the lawgiver; the jury must follow the judge's instruction. If the jury acquits, the defendant goes free. If the jury convicts, the judge can still overrule the jury and acquit. It is the defendant's choice whether to have a trial by jury or one only before the judge. (In Texas the defendant can even choose whether he wants the sentence imposed by the jury or the judge.) Most choose a trial by jury. When the trial is only before the judge, he or she wears two hats: as the fact finder as well as the lawgiver.

And the victim? The victim is not a key player and generally hardly participates at all. The district attorney is the lawyer for the state, not for the victim. As a matter of course, many district attorneys pay close heed to a victim's wishes, but many still do not.

Furthermore, in most places, victims do not even have the right to attend the entire trial. They can be excluded three ways. First, clever defense lawyers will keep victims on a witness list, so victims can be present only when they testify. Second, juvenile proceedings are generally closed—even closed to the victims. Third, parents of murdered children have even been excluded because allegedly their mere presence would prejudice the jury!

Times are changing slowly. Some states are trying to make the victim part of the process. Alabama now has a law which permits the victim to be present at all proceedings and even to sit at the counsel table. Wisconsin now allows the victim—or, in murder cases, the victim's family member—to be present at the entire trial. So even if victims are subpoenaed by defense lawyers in Alabama or Wisconsin, they cannot be excluded. California has moved to open up juvenile proceedings—not to the public, but at least to the victim.

Finally, an old rule may be coming back. Some states, such as West Virginia, permit the victim to hire a lawyer to assist the prosecuting attorney. The expensive "private prosecutor" system is rarely used, but if district attorneys are insensitive, it is an opportunity that victims may wish to consider. Even the threat of using a private prosecutor, whom district attorneys view as a challenge to their turf, could make the prosecutors more responsive.

The most important ingredient for success at trial is not what the lawyer or the witness does at trial, but as in sports, how they prepare for the big event. As a witness, you need to pay close heed to the instructions and advice of the district attorney, who has the responsibility not just to present the case and argue the law, but also to prepare the witnesses.

At the start of a jury trial, the jury is chosen from a pool of prospects. Jurors are asked questions to ensure their neutrality and objectivity about the case. These questions are called *voir dire* (French for "to see, to hear"). Jurors are excused "for cause," that is, for having either knowledge of the case or a background that would make them unsuitable for this particular case.

Referring again to *Presumed Innocent* will illustrate the position a juror must take. At the start of Rusty Sabich's murder trial, the judge asks the first prospective juror whether he thinks the defendant is innocent or guilty. The man answers what 90 percent of us would: "I don't know—I'd have to hear the evidence first." The judge immediately excuses the man from jury duty, then addresses the rest of the jury pool with the admonition that the defendant walks into the courtroom an innocent man, and all jurors must consider him innocent until he is proven otherwise, beyond a reasonable doubt.

After jurors are excused for cause, then both the state and the defense can excuse a certain number of jurors whom they simply don't want. This rejection is called a "peremptory strike." The choice of jurors has evolved in recent years from an art, based on hunches, to a science. Wealthy defendants will hire sociologists and psychologists to advise whom to strike, based on the person's *voir dire* answers, demeanor, occupation, age, and socioeconomic status, and even the opinion of neighbors.

The jury consists of twelve people in the federal courts and in most states. Some states now use smaller juries—Louisiana uses six people, for example. In a few states, a less-than-unanimous verdict is permitted.

At the start of the trial, the prosecuting attorney will make an opening statement, explaining the nature of the case and what the witnesses will be expected to say. Then the defense lawyer will make an opening statement (although some defense lawyers choose to wait and give their opening statement at the start of their case). The lawyers are not allowed then—or at any other time—to explain the law to the jurors. Only the judge has this prerogative.

The state, by its witnesses and exhibits, must prove that the defendant is guilty beyond a reasonable doubt. The term "reasonable doubt" continues to elude a precise definition by scholars and judges. In general, it means that jurors must be convinced—not beyond the shadow of a doubt, but at least to a moral certainty—that the defendant is guilty.

The state must first prove that a crime occurred, which is obvious in some cases, but could be difficult in a case of sexual assault, child abuse, or homicide if the body is missing. Then it must prove that the defendant committed the crime. Sometimes the state has direct evidence, such as witnesses who saw the crime or an admission by the defendant to a friend. At other times, the state must rely on circumstantial or inferential evidence: evidence that allows the jury to infer that the crime occurred, such as the defendant's ownership of the gun used in the crime, or the defendant's being seen near the scene of the crime. While direct evidence may be "better," there is nothing wrong with circumstantial evidence, which we use constantly in our daily lives. (If we wake up and see snow on the ground, we infer that it snowed during the night.)

In addition, the state must prove intent. Did the defendant intend to commit the crime, or was the action or the consequence accidental? In Kanawha County, West Virginia, a black man was tried and convicted for murder in a situation where, late at night and after a round of drinking, he lit a match to give his passed-out friend a hotfoot. The fire got out of control, the house burned, and a baby upstairs died. A tragedy occurred, yes, and perhaps some crime as well. But bringing a *murder* case, which fortunately a higher court reversed, was an example of a prosecutor's seeking headlines instead of justice.

The state may not introduce evidence of the defendant's bad character—his or her character is not on trial. But if the defendant introduces evidence of good character, the state may rebut it on cross-examination or with witnesses on rebuttal. Nor may the state introduce evidence of prior crimes of the defendant, except in narrowly tailored situations of similar crimes which help to show the *modus operandi,* the method of carrying out the crime.

After the state finishes its case, it is the defense's turn. The defendant doesn't even have to present a case because the burden of proof is on the state. Generally, however, the defense will want to present its version of events.

The defendant's case could proceed along several lines:

• You got the wrong person. Someone did this dastardly deed, but I have an alibi—I was elsewhere at the time.
• I did something, but it wasn't what the state says it was. In a murder or assault case, it may be self-defense. In a rape case,

there may be a dispute about consent. In the case of two defendants, one defendant may say that the other was the triggerman.

• I did it, but I didn't intend to. The most common category here is insanity, but others include coercion (Patty Hearst, who had been kidnapped, used this defense to a string of bank-robbery charges) and entrapment (often used in drug cases, where defendants claim that law-enforcement officials enticed them into acting).

The insanity defense is quite controversial—no, it's more than controversial. Since the two masters of malapropisms, movie producer Sam Goldwyn and Chicago Mayor Richard J. Daley, are dead, and since other lawyers are afraid to say it, I will: The insanity defense is crazy. There is nothing wrong with pronouncing someone guilty but mentally ill. But an *acquittal* based on insanity says, "Since you are crazy, we release you back to the streets, so you can do it again and come back and win another insanity acquittal." Poor people almost never win an insanity plea. Does this mean that rich defendants are crazier than poor defendants—or doesn't it mean, rather, that the wealthy are more likely to bring in persuasive psychiatrists and lawyers? The writer Ambrose Bierce, in his *Devil's Dictionary*, notes with irony that a poor person who steals is a thief, while a rich person who steals is a kleptomaniac.

After Americans found that a man could shoot the President of the United States and be acquitted on grounds of insanity, as John Hinckley, Jr. was after shooting President Reagan, common sense started to reenter the picture. The federal government and some states moved toward a "guilty but mentally ill" approach.

Sure, let's incarcerate mentally ill criminals in a place where they can be treated. But it is fundamentally wrong to acquit them; it puts the community in grave danger. The Milwaukee mass murderer Jeffrey Dahmer tried to raise the insanity defense for killing and cannibalizing his victims. Instead, the jury fortunately found him guilty. A finding of insanity could have meant that Dahmer could return to haunt other Wisconsin residents in a few years; the verdict of guilt means he will not.

The defendant may choose to testify but, because of the Bill of Rights, does not have to speak. If defendants do not testify, the state cannot use their failure to speak against them.

When the defense concludes its presentation of witnesses ad

exhibits, the state may present a short rebuttal case to counter what the defense presented. Then both sides will "rest their case," and the lawyers on both sides will give their closing argument to the jury.

The closing argument is the time in the trial when the lawyers' skills are most on display because it allows both sides to argue why the jury should rule their way. For rural juries, lawyers who wouldn't know which end of a cow to milk will be magically transformed into experts on country expression. Lawyers who come in from out of town will reveal themselves as incredibly knowledgeable about local folklore. Both sides will fall all over themselves complimenting the skill of the other lawyer(s), which is a smart tactic as well as professional courtesy—if the other side's case is that bad even with a great lawyer, think how quickly the jury should rush in and deliver a verdict against them.

Every lawyer has stories about a dramatic closing argument. My favorite is from the former attorney general of Oklahoma, Mike Turpen, also a leading victims'-rights advocate:

As a young district attorney, Turpen had to prove a murder case where the body had never been found. At the closing argument, the defense lawyer gave a compelling argument about the absence of a body: "There was never a murder here. The victim did not die. Not only did he not die, but in thirty seconds he will walk through the back door of this courtroom." The lawyer looked at his watch and counted to thirty. The jury, the judge, the spectators all looked to the back, wondering whether the doors would really open. Even Turpen found himself looking over his shoulder. The doors did not open and the victim did not appear, but the defendant's lawyer then gave this wrap-up:

"Ha! Even though he didn't come in, you thought he might. So you, the jury, have a reasonable doubt about whether the defendant is dead. Therefore, you must acquit my client of murder."

Turpen, crestfallen, awaited the result. He was astounded a short time later, when the jury announced it found the man guilty of murder, a victory for him and for the State of Oklahoma. Puzzled, he asked the jury foreman why. The reply: "Easy. Everyone else looked to the back door—except for the defendant. He kept looking forward!"

After the closing argument, the judge gives the jury instructions: an explanation of the law and direction on how to apply it. The jury then retires to consider its verdict. It can take any exhibits it wants with it and can come back to have testimony read to it, or to get more clarification from the judge on the law.

The jury can do five things: (1) It can acquit, which ends the case. (2) It can convict, which, if the judge allows the verdict to stand, means the defendant is guilty. (3) It can acquit on some counts and convict on others, a result that usually is considered a victory for the state. (4) It can absolve the defendant on the grounds of insanity. (5) Or it can hang, meaning that the jurors could not agree among themselves what to do; this result is generally considered a victory for the defense. A hung jury results in a brand-new trial at a future date, if the judge orders it. Alternatively, at that point, the judge can simply dismiss the case, a ruling that is appealable by the state.

Being a witness

Any surviving victim is almost certain to be called as a witness. *You* offer the primary proof that a crime occurred, and you may well be the key witness in proving that it was the defendant who committed it.

Prepare for your testimony. Become familiar with the court-room before the trial. Have the victim/witness coordinator or the assistant district attorney take you into the room where the trial will be held. Sit in the chair where you will be sitting. Spend time discussing your testimony with the assistant district attorney. Find out not only what type of questions you will be asked by the state, but what questions to expect from the defense. Then sit with your spouse or a close friend who is not involved in the trial and talk through what you have learned. Things always sound better if they have been said before. Don't worry about the question some defense lawyers will ask: "Have you gone over your testimony with the district attorney?" Of course you have, and that is nothing to hide—a district attorney would be remiss if he or she did not sit down with you and review your testimony in full.

For the trial, dress up and dress conservatively. Men should wear a dark suit, and women a dark suit or dress.

The lawyer who calls you as the witness—presumably the district attorney—does *direct examination*. The opposing party—probably the defense—does *cross-examination*. The two types of examination are quite different.

Direct examination

On direct examination, the witness tells his or her story. The lawyer asks straightforward open-ended questions, and the witness answers directly. When I do direct examination of a witness, on my notes I write the *answers* I am looking for, not the questions I want to ask. That way, I keep asking questions until the witness conveys all of the information on my notepad to the judge, magistrate, or jury. But questions that suggest the answer, known in the law as *leading questions*, are not allowed in direct examination.

Cross examination

Cross examination is different. Here the opposing side tries to poke holes in the testimony of the witness, and usually does so by asking leading questions. The legal term is *impeaching* the witness. There are several approaches lawyers use, depending on the circumstances, including:

1. showing that the witness's memory is faulty or imprecise, so that the witness is guessing or speculating about key facts;
2. showing that the witness is biased, e.g., because the witness has a blood dispute with the defendant or has an economic stake in the outcome;
3. showing that the witness is lying to or misleading the jury, e.g., by pointing to prior inconsistent statements the witness made;
4. showing that the witness is not giving independent testimony, e.g., by demonstrating that there was coaching by the district attorney.

Despite what you have seen Perry Mason and Matlock do on TV, the most common way to impeach a witness is not to show that he or she is an outright liar—that rarely happens. Indeed, I don't know a lawyer of any age who can recount "Perry Mason"-type experiences every week, where a chief accuser of his client breaks down and confesses in front of the judge, jury, and press that he—not the defendant—committed the dastardly deed. No, the chief method of impeachment is the first one, where the lawyer picks at small bits of the testimony to show that the witness, even with the best of motives, could not substantiate all the testimony given on direct examination.

But when lawyers can do so, they will directly attack the witness's motive, or the witness's ability or willingness to tell the truth.

Cross-examination skills are among the hardest to develop. Few can do it to perfection. One who apparently could was a country lawyer of the previous century in Springfield, Illinois. Representing a family friend charged with murder, whose poverty-stricken mother had begged him to represent her son, the lawyer took the case, one of many he did for free. On direct examination, the chief accuser told how he saw the murder committed in cold blood. On cross-examination, the lawyer asked the time of the murder, to which the witness replied, "Midnight."

"So how could you see this action so clearly?" the lawyer asked.

The witness answered, "The light of the moon shone so brightly that night that I could see it all." Whereupon, Abraham Lincoln pulled out the *Farmer's Almanac,* which showed there was no moon on the night of the murder. Not guilty.

In cross-examination, lawyers should not ask any questions—or at least any important questions—to which they do not already know the answer. It is better to get a little adverse information from the witness and then argue from that point in the closing statement to the jury. Law-school professors point out the great pitfalls of asking one question too many; and one, the late Professor Irving Younger, told my class this story. A man was charged with biting off the ear of another man. A third man testified against the accused. On cross-examination, the defendant's lawyer asked the witness:

"Did you see my client bite off the man's ear?"

Answer: No.

Now, if the lawyer had stopped there, just think of the good argument he could have given to the jury in the closing statement. Instead, he asked one question too many:

"Then how do you know he bit off the man's ear?"

Answer: Because I saw him spit it out!

That lawyer was no Lincoln.

As a witness, you need to listen closely to the questions by the district attorney. If you are cut off from explaining something, tell the judge you didn't finish—you will almost always be allowed to answer, and the defense lawyer will look disrespectful before the jury. Some questions cannot be answered by a simple yes or no.

Having said that, let me emphasize that you give short answers. Long answers only open up new areas for the other side's attorney.

You want to say as little as possible on cross examination, to give the defense lawyer as little ammunition as possible on closing argument.

The district attorney should be alert to helping you, both by objecting to irrelevant or inappropriate questions, and by making sure the defense lawyer doesn't berate you. Sometimes when I object to a question, I am also sending the witness a message on how to answer the question. Listen to what your side's lawyer says in the objection.

Be respectful to all. True, the trial can be traumatic, but, in Martin Luther King, Jr.'s, words, keep your eyes on the prize: justice for the victim and security for the community. You can go to the gym later and hit the punching bag.

TIPS ON TESTIFYING

Preparation
- Tour the courtroom in advance, and sit in the witness chair.
- Dress conservatively. Men should wear a dark suit. Women should wear a business suit or a simple dark dress.
- Review your testimony with the district attorney and by yourself, but do not memorize it.
- You may take notes with you to the witness stand, although the other lawyer and jury may look at them, and if you look at the notes a lot, it could damage the impact of your testimony.

Examination by the district attorney
- Listen to the question and answer it.
- Tell only what you know to be true.
- Describe what happened. The jury and the judge—not you—will draw the conclusions.
- Speak clearly. The jury and the judge are interested in what you have to say.

Cross-examination by the defendant's lawyer
- Listen to the question and answer it.
- If you do not understand the question, simply say so. If you do not know the answer, say so.
- Maintain eye contact with the attorneys, the jury, and the judge.

- Stop and listen if the district attorney objects. He or she may be sending you a message.
- Be courteous. Remember the advice from the Bible about being slow to anger. Anger, arguments, and discourtesy hurt your case.

Stage 6: Sentencing

Sentencing continues to baffle victims, but they are not the only ones astounded by the great disparities and surprising results. Lawyers, scholars, and judges themselves are often the harshest critics of sentencing policies in American courts.

Here are the problems with sentencing:

1. Sentences are not proportional to the crime. Sentences should ensure that the most dangerous criminals stay off the streets a long time. First-time offenders committing less serious crimes should not be clogging up prisons; ultimately, they should be given a second chance.

2. Sentencing for different segments of the population is not proportional. Studies continue to show that African-American, Hispanic, and poor white defendants fare worse for the same crime than the rest of the population.

3. Sentencing choices are too limited. For first-time nonviolent offenders, prison is often not the right choice, but neither is no punishment at all. We need required community service, restitution, weekends in jail, and similar "in between" choices.

Solutions are not easy. Sentencing has a variety of goals, all legitimate, and these goals sometimes conflict in application. They include:

Punishment—the price a convicted person must pay for the crime.

Community safety—sending a violent person to prison in order to keep the streets safe.

Community deterrence—a message to the community of what will befall those who commit such a crime.

Deterrence of the individual—a punishment that attempts to dissuade the violator from a future life of crime.

Rehabilitation—a sentencing program that improves the individual vocationally and emotionally.

It is easy to see how the goals can collide. For example, it may be advisable to give a substantial sentence for a crime to deter others from doing the same thing, but such a long sentence in a typical prison may reduce the chances for rehabilitation. (Rehabilitation is not something that American prisons have been very good at— former Attorney General of the United States Ramsey Clark called them "schools for crime.") Another example is white-collar crime. If the main goal of sentencing is community safety, then there is probably no need to send a white-collar criminal to prison. But if the goal is punishment, it is hard to think of someone who brought more economic ruin to people's jobs and lives than financier Michael Milken.

Even letting the punishment fit the crime is easier said than done. Should the punishment be the same for a gas-station robbery, whether the defendant is a nineteen-year-old first-time offender with a clean record or a thirty-five-year-old career criminal? I would vote not.

We send more people to prison than any society in the world. On the other hand, we have more violent crime than any other large country. Is there a way to get violent people behind bars and keep them there, and yet reduce our prison population?

I feel there is. As mentioned above, the American sentencing system lacks creativity. Most of the time, the choice in sentencing is between prison and nothing. What we need are more alternative punishments.

A study of the attitudes of the people of Alabama by the Edna McConnell Clark Foundation is instructive. The study found broad public support for alternatives like boot camp for young people, incarceration in the home (while wearing an electronic locator device), weekends in jail, and extensive community service, for crimes that now send people—especially young people— to prison.

Our prisons are overflowing. We need to keep them full of violent criminals serving long sentences; there are viable alternatives for other lawbreakers, options that cost much less taxpayers' money. In addition, an emphasis on community service for nonviolent offenders can do a great deal toward helping our needy and cleaning up our environment.

When I was attorney general of West Virginia, I decided to face the dilemmas of sentencing head-on, by creating a state Uniform

Sentencing Commission. We brought together representatives of all aspects of policy making, from police chiefs, judges, and state legislators to the Council of Churches. West Virginia had some bizarre notions of sentencing. For example, second-degree *murder* and *unarmed robbery* draw the same sentence. And eligibility for parole for first-degree murder, with mercy, often comes before parole eligibility for armed robbery. I was never sure why. Either the laws written 100 years ago were at a time when the lawmakers felt crimes of property were more serious than crimes of violence, or the sentences were drawn with no rhyme or reason at all. We proposed sentencing laws that (1) punished violent offenders the most severely (which meant increasing some sentences and decreasing others), (2) punished repeat offenders more severely than first-time offenders, and (3) inserted alternative-sentencing options for judges to consider.

I'd like to say that our four-year effort had a good ending, but it did not. The judiciary committees of our state legislature were packed with criminal-defense lawyers who saw no reason to disturb the status quo, and the county prosecutors saw the bill as a threat to their practices of negotiating sentencing and pleas with local lawyers. Each year, the bill died.

The Role of Victims in Sentencing

Sentencing comes after either a conviction or a guilty plea. After a trial, the judge generally sets a date for sentencing. After a plea bargain, practices vary: in some courts, the sentence is pronounced immediately, and in others at a future date.

Find out what the practice is in your county. If sentencing is imposed immediately, you may be faced with giving your views about sentencing at the same time as your views on the plea bargain.

In most places, however, you as a victim can expect the question of sentencing to be referred first to the probation officer, who will prepare a report to the judge. Some states now require that victim-impact statements be included as part of the presentencing investigation. Even if that is not the practice where you were a victim, it is now appropriate for the victim—and the victim's family or support group—to take action.

You may fill out a form for the probation officer, write a letter to the judge, or testify in person before the judge. Keep in mind, as stated earlier, that laws and customs vary from state to state, from county to county, and even from judge to judge. If neither the district attorney nor the judge is cooperative, you may need to go to the newspaper and other media to publicly show that you are not going to be deterred from expressing your views as a victim of crime.

There are at least four reasons why the victim may wish to advise the judge, in person or by letter, on the sentence. First, the victim may wish to urge the judge to let the punishment fit the crime. (Such a letter could urge severity or leniency; victims have been known to go either way.) Second, victims may wish the judge to know the impact of the crime on them and their families. Third, the victim legitimately may be in fear of the defendant if he or she is set free. Fourth, the victim may desire court-ordered restitution; that is, money, from the lawbreaker. In some states, judges have a great deal of discretion in sentencing; in other states and the federal system, their choices are quite limited.

It doesn't hurt—and it may help—for friends and family to attend the sentencing. Part of the success of Mothers Against Drunk Driving has been the group's willingness to pack the courtroom on sentencing day. It's no wonder, then, that their attendance coincided with judges starting to give more drunk drivers jail sentences!

Whether victims could legally testify at sentencing hearings became in doubt in the late 1980s, when a Supreme Court opinion, *Booth* v. *Maryland*, held that victim-impact statements violated defendants' rights in death-penalty cases. But in 1991, in the case of *Payne* v. *Tennessee*, Charles Burson, the attorney general of Tennessee, persuaded the Supreme Court to reverse *Booth*. Now victim-impact statements are legal in capital and noncapital cases. In the Tennessee case, the defendant had killed a woman by stabbing her repeatedly. Then he stabbed her two-year-old daughter to death, and stabbed but did not kill her three-year-old son. After the conviction, the grandmother testified at the death-penalty hearing that the little boy still wandered around the house wondering why his mother and baby sister didn't come home. Although a lower court felt that such comments prejudiced the jury, which then voted for the death penalty, the Supreme Court found them perfectly appropriate to describe the family holocaust.

Opponents of victims' rights claim that victims always want the worst possible sentence for defendants and have no compassion or objectivity. A story from Georgia belies this claim. In 1991, one day away from his electrocution, a murderer's life was spared. The reason: the victim's family had come before the Georgia parole board and asked for a commutation, saying that they had talked about it and prayed about it, and believed that the death penalty was not the right answer for the man who killed their relative.

Stage 7: The Appeal

In civil cases, either side that loses can appeal. But in criminal cases, jury verdicts of acquittal cannot be appealed. The defendant may appeal a guilty verdict.

Once in a while, the state may seek an appeal if (1) the judge throws out the case before it starts, e.g., by excluding evidence the state needs for a conviction, (2) the judge makes a ruling on the eve of trial and an appeal is taken, perhaps with the permission of the judge, who seeks legal guidance from a higher court, or (3) the sentence is not severe enough. That last category—appeal of a sentence—was extremely rare until recently. In federal court, either side may appeal if the sentence falls outside the United States Sentencing Guidelines; some states are starting to adopt a similar approach. Illinois, for example, does allow for an appeal of the sentence.

But, as stated, most appeals are made by a convicted defendant. In some states, such as Rhode Island and Montana, there are only two tiers:; the trial court and the state supreme court. In more heavily populated states, such as Indiana and Colorado, there are three levels of courts, with several courts of appeal sitting around the state, acting as the first level of appeal. Final appeal would then be made to the state supreme court.

The names of these courts vary considerably. The trial court has names like District Court (California, Texas), Common Pleas (Ohio, Pennsylvania), or Circuit Court (Virginia, West Virginia). The highest court in the state is known as the Supreme Court in forty-three states. In the other seven, it goes by different names: in Connecticut, the Supreme Court of Errors; in Maine and Massachusetts, the Supreme Judicial Court; in Virginia and West Virginia, the Supreme Court of Appeals; and in Maryland and New York (and in the District of Columbia), the Court of Appeals. The states with intermediate courts call them courts of appeal

(California) or, more commonly, courts of appeals. Texas has separate courts of criminal and civil appeals.

New York has the most confusing set of names. The trial court is called, oddly, the Supreme Court; the intermediate court is the Supreme Court, Appellate Division; and the highest court is the Court of Appeals.

The number of judges on the state's highest court is commonly seven—the number in California, New York, and Ohio—but it varies from five in many smaller states, such as West Virginia and Nevada, to nine in states like Maryland, Missouri, Texas, and Washington.

The United States Supreme Court has had nine Justices for the past 120 years. During the Civil War, Congress gave President Lincoln a tenth judge, to counter the weight of slavery advocate Chief Justice Roger Taney. When Andrew Johnson was President, every time a Justice died, Congress reduced the size of the court, rather than give a man they despised the power to appoint. Then Ulysses S. Grant took over and the number was restored to nine.

During the Great Depression, Franklin D. Roosevelt became disgusted with the Court's conservative opinions and tried to pack the court by asking Congress to increase its number to sixteen. Roosevelt's floor leader, Senator Robinson of Arkansas, had a heart attack and died while debating the bill. Fearing that God had decided that nine was the right number, the Senate overwhelmingly defeated the bill, and the issue, like Senator Robinson, is dead forever.

Appeals focus on errors of law. Higher courts will reverse if the trial judge made a significant mistake in a ruling. A minor mistake by the judge will be called a "harmless error" and will not cause the conviction to be reversed.

In the 1950s through the 1970s, the United States Supreme Court reversed many cases on appeal from state supreme courts, adopting new constitutional principles. In the 1970s and 1980s, many state supreme courts started reversing appeals by adopting their own principles from their own state constitutions. As a result of changing public moods about crime, the appointment of new Supreme Court Justices by Presidents Reagan and Bush, and the electoral defeat of some state court judges, most spectacularly California Chief Justice Rose Bird, the reversals of criminal convictions by announcing new rules is less common now.

It is hard for victims to present their views in criminal appeals.

Normally, only the lawyers for the parties may present oral arguments before the judges, and the parties are the state and the defendant. But victims may present a written memorandum to the court which is known as a "friend-of-the-court" brief. Victims'-rights organizations, especially the San Diego–based Victimology Center and its director Judy Rowland, have been increasingly active in presenting such briefs.

Stage 8: Parole

Parole is the release of an inmate under supervised conditions before the entire sentence is served. It is not to be confused with probation, which is the decision to allow a guilty person to remain free *instead of* going to prison, subject to certain conditions.

Few prisoners serve their entire sentence. They either are released on parole after serving a fraction of the sentence, or are released early because of good time served. The decision to parole a prisoner early is made by a commission created for that purpose: the state parole board.

The power of parole boards is enormous. To understand why, you need only look at the normal sentence: it has a range of years. Whether the prisoner serves in the low or the high range is up to the parole board. In fact, in many states, the prisoner becomes eligible for parole before the *minimum* is served; in West Virginia, the prisoner is eligible after serving one-fourth of the maximum, an amount which is usually less than the minimum. In other states, the good-time rule makes for early parole eligibility; in Illinois, prisoners get one day reduced for every day served, provided they don't misbehave. In many states, life sentences do not mean life: they mean that the prisoner *might* serve life, or might get paroled after a certain number years.

The parole process has drawn a number of critics: those who believe the process makes sentences too discretionary and inconsistent, those who believe it allows judges and prosecutors to make decisions that should be made at the time of sentencing, and those who believe that victims are deceived by the sentence term given the prisoner. Several states, such as Oregon and Washington, and the federal system, are phasing out the use of the parole system. New Hampshire has adopted a Truth-in-Sentencing Act: now the sentence given an individual is the time that will be served. But the parole process remains in the great majority of states.

Many victims fear an early release of prisoners, and often their fears are justified. The tragic saga of Lisa Bianco of Indiana illustrates the point. Bianco was beaten consistently by her husband, who also once kidnapped their children to Florida. After the divorce, when he beat her again savagely, she had him arrested. In videotaped testimony, she told the prosecutors that he promised to kill her if she prosecuted, and she begged them to protect the safety of her and her children. After his conviction, he was sent to prison for a lengthy term. He applied for an eight-hour furlough, and his mother called Ms. Bianco to tell her about it. Ms. Bianco called the district attorney, who contacted the corrections department and asked for a hearing. The furlough was canceled, and the district attorney asked for prior notification of any future furlough.

Due to an administrative error, the next time her ex-husband applied for a furlough, neither the district attorney nor Bianco were notified. Her ex-husband went straight to Lisa's house, chased her to a neighbor's door, and killed her, right in front of their two children. Ironically, Lisa Bianco was then working for a battered-women's shelter.

The Bianco tragedy illustrates the need for corrections departments and parole boards to listen—and listen closely—to victims, lest there be a second victimization.

Amazingly, half the states still do not allow victims to testify at parole hearings, an area in which state legislatures need to act. All states, however, do allow victims, district attorneys, and all others to write letters to the board.

If the parole hearing is important to you, contact the state parole board and find out when the perpetrator is scheduled for a parole hearing. As elsewhere in government, the result will vary: some boards will notify victims in advance of the hearings, while others will not be cooperative. Before the hearing, you may wish to write the parole board and enlist the help of friends, the district attorney, and the media. California, in particular, has had highly publicized parole hearings, such as for Charles Manson and Sirhan Sirhan. Victims should also find out whether oral testimony by someone other than the prisoner is permitted. Letters or testimony should deal with the severity of the crime, the impact of the crime, or fear of the prisoner.

The Cincinnati-based Parents of Murdered Children organizes letter-writing campaigns on behalf of families of murder victims. To date, this outpouring of support has had its desired effect each time the group has gotten involved. Other, more local groups have taken up the cause for victims and their families. Parole boards are appointed by the governor. Like other agencies of government, they can count noses; the more letters sent, the more likely they will be noticed.

The best program would allow for (1) *notice in advance* to all victims of the date a parole hearing is scheduled, (2) *the right to testify in person for victims and others,* and (3) *notice in advance* when/if an inmate is being released or furloughed. Maybe if enough parole boards read about the tragedies in this book, or in the newspapers in their own state, all fifty states will have such programs in the near future.

Juvenile-Delinquency Cases: A Different Set of Rules

Most crimes by juveniles—children under eighteen years of age— are handled very differently from crimes by adults, and for some very good historical reasons. Up until this century, children were warehoused with older criminals, making their chances of becoming productive adult citizens virtually nil. Juvenile courts were first introduced in 1899 in Illinois, and spread elsewhere quickly. California, for example, followed suit in 1909.

Today, in every state, separate procedures govern the handling of juvenile delinquency, procedures which emphasize treatment and rehabilitation for children under age eighteen. The goal of juvenile courts is turning youth away from a life of crime and toward becoming productive, law-abiding citizens. In many cases, it has been successful. John Hey, a popular judge in Charleston, West Virginia, spent several of his teenage years in a detention facility in Rhode Island; he often asserts that the juvenile-corrections system turned him away from a life of crime and allowed him to start his adult life unencumbered by the stigma of an adult criminal record.

The focus of the juvenile courts is to decide the "best interests" of the minor. The hearings are closed and court records are sealed. Juvenile violations do not become part of a permanent record.

Some aspects of the juvenile-court system are not controversial. First, they are a method of dealing with petty theft, pranks that turn into vandalism, and status offenses (acts that would not be crimes if committed by adults, such as school truancy and curfew violations).

A second value of the juvenile-court system is that impressionable young people are not incarcerated with seasoned criminals. Juvenile courts view detention as a last resort. When it is ordered, youth are kept separate from the adults. Having taught school in both juvenile and adult prisons, I can personally testify that this is a very good idea, and one that should not change no matter how tight state budgets get. Still, separate facilities can mean a range of options. Florida and Michigan, among other states, send youths who need discipline and training to boot camp, a regimented life comparable to being in the marines.

But problems exist with using the juvenile courts to address major violent crime by young people. How do we reconcile this system of secrecy and the goal of the best interests of the juvenile with the goals of victims' rights and the need for a safe society?

One solution is to treat the youth as an adult, and every state allows this. The district attorney can make a motion to the judge to bind the youth over to the adult courts. The decision of the judge would depend on the seriousness of the offense, the age and sophistication of the juvenile, and his or her prior history of delinquency. Amy Fisher, the "Long Island Lolita," was only seventeen when she shot and critically injured her paramour's wife. The judge granted the New York district attorney's motion to try her as an adult. She pleaded guilty, and was sentenced to fifteen years in prison, a term that would have been much shorter had she been left in juvenile court.

Most states have a minimum age at which a juvenile may be tried as an adult; in California it is sixteen. Florida has a minimum age of fourteen, except for crimes for which the penalty for adults is life imprisonment or death; for these there is no minimum age. Pennsylvania has no minimum. Recently a nine-year-old boy intentionally shot a seven-year-old girl to death while she was riding a snowmobile. The courts wrestled with trying so young a child as an adult; the state supreme court ruled that it would depend on what the judge found out at a hearing. Ultimately, the child was not incarcerated; he is being kept on probation until age eighteen and cannot attend the local school where the little girl's siblings go, and his parents cannot keep any guns in the house.

Victims' rights have not progressed as rapidly in juvenile courts as in adult court. Victims often have been excluded from the hearing, except perhaps for their testimony. Indeed, many victims do not even know the disposition of the case against the perpetrator. Through 1989, only thirteen states had victims'-rights legislation that specifically addressed victims of juvenile crimes.

Some states are now opening up juvenile proceedings to their participation by victims and observation by the public. California is one that has opened up juvenile courts for major juvenile crimes. The press and the public, as well as the victim, may attend. The exception is cases where the victim is a sexually assaulted child, in which case the court is closed when the child testifies, and the entire proceeding may be closed at the request of the child's guardian. Victims may attend the disposition (sentencing) proceeding or may find out what happened by contacting the probation department. Afterward, the court records are sealed.

Florida also has a law that opens up juvenile-court proceedings, but the judge has the total discretion to close them "when the public interest and the welfare of the child are best served by so doing."

In most states, juvenile courts remain an unconquered outpost for victims' rights. Talk to the district attorney or the victim/witness advocate about your rights in juvenile proceedings—and be prepared to learn that in your state they may be nonexistent. But more than action on individual cases is needed. We need media attention, then action by state legislatures, to make sure that victims have the opportunity to participate in juvenile proceedings.

Part III

Money for the Victim: The Opportunity for Financial Recovery

CHAPTER 4

The Primary Sources: Victim Compensation, Insurance, and Employee Benefits

Crime costs you money. Some losses for a victim of crime are easy to measure: stolen or vandalized property, hospital bills, lost time from work. Other losses, such as future medical bills, are harder to calculate. A victim may require physical therapy or counseling for years to come. Then there is the impact of pain, fear, or emotional trauma. Referred to as "general damages," these are losses the law will try to measure—often with great difficulty.

Victims can recover for losses on three levels: costs to date, future costs, and general damages.

The avenues available for victims to assert their rights for damages are often blocked by the financial insolvency of the wrongdoers, legal intricacies, and indifference by the criminal-justice system. Yet many victims have fought back—and succeeded. Victims have won cash awards through several different routes, and the number of victims fighting back and winning is increasing each year.

There is a good chance that some—or all—of your losses can be recovered.

Money for Victims of Crime:
Sources for Financial Recovery Available to You

---

❶ **State Crime Victim Compensation Board:** Covers a variety of
medical bills and other losses, resulting from violent crime, not
covered by insurance.

❷ **Your Insurance Policies:** Health, life, disability, auto, homeowner's,
professional, commercial, and any other. Read the fine print.

❸ **Insurance of Others:** Auto, homeowner's, professional malpractice,
and commercial.

❹ **Employee Benefits:** Health care, disability, medical leave, life
insurance, retention of health insurance at conclusion of employment,
provision for employing handicapped.

❺ **Restitution from Criminal:** Money the defendant will pay to the
victim as part of the sentence or plea agreement.

❻ **Suing the Criminal:** Making the criminal pay—in cash.

❼ **Suing a Third Party:** Seeking money from someone with a
responsibility for your safety who acted, or failed to act, in a manner
that resulted in the crime.

A. Victim Compensation: Your State May Foot the Bill

Have you heard about the law which said that if you are robbed or
murdered, the city in which the crime occurred would have to
compensate you or your heirs? Why not? If the government
doesn't keep the streets safe, then it should pay the medical bills.
You might think that such a commonsense law is fairly new
because it is not something the government did in our parents' or
grandparents' day. Actually, such a law was part of the oldest legal
document ever found: the Code of Hammurabi, written in
Babylon in about 2000 B.C.

The Babylonians were not alone. Most ancient societies, such as
the Israelites, developed their system of justice around the victim.

In the early days of the American republic, too, justice for the
victim was emphasized. Somehow, in our modern zeal to construct

a system protecting the rights of the defendant, we neglected the advice of our ancestors—and the rights of the victim.

The greatest single advance for victims' rights in this century was adopting the system used by King Hammurabi: compensation by the state for victims of violent crime. First enacted by New Zealand in 1963, then by California in 1965, the program acts as an "insurance company of last resort" for victims. Ultimately, all states followed suit, until by 1992 all states, the District of Columbia, and most territories have victim-compensation boards. Directory A lists the addresses and telephone numbers of these boards. Victim-compensation boards exist only for victims of violent crime. Losses from burglary, robbery, and white-collar crime are not covered.

Who is Eligible

To be eligible, a victim must:

❶ Report the crime to the police within the state's time period, usually 48 or 72 hours (although many states allow an exception for "good cause")

❷ Cooperate with law enforcement authorities in solving and prosecuting the crime

❸ Be an innocent victim; and

❹ Make claims to the state crime victim compensation board in time. The period is usually one year after the crime occurred, with the exception of 15 states and the District of Columbia:

60 days: Maine, New Hampshire

6 months: District of Columbia, Georgia, Iowa, Maryland, Oregon, South Carolina, Virginia

18 months: Hawaii

2 years: Alaska, Connecticut, Indiana, Nebraska, New Jersey, Virgin Islands, West Virginia

3 years: Rhode Island

No set period: Vermont

For all states not listed, the time period is one year.

Note: Most states allow children a longer period to report.

Who is eligible?

To be eligible, a victim must report the crime to the police in a timely manner, must cooperate with the authorities in solving and prosecuting the crime, must be an innocent victim, and must make the claim to the state crime-victim-compensation board in time. Some states also have a "good cause" exception to the time requirement for adults, and most allow children a longer time to file. All states require proof of financial losses or incurred expenditures. See the chart "Who Is Eligible" on page 67.

One thing *not* required is that the criminal be convicted—or even identified.

If health insurance, or the defendant, or a liable third party pays for all the losses, victim-compensation boards do not have an additional obligation. If insurance or other sources pay part of the cost, say 80 percent, then the victim compensation board will cover the other 20 percent. Nine states also require that the victim suffer "financial hardship" to qualify for money.

You are covered by the state in which the crime against you occurred. You do not have be a resident of that state to apply for compensation (except in Nevada, which covers only its own residents if a crime occurs there).

What may a victim recover for?

Medical bills and *lost wages* are always included, as are *funeral costs* and *replacement-service costs* (the cost of services the victim can no longer perform). A general death benefit is usually permitted, sometimes including payments to minor children. Counseling for victims, needed in the aftermath of a crime, is now covered by every state.

Twenty-four states allow recovery for certain crimes even if there is no physical injury, such as therapy for a victim of sexual assault. Illinois allows a child who witnesses a sex crime to receive money for counseling, which makes sense; in this situation the child is also a victim.

Pain and suffering, a general award on top of medical bills, is not allowed in forty-seven states—Hawaii and Rhode Island award money for pain and suffering, and Tennessee does so for sex crimes.

All states except New York and Washington have a ceiling on compensation payments. The maximums for each state are indicated in the chart on the next page.

Twenty states have a minimum level of damages before someone may apply, ranging from $25 to $200, while seven states have a $100 or $200 deductible.

Eleven states allow victims to recover from some property losses occurring in the course of violent crime—see chart on page 71.

Where does the money come from?

In three-fourths of the states, most or all of the revenue to run the program comes from "abusers' taxes"—a surcharge on fines or penalty assessments—rather than reliance on general revenues

Maximum Allowed by State Crime Victim Compensation Boards	
Limit	**State**
Unlimited	New York (Medical & rehabilitative) Washington (medical)
$35,000 to $50,000	California, Maryland, Minnesota, Pennsylvania, Utah, West Virginia, Wisconsin
$20,000 to $25,000	Arkansas, Connecticut, Delaware, District of Columbia, Idaho, Iowa, Kentucky, Massachusetts, Montana, New Jersey, North Carolina, North Dakota, Ohio, Oregon, Rhode Island, Texas, Utah, Virgin Islands.
$10,000 to $15,000	Alabama, Arkansas, Arizona, Colorado, Florida, Hawaii, Indiana, Kansas, Louisiana, Michigan, Mississippi, Missouri, Nebraska, Nevada, New Mexico, Oklahoma, South Carolina, South Dakota, Vermont, Virginia, Wyoming
$5,000	Maine, New Hampshire, Tennessee
$1,000	Georgia

Note: The National Commission for Uniform State Laws has recommended that every state have a minimum of at least $25,000.

and law-abiding taxpayers. The other states still rely on so-called general revenues, a code word for the taxpayers like you and me.

The federal government, which picks up 40 percent of the tab, gets all of its money from fines and penalties levied against law violators. Federal money in this program now exceeds $150 million per year. Large sums for the program have come from fines paid by Exxon for its oil spill in Alaska, and from corporate criminals like Michael Milken for his Wall Street sleight-of-hand.

Victim compensation is an important part of our system of justice. There is nothing new or radical about this concept—it is backed by a 4,000-year-old tradition.

B. Insurance: Coverage You May Not Know You Have

Insurance coverage on a widespread scale represents one of the great gains of the twentieth century. When my grandfather's feed store in rural Georgia burned in 1920, he had no insurance and therefore was effectively wiped out. With insurance, such catastrophes no longer create the same financial devastation. Most people have become willing to pay a little each year to protect themselves from disaster.

You will read a lot about insurance—yours and other people's—in this book. This section covers *your* policies. In Chapter 5, we examine the criminal's insurance; then, in Chapter 6, we look at the insurance policies of third parties. (By "third parties" I mean someone who is not the criminal but whose reckless or careless actions, or inactions, allowed the criminal to commit the crime.)

1. Car Insurance
Your car insurance provides financial protection when you are at fault in an accident. The policy probably contains health insurance to cover some or all of your medical bills as well. In states with no-fault insurance, certain bills are covered by each driver's insurance, regardless of fault.

In addition, your insurance policy may contain provisions to protect you when the other party is at fault, but cannot fully compensate you for your losses:

• *Uninsured-motorist coverage* applies when the other driver is at fault, and does not have insurance or cannot be located (such as a hit-and-run accident).

States That Allow Some Property Losses

Alabama:	Up to $400 for loss of cash; up to $1,000 for loss of essential property.
Colorado:	Emergency money to replace doors, locks, and windows
Indiana:	Up to $500 for property reimbursement.
Louisiana:	Up to $10,000 for destruction of a house.
Minnesota:	Financial assistance for dental products and prosthetic devices.
Nevada:	Up to $1,000 for property essential to physical or mental health.
New York:	Financial assistance for (1) "critical property," such as glasses and hearing aids, (2) necessary transportation, and (3) replacing necessary property (for the elderly only).
Pennsylvania:	Reimbursement if robbed of proceeds of Social Security check.
Utah:	Coverage for "essential personal property"—no limit
West Virginia:	Payment for the cost of eyeglasses.
Wisconsin:	Clothing and bedding, plus $200 for other property.

● *Underinsured-motorist coverage* applies when the other driver is at fault, but has *insufficient* insurance to cover your losses.

If you don't have uninsured and underinsured motorist coverage, I strongly recommend getting them. (In some states, such as Virginia, the two are part of the same policy; in other states, such as West Virginia, you buy them separately.) Victims are generally more successful in trying to collect the insurance than in trying to acquire the driver's assets. Many—probably most—drivers do not carry limits to cover a serious accident, and a frighteningly high number drive without any insurance at all.

2. Homeowner's Insurance

Homeowner's insurance covers damage to your home, theft of property, and unintentional acts that result in injury to others. If you are a victim of arson or burglary, such a policy covers or at least cushions the losses. A more narrow policy for tenants is *renter's insurance* or *contents insurance,* which insures the contents of the house or apartment.

As discussed later in the book, your homeowners' insurance may cover you if the crime occurred in your home.

3. Health Insurance

As an employee, retiree, or purchaser, you may have one or more health-insurance policies. Read the fine print; you can be sure that the insurance company will. All health-insurance policies, along with Medicare, should be analyzed to determine the extent of coverage.

Increasingly, an important part of health insurance is the extent of *mental-health coverage,* and what type of mental-health counselors your policy will cover. More-enlightened policies cover counseling by clinical social workers as well as by psychiatrists and psychologists because social workers often have the specialized training to match the other professionals.

4. Life Insurance

In addition to a regular life insurance policy, your family member may well have a separate policy related to a business, employment, or fraternal membership.

He or she also may have credit life insurance attached to a loan, most frequently on a car. I do not recommend buying these policies—credit life insurance is almost always a ripoff—but they are often required with a loan. If a family member dies, check whether there is such a policy attached to a loan, because it automatically pays the debt.

5. Disability Insurance

Many employees are covered by disability insurance, but many others have to buy a separate policy. In some cases, credit life insurance or other contracts may contain a disability clause.

Obviously, what constitutes "disability" may not be something that you and the insurance company see eye-to-eye on. Don't be in a hurry to accept the company's judgment; it won't be in a hurry to accept yours!

6. Other Insurance

Name a catastrophe—cancer, drought, being hit by a meteor—and someone will sell insurance on it. No one ever seems to collect, at least not without a major effort, on some of the more offbeat policies; midwestern farmers had to bring a class-action lawsuit to receive payment on their drought insurance policies in the late 1980s. You could be the talk of your neighborhood if you are one who does collect.

Dealing with Insurance Companies

Too many insurance representatives are trained to say no, even if the right answer is "yes" or "maybe." Others make it a point never to volunteer anything. Insurance agents represent the insurance company; they are not *your* agents, regardless of what the television commercials suggest. And few insurance companies go out of their way to award big claims. So don't give up just because the first answer from an insurance company is "no."

A cardinal rule of insurance law is that any vagueness or

Tips in Dealing with Insurance Companies

• Agents represent the company's interests. Don't expect the company to offer to pay, and don't assume a negative response is final.

• Check every policy you have.

• All ambiguous language will be decided in the consumer's favor.

• Contact the state insurance commissioner for assistance.

• Contact a lawyer if you need help interpreting the policy or if you think the insurance company is acting in bad faith.

ambiguity in the language of the policy is interpreted *in favor of the consumer* and against the insurance company.

If you feel that your claim has been wrongly denied, contact your state insurance commissioner. Many have toll-free lines.

If you are unclear about anything, sit down with a good lawyer to review your policies. Some people have won big lawsuits because their insurance company dealt with them in bad faith: by denying coverage when it should have paid up right away.

C. Employee Benefits: You May Have More Than You Realize.

If you or a family member are victims of crime, check with your employer at once. Larger companies usually have a manual to describe employee benefits. Others may have a helpful personnel manager or department. Note: These benefits are not triggered because you or your family member are victims of crime; they would be available to any employee or family member who had an injury or illness.

1. *Health insurance,* if your employer has it, is the starting point. Note the amount of coverage, the deductibles, and the services provided for (for example, whether mental-health counseling is a covered service).

2. *Sick leave* and *vacation leave* provide an automatic right to a period of time away from work—with pay.

3. *Disability insurance* is offered by many companies. The employee could go on extended leave, at reduced pay.

4. *Extended sick leave* permits a leave of absence, without pay, with the right to return.

5. If your family member is murdered, there may be a *life insurance* policy on each employee. In some policies a violent death, which is treated as accidental death, pays double.

6. *Individual health insurance upon exiting* is probably available. Laws now often provide that when people leave their employment, they may buy low-cost health insurance through the employer for a period of time.

7. *Disability rights* prevent employers from discriminating in the hiring or promotion of handicapped people. In 1991 Congress passed the Americans with Disabilities Act, the most sweeping civil-rights bill for the disabled ever. Before then, rights for the

disabled were a hodgepodge, with fairly strong laws in some states and weak or no laws in others. Now there are national standards for the expanding rights of disabled Americans. Employers must now make "reasonable accommodations" for the disabled. That means that medium-sized and large companies must take steps to ensure that their workplace is one in which the disabled may work, even if it means making capital expenditures to improve physical access.

Furthermore—and this is important for crime victims—the law applies to those who *become* disabled. Thus, if crime disables you or a family member, you *may* have the right to compel the employer to make workplace adjustments to permit you or your family member to keep the job. Contact your state or city human rights commission, or the United States Equal Employment Opportunity Commission. 1801 L Street, N.W., Washington, D.C. 20507 (telephone 202-663-4264).

CHAPTER 5

Make the Criminal Pay— in Cash

It's time to blow three myths out of the water, once and for all.

Myth #1: When crime takes a financial bite, there is nothing you can do about it.

If you did believe it—and such thinking is encouraged by many of those *inside* the court system who ought to know better—you probably don't anymore. Financial recovery, while not at all guaranteed, is certainly worth the fight. Victims are making financial recovery—from victims'-compensation boards, from insurance companies, from criminals or their accomplices, or from negligent third parties—with increasing frequency and success.

Cullen Bryant, a Texas multimillionaire, was acquitted of murdering his stepdaughter and his wife's lover, despite incredibly strong eyewitness testimony. (He had the best-known lawyer in Texas representing him, Richard "Racehorse" Haynes.) The families then went after his assets, and this time they won in an out-of-court settlement.

Myth #2: If the person who commits the crime isn't convicted, there is no way to make him or her pay monetary damages.

We have two types of courts: civil and criminal. If a defendant pleads or is found guilty, the job of the criminal court is to mete out a sentence in the interests of the public, the criminal, *and the victim.* The job of the civil court is to give victims money for their losses or to provide court orders to correct problems. In the civil courts, the burden of proof is much less. Whereas a defendant must be proved guilty beyond a reasonable doubt in criminal court (and this is how it should be), in a civil court the question is, who is 51 percent right? In cases that are difficult to prove, such as rapes and molestation, the civil courts may be the *only* place that victims can get justice.

The man who shot President Reagan and gravely wounded his press secretary James Brady was acquitted on the ground of insanity. But Brady and his wife Sarah prevailed in a court ruling in a subsequent civil case, where the court held that the would-be assassin, John Hinckley, Jr., could be liable to damages.

Myth #3: All criminals are poor, so there is no reason to try to collect.

What an insult to poor people such a statement is! First, being poor does not make you a sinner, any more than being middle class or rich makes you a saint.

The late Frank Carrington, the dean of victims'-rights lawyers, assailed the "myth of uncollectability." Don't listen to people who say that there is no reason to pursue the criminal for money. I'm not saying there is, but I am saying you should look at all options to get money: the criminal's assets, wage garnishment, the assets of aiders and abetters, the possibility of insurance, and future assets that the criminal may collect. Some criminals have lots of assets—your goal should be to make sure they are a lot poorer when you are done with them!

Say goodbye to the myths; let's start looking at the facts.

The Decision to Go to Court

I hope that all needy victims will first avail themselves of financial remedies that are available without the hassle of going to court, such as victim-compensation boards, insurance policies, and government benefits. The issue of filing a lawsuit to obtain financial recovery is much more complex, and one in which you should weigh the pros and cons.

Here are three good reasons to go to court in order to obtain financial compensation.

1. *Financial Needs:* Victims often find themselves with bills, lost wages, and stolen property, all taken from them by a criminal act. Economic necessity alone may cause victims to seek financial recovery.

2. *Regaining control:* Victims often feel that they have completely lost control of their lives. Going through the judicial process often helps victims bring a sense of order back to their lives.

3. *Accountability.* The criminal-justice system may fail to enforce adequate measures against perpetrators. In such situations, financial sanctions can at least partially remedy the situation and bring accountability to the actions of criminals, and to negligent third parties as well (see the next chapter).

Here are three good reasons *not* to go to court:

1. *Physical and Recovery:* Because the basis of recovery is the amount of damages, victims may consciously or unconsciously not want to work toward emotional recovery or physical rehabilitation, in order to show the jury how bad things are.

2. *Time:* The courts are painfully slow. Be prepared for several winters of discontent before your case is concluded.

3. *Winning and collecting:* You have to win, and you have to collect the money. Your lawyer can guide you in this area, but the best he or she can do is give you the odds; there is no certainty.

The decision of whether to proceed is yours and your family's. Don't ask your barber whether you need a haircut. Don't ask your lawyer whether to go to court.

Obtaining Restitution

There is an alternative to filing a lawsuit yourself: a judge may be able to deal with your financial losses while sentencing the criminal. Included in the sentence can be a judicial order that the convicted criminal make restitution to the victim.

This is how restitution works. After agreeing to plead guilty, or being found guilty, the defendant will receive a sentence from the judge. Hoping for a lighter sentence, the defendant may agree to pay back the victim. Even if the defendant doesn't want to compensate the victim, the judge can order restitution.

The moment of sentencing is an ideal time for the victim to gain restitution. Many defendants are pleased to agree to pay money, believing they may get less time—or no time—in jail. The order of restitution means that victims will not have to go through a civil proceeding to get their money. The sentence and the restitution are tied together in one package.

But having an order of restitution means that you are only partway there; you still have to get the money! The next step is putting liens on assets, garnisheeing wages, or asking that the defendant be placed in contempt of court (if he has even some of the money to pay). A lawyer, or the judge's clerk, or the victim/witness advocate, should help you enforce the restitution order.

Several thorough studies of the effectiveness of restitution have been conducted in South Carolina, in New York, in California, and in a multistate survey by the American Bar Association. These studies show that restitution is a lot more common than it used to be and that some district attorneys and judges have conscientiously implemented programs that award victims fairly.

But there's bad news, too. The South Carolina study, conducted by Dr. Dean Kilpatrick of the Medical College of South Carolina, demonstrates that only 22 percent of guilty pleas or verdicts contained an order of restitution, and only 10 percent of crime victims in cases with guilty defendants actually received *any* money from the perpetrator. So restitution is still (1) usually not ordered, and (2) when ordered, usually not paid.

The California and New York studies found that restitution was frequently not provided for, even in many cases where it clearly should have been; and that restitution, when it is ordered, varies considerably from one court to another.

Today, twenty-seven states and the federal government *require* restitution if there is no jail time (and some even if there is), unless the judge states reasons why such an order is not appropriate. Unfortunately, in many American counties, the courts are not only failing in a moral sense to help victims, but are also circumventing the law. As these studies show, they are not even *trying* to obtain restitution for the victims in their courtrooms.

Victims want restitution. The South Carolina study found that over 90 percent of victims believe they are entitled to it. All that is needed now is for the court systems to catch up: for judges, district attorneys, and their staffs to turn restitution from a good idea into a consistent reality.

The sad truth is that many offenders don't believe the judges take restitution seriously. While many offenders are not well off financially, the New York study found that 92 percent of probation departments felt offenders usually or always had the financial resources to pay *something*. Interestingly, the American Bar Association found—and the other studies support this finding—that the most important reason offenders don't pay is that *they believe they won't be punished* by the courts.

Meanwhile, some judges and some victims are leading the way toward greater restitution. A few years ago in Virginia, a girl was killed by a drunk driver. The child's parents agreed to settle their financial claim against the driver after he promised to write a check for one dollar per week, every week, until their daughter would have been eighteen. This couple, aware of the frequency of repeat offenses by drunk drivers, felt it was the best way of reminding the man of his crime and preventing him from committing it again. In early 1989, the payments stopped; in 1990 the parents went to court with a motion for contempt. Seeking to show that his orders for restitution had teeth, the judge sentenced the man to a year in jail. The case is now on appeal.

Here's another important court ruling. In a child-molestation case in California, the defendant was ordered to pay the child's counseling fees. Later, without any notice to the victim's family, a judge terminated the defendant's financial obligation. The child's family appealed, and the higher court ruled in favor of the victim. The California "Victims' Bill of Rights" requires notice to the victim in advance of a hearing.

Is restitution unfair to criminals who are poor? Absolutely not. It gives the criminals the opportunity to work and pay off their crime, rather than sitting in jail living off the taxpayers, while the victim gets nothing. By acting as a reminder to the defendant, restitution may deter future criminal activity, especially if the defendant is a nonviolent offender or a kid who made a dumb mistake.

Restitution can be made to work. For example, no defendant should be released on probation or parole until the court is satisfied that he or she has made all restitution economically possible. The federal courts use such a system now. Another workable approach is wage garnishment: money is deducted from the defendant's paycheck and sent directly from the employer either to the court or to the victim. Under such circumstances, defendants cannot stop paying even if they wanted to. Wage garnishment has long been used to repay bank loans and is now a more frequently used tool to enforce child-support payments; yet it is used rarely to redress obligations owed to crime victims. One of the goals of this book is to encourage the widespread use of wage garnishment as a means of restitution.

Restitution is no substitute for prison terms resulting from crimes of violence. Violent criminals belong behind bars, where they cannot again prey upon law-abiding citizens.

Suing the Defendant

Restitution is one way of getting money from the criminal. The other is a lawsuit. Some defendants have money; others have applicable insurance coverage. It's only fair that victims and their families be first in line to recover.

The following examples illustrate the success of victims in getting financial compensation from the perpetrator.

Suing a spouse: Some cases sound as if they came straight from hell. A Louisiana doctor was accused of drugging his own minor children, then sexually molesting them. The children were allowed to bring a lawsuit against him, and so was his former wife.

As part of preserving the family unit, courts used to prohibit spouses from suing one another. But shocking acts of violence have caused a reassessment in the past two decades. For example, courts in Mississippi and Wisconsin ended the old doctrine of wife-husband immunity. In one case, the wife was brutally assaulted; in the other, she was murdered. The woman and the murdered woman's family were allowed to sue to get the asets of the husbands.

(Remember, previously I mentioned that judges can overrule earlier case law. Future courts are not bound unto eternity to follow earlier decisions. In the above cases, the Mississippi and Wisconsin courts decided that husband-wife immunity was out-of-date, at least when it comes to violent crime. So they overruled their judicial forebears and changed the law.)

Suing for sexual abuse: Health providers who sexually assault their patients have been sued successfully. In California, two mothers who found their children had been sexually molested by the psychologist treating them prevailed in a civil-liability case.

There is increasing publicity about professionals of all types who use their position to leverage their adult patients or clients into forced sex. Because of the emotional harm often done to the client, damages are needed to pay for counseling and other readjustments, and professionals usually have assets. Furthermore, there is nothing like a highly publicized lawsuit to deter other professionals from engaging in similar criminal conduct.

In Texas a few years ago, a teenage girl sued her stepfather, a wealthy rancher. For years, he had forced her to have sex with him. If she wanted to go to cheerleading practice, for example, she would have to perform a sex act with him. After years of abuse, she sued; the jury decided in her favor and gave her his ranch.

The statute of limitations—the period of time after a crime or tort (a wrongdoing) that an aggrieved party has to file suit—may be a barrier to adults who seek civil liability for molestation they suffered as children. Minors usually have until the beginning of their adulthood, age eighteen, before the statute of limitations begins to run. While many victims of abuse decide that their lives would not be improved by a lawsuit, others feel that such a course of action is necessary. Molestation victims may not realize what happened—or the impact of such trauma—until much later in life.

For that reason, California now permits some victims to wait until age twenty-eight to assert their rights, for sexual abuse that occurred as children. Other states may be following suit. A Virginia law permits child sexual-abuse victim to sue within two years after they *realize* the damage they have suffered, so long as they file by age twenty-eight. A Supreme Court of New Jersey opinion broadens the opportunity of child-molestation victims to sue after reaching adulthood.

And don't forget the *people behind the crime*. Consider the aider and abbetter, such as the friend who hands over the weapon; the coconspirator, who doesn't participate in the actual crime but who helps plan it; or the mastermind, the professional criminal who stays behind the scenes so that only the stooge gets caught. All can be held liable for damages.

One such mastermind was Tom Metzger, the leader of the racist White Aryan League, who encouraged his young skinhead followers to terrorize African-Americans and Jews. In Oregon, the estate of a young Ethiopian sued both the boys who killed him, and also Metzger. Represented by the brilliant lawyer Morris Dees, who had earlier put the Alabama Klan out of business with a lawsuit (an all-white Alabama jury awarded the mother of a black murder victim $7 million), the plaintiff won $10 million, which silenced this merchant of hate.

Getting the Assets

Go hunting where the ducks are. Determine whether your perpetrator (1) has assets, (2) is covered by insurance whose policy may cover what happened, or (3) will get assets. If the results are negative, turn to the next chapter, on third-part liability.*

1. Finding the Assets:

In every area of crime, some of the violators have assets. (Burglars, for example, may be part-timers while holding a legitimate job.) Although some types of crime are more likely to have defendants who have assets, any type of criminal could have assets worth going after.

Chris Edmunds of the National Victim Center, coauthor of *Legal Remedies for Crime Victims Against Perpetrators* (1992), the best handbook available in this area, has grouped the crimes in which recovery is most likely into three areas, referring to them as the three C's:

• *Concealed crimes,* most commonly child molestation, in which the perpetrator violates someone who does not yet know that a crime has been committed;

• *Concealable crimes,* most commonly domestic violence, in which the victim may have to weigh a number of factors, including her family's security and her own, before she presses charges; and

• *Covered-up crimes,* most commonly acquaintance rape, in which the perpetrator usually claims consent and the victim may be left with the difficult and painful choice of whether to prosecute.

Each of these crimes is frequently committed by a person with money and a community reputation; in short, with a hell of a lot to lose. Some may pay damages very quickly for fear of losing a publicized civil case. Others will deny the allegations forever, and the case may well turn out to be one person's word against another's.

The choice of terms above for the 3 C's is not accidental. Only recently have such crimes been taken seriously by society. But they

---

*Recognize that chapters 5 and 6 deal with lawsuits, which can permit large recoveries. Don't forget all the options in chapter 4—crime-victim compensation boards, employer benefits, your own insurance—where recovery may be more likely, but whose benefits may be less than your losses.

remain difficult to prove, and victims should consult both a lawyer and a counselor before embarking on what may be a very difficult course of action. But at least today, in the 1990s, people will listen.

2. Going After the Insurance:

Sometimes the perpetrator has coverage that will pay for the victim's losses, especially in cases involving automobile accidents, homeowner liability, and professional malpractice.

Car insurance most commonly applies in situations of drunk driving; most of the time, the drunk driver will have car insurance. Someone else's car insurance might also apply. For example, if a teenager is driving his father's car while drunk, in many states his father's insurance can also be tapped, under the legal theory that he was negligent to entrust his car to an irresponsible driver. In addition, as pointed out in Chapter 1, the victim's uninsured- or underinsured-motorist coverage could provide funds.

Homeowner's insurance generally excludes intentional acts, but many judges now say that homeowner's insurance must pay the damages if *the injury was not intended,* even though the act was intentional. In a Louisiana case, a man named Schexnider was visiting the home of his friend McGuill. McGuill playfully gave Schexnider an "unpremeditated short jab," causing massive damage to his friend's cheekbones. The court held that McGuill's homeowner's policy should pay for his friend's injury. Although McGuill obviously intended to hit Schexnider, he did not intend to injure him.

In a case where a black cadet had been hazed and assaulted by white cadets, a South Carolina court held that the plaintiff could reach the homeowners' insurance of the parents of the defendants. Even though homeowner's insurance excludes "intentional acts" from coverage, the law in South Carolina requires that both the acts causing the injury and the injury itself be intentional.

The more common approach, however, is to deny coverage when the defendant committed the act intentionally. In Wisconsin, three men, in the process of holding up a store, shot and killed the clerk. The fourth conspirator, a man named Moe, stayed in the car, then drove the other three away with the loot. The clerk's father sued to collect under Moe's homeowner's policy. The jury ruled for the father, deciding that, although Moe was part of the conspiracy that caused the clerk's death, he had not intended for the clerk to be killed. But a higher court reversed the decision, ruling that homeowner's policies were never intended to cover conspirators in criminal behavior.

But if an act that harms someone is done in self-defense—ordered a Florida court—the act is not "intentional," and the homeowner's insurance policy must pay for the damages.

Victims sometimes have recourse against malpractice policies of health providers or other professionals. After a New York doctor sedated and raped a hospital patient, the judge ruled that the hospital's malpractice policy applied.

3. Tracking Future Assets:

If you are poor now, do you want to stay that way? Neither does the criminal. There are many ways for someone who doesn't have money to get it. One is the old-fashioned way to get rich: *inherit* it. Another is the newfangled way: *win the lottery*. Don't laugh—a criminal in California did just that, and the victims went after the winnings.

And how about *bail money*. It's funny how so many people with apparently no assets seem to come up with cash bonds to get out of jail. Once posted, this money resides with the court until the trial is over. Petition the court to hold the money and then turn it over to you!

Then there are criminals who *win lawsuits*. Hardly a week went by when I was attorney general of West Virginia that I wasn't served with papers by some prisoner who sued the state over unsafe conditions, or over access to the jailhouse lawyer, or over his allotment of cigarettes, or over a dozen other things. I can't think of any who won during my watch, but I have read about many who did in other states. If the prisoner wins a suit for damages over living conditions, or for any matter whatsoever, that money should immediately be up for grabs, with the victim getting first crack at it.

A few criminals try to get rich by *writing a book* about their exploits. More than forty states passed laws that allow *victims* to obtain payment from the book or movie. These "Son of Sam" laws—named after the notorious New York serial killer—were aimed at preventing the criminal from cashing in on crime.

The Son of Sam law worked for the benefit of a New York widow in a 1990 jury verdict. A decade ago, Jack Abbott, a convicted murderer in a Utah prison, wrote a book of such literary merit that Norman Mailer and other top writers pressed for his early

release, which was granted. Barely two weeks out of prison,
Abbott stabbed a young New York City waiter to death. Back in
prison, he wrote a second book, *My Return*. In the book, he
audaciously suggested that he killed the young man because the
latter "showed disrespect." The victim's widow sued, and, a decade
after the crime, won the proceeds of the book. But her victory was
short-lived.

Unfortunately, the Son of Sam laws were declared illegal in 1991.
The book publishing and movie industries—both ever willing to
exploit violent crime for megabucks—challenged this law, claiming rights of freedom of speech under the First Amendment. The
United States Supreme Court agreed, ruling the New York Son of
Sam law unconstitutional. The Court invited New York and other
states to go back to the drawing board and write a better law.

In light of this ruling, lawyers in the victims'-rights movement
have recommended that states draw up laws to say that victims
would have the right to sue criminals who got rich in *any* fashion:
inheritance, lottery, lawsuits, *or* through writing.

We could design a system in this country, built around restitution, where criminals, at the time of sentencing, would be obli-
gated to reimburse their victims and would not be permitted to
get out from under this obligation through bankruptcy. The
courts would automatically intercede to help victims with financial recovery. We have made great strides toward developing such
a system, and in the decade of the 1990s, I think we can complete
it—and make it work in all courts.

But we aren't there yet. So remember, if you are a victim, you
have the right to sue to recover what you lost. However, under
today's rules, you will have to come forward and fight for just and
fair compensation.

Choosing Your Lawyer

Many people have been denied justice because they chose the
wrong lawyer. Look for lawyers with reputations as "trial lawyers."
Cases to establish third-party liability, or to pinpoint liability on
the party with insurance or deep pockets, are beyond the ca-
pability of many lawyers. Try to find a lawyer who specializes in

personal-injury cases, or has a strong background in the field of victims' rights.

Two organizations are worth mentioning here. One is the Coalition of Victims' Attorneys and Consultants (COVAC). This informal network, begun by the late Frank Carrington and Anne Seymour of the National Victim Center, keeps up with developments on victims'-rights law in all the states. The organization will refer you to a lawyer in your state who belongs to the COVAC network and who stays abreast of developments in victims'-rights law. COVAC is now run directly by the National Victim Center; if you would like a referral, call NVC at (703)276-2880, or write to 2111 Wilson Boulevard, Suite 300, Arlington, VA 22201.

The Association of Trial Lawyers of America (ATLA) is the nation's premier organization of lawyers who specialize in representing the "little guy." This organization, with chapters in every state and over 100,000 members, conducts a wide variety of training programs for its members. You can contact the national office in Washington, D.C., at (202)965-3500, to get the names of ATLA lawyers in your community. Or write ATLA at 1050 31st Street, N.W., Washington, D.C. 20007.

Look for three traits in a lawyer: (1) talent and experience, (2) an indication that this case is important to the lawyer, and (3) good chemistry between you and the lawyer.

Experience:
Find out the type of cases this lawyer has tried. Even if he or she is a member of COVAC or ATLA, ask about the lawyer's area of specialization and the successes obtained in that area. As mentioned above, you probably want a lawyer who has done personal-injury or "little guy's" civil litigation.

Hard work:
Mark Twain said it best: "The harder I work, the luckier I get." Does this lawyer indicate a willingness to work hard for you? Sometimes the young and hungry lawyer will beat the older one who sees this one as just another case.

Your relationship:
My father, a doctor in Mansfield, Ohio, had a successful family medical practice for almost fifty years. A major reason people

kept going to him was that he would spend time talking to them, showing a sincere interest in them and their lives. Such a style also made my dad a better doctor; the more he knew about his patients, the better he could diagnose them. Pick a lawyer for this reason, too. To win, cooperation is the key to digging out all the facts and presenting them in the courtroom. Indeed, if a lawyer cannot communicate successfully with you, how well do you think he or she can talk to a jury?

For an important case—and if it is *your* case, it is important— try to interview three or four lawyers. For a personal-injury matter, many lawyers do not charge for an initial interview; others may charge only a small fee.

What will a lawyer cost? Maybe nothing up front. In the American system of justice, lawyers frequently take cases on a contingency basis. If so, you might pay nothing if the lawyer recovers nothing. (However, lawyers may charge you for their out-of-pocket costs, such as travel and deposition fees, whether or not they recover anything.) If the lawyer recovers money, he or she keeps a percentage, often one-third.

The lawyer will probably give you a contract, or "retainer agreement," to sign. The contract should state both the fee and the work the lawyer is to do for you; make sure you understand both. Feel free to suggest changes and to take it home and read it. (Be suspicious of a lawyer who pushes you to sign it right then and there.)

Willie Keeler, an early baseball star in the period before players hit many home runs, said the secret to his high batting average was that "I hit 'em where they ain't." Good lawyers are equally creative in finding ways to recover for injuries. Like Willie Keeler, their batting average depends on their skill in finding holes in the other team's defense.

CHAPTER 6

See If Others Are Liable

During the last ten years, judges and juries across the nation have granted sizable cash awards to victims based on third-party liability.

Third-party liability exists when a person or company that is not actually the criminal is responsible, directly or indirectly, for the victim's injury. Because this party had no intent to cause harm to the victim, there is no question of guilt in a criminal sense. But even though the third party (so called because he is neither the victim nor the criminal) may not have acted criminally, liability exists and money is owed because the third party failed in a legal duty to *protect* the victim.

Most third-party liability cases fall into the category of what we commonly call *tort* law. "Tort" is a Medieval English and French word for *"wrong."* In American law, a tort occurs when someone:

1. has a duty to protect you—that is, should act in a prudent manner in circumstances that affect you; and
2. is negligent—that is, fails to exercise reasonable care or precaution—and you are harmed as a result.

Both parts must be proved: the third party must have that duty to the victim and must have acted negligently, causing the victim harm.

In a common example of a tort, a shopping mall is open at night, but fails to provide adequate lighting in its outdoor parking lot, or to hire guards for the outside premises. A woman is assaulted one night in the mall's parking lot, an action that probably would not have taken place if the area had been properly lit and if security patrols had been making regular rounds. In most states, the victim may sue the company that operates the mall. The company and its employees did not want the customer to be a victim of a crime, so it could not be charged with a criminal act. But the mall owes a duty to its customers during business hours. So the victim can take the mall to civil court and win damages, if she can prove that, as a customer, she had the right to expect adequate security, and that the mall's failure to live up to its duty contributed to the crime. On the other hand, if a couple parks their car in the parking lot long after the closing hour, the mall would probably have no liability because it would not expect its customers to be present then.

An alternative avenue to third-party liability is *contract* law. Let's say you buy a burglar alarm, and the company installs it. You are given a one-year warranty. One night, when you are away, a burglar breaks in, and the alarm malfunctions. You can bring a lawsuit to recover the value of your stolen property against the burglar-alarm company because it contracted with you to provide an alarm that would work. Again, intent does not matter. Certainly the burglar-alarm company did not want you to be robbed. Regardless of the *intent,* the company has a *duty* to provide a product that lives up to its promise.

This chapter reviews examples of situations in which victims may be able to obtain financial recovery against liable third parties. As discussed previously, you can obtain damages for out-of-pocket losses, expected future losses, and general damages, such as pain and suffering. Once in a while, a jury or judges will tack on an additional amount for *punitive damages,* if there is evidence that the third party acted so recklessly and irresponsibly that it should be punished—as a message to that company and others.

In discussing legal cases, we need to remember four points:

1. *Laws vary from one state to another.* An Illinois court may determine that it doesn't like the way a certain issue was decided in New Jersey or Tennessee, and may therefore rule differently. Every state may write and interpret its laws individually, within the boundaries of federal law and the United States Constitution. So just because a victim's case was raised and defeated in one state doesn't mean the result will be the same in another.

For example, in the past, most states did not hold a restaurant or bar liable if it served an intoxicated person who then caused a car wreck. Illinois, however, took a different position decades ago. In recent years, courts in most states that addressed the issue have agreed with Illinois, that "serving one for the road" has produced countless victims of drunk driving. Increasingly, victims have been winning cash awards against establishments that serve alcohol to intoxicated patrons.

2. *Laws can be changed by legislatures and by the people.* If the Supreme Court of Arizona or Minnesota rules that shopping malls are not responsible for the safety of their parking lots, the legislature can change the law to make shopping malls liable.

In Maryland, for example, a teenage girl was raped by a custodian in her local synagogue. Besides their concern about severe emotional harm to the child, the parents wanted to know whether the rapist had AIDS. But Maryland law stated that the defendant's blood, and the existence or nonexistence of AIDS, is a matter of personal privacy. As a result, the girl's parents were legally prevented from discovering this crucial information. In 1992 the Maryland legislature removed this obstacle for future victims by requiring that a rapist's blood sample be tested and the results given to the victim.

3. *Courts can and do change their minds to reflect community needs and expectations.* Our judges are human beings—members of this society—and, as the movement for the rights of the victim sweeps across the nation, many of them have become more sensitive to the victim's financial needs. Already, courts are more likely to be sympathetic to the victim than they were just five or ten years ago.

For example, the "battered-woman" defense is now looked on with much greater sympathy than in the past. This doctrine permits abused spouses to assert that the killing of their husband (or wife) was committed in self-defense, not only because of what happened that moment, but *because of what had been happening for months or years.* Judges used to rule that self-defense applied only to the moment at hand, but now usually will permit evidence about the history of the relationship. Failure to allow the defense in the past caused Governor Celeste of Ohio and Governor Schaffer in Maryland to grant pardons to a number of women who killed their husbands or boyfriends.

Incidentally, the new rulings on the battered-woman doctrine are probably *more* consistent with the law of self-defense than the older rulings. The law on self-defense is that everyone must try to retreat before resorting to force, but there has never been such a duty to retreat from your own home. So, for the battered spouse *at home,* there really is no place to retreat to.

4. *The law gives only the framework—the facts matter most.* In many of the cases discussed here, a higher court has ruled only that a "cause of action" exists, meaning that if the plaintiff can prove his or her case, he wins. The judges have not said that defendants are automatically liable. Facts are usually—and best—decided by juries. So, just as every plaintiff gets his or her day in court, so does every defendant!

Why would victims pursue a case against a third party when they could simply proceed against the perpetrator? The answer is that if the damages are great, victims need to find parties with adequate insurance, or with deep pockets, to cover their losses. When asked why he robbed banks, Willie Sutton, a much-publicized criminal of the 1950s, replied, "Because that's where the money is." When the financial losses are great, victims also have to go where the money is.

Under certain circumstances, a wide variety of third parties may incur liability.

Hotels and Motels

The Connie Francis case established that hotels and motels must provide a safe and secure environment for their guests. The famous singer was brutally raped and assaulted in her Long Island, New York, hotel room by a man who gained entrance through a defective sliding glass door. She filed suit and, after a highly publicized trial in 1976, the jury awarded her $2,500,000.

The case caused many hotels and motels in America to tighten their security and add deadbolt locks. In winning her suit, Ms. Francis received compensation and—in the process—made hotels a lot safer for the rest of us. A precedent-setting, or breakthrough case often heightens awareness and benefits society as a whole.

Since the Connie Francis case, people robbed or injured by crimes where hotel security was inadequate have prevailed in many states, including California, Florida, North Carolina, and Texas. In one southern state, a *visitor* of a motel guest was raped after leaving a motel lobby. Because of security questions, the judges allowed the case to proceed to the jury.

Hotel and motels are not *automatically* liable when a crime occurs on their premises. Although victims have won judgments against public accommodations facilities, hotels and motels have prevailed many times because they have demonstrated that they had taken all reasonable security precautions.

Landlords

When tenants have provided evidence that inadequate security resulted in a crime, they have been able to win monetary awards against landlords. In Nebraska, Oklahoma, and Pennsylvania, tenants have won cases because assailants entered as a result of defective locks. In Texas, the judgment came about because of a failure to put on a deadbolt lock when requested and, in Missouri, because of a defective window. A landlord was liable in Florida because a rapist took a ladder from an unlocked shed and used it to reach an upper-floor apartment. In a case where the crime was committed by a tenant in the same building, another Florida court ruled that the landlord can be responsible for paying damages to the victim.

If they are victimized owing to lax security, office tenants also have the right to proceed against the landlord, according to recent cases in Illinois and Missouri.

Bars and Restaurants

It is against the law for a bar or restaurant to serve someone who is already intoxicated. Some victims of drunk driving have been able to win money from bars that continued to serve a patron who had too much to drink. These cases, known by the term "dramshop," (an archaic term for "barroom") have become increasingly frequent in recent years.

The message for bars and restaurants has become clear: *if you serve a drunk and he or she causes an accident, then you get sued.* Once a direct threat to their pocketbooks began, many restaurants and bars saw the light, encouraging "designated drivers" and refusing service to intoxicated patrons. Several tavern owners have told me in recent years of their fears, and also acknowledged that the dramshop cases have caused even some of the sleazier joints to clean up their act.

Victims injured by drunk teenage drivers have also looked to deep pockets and have found them in the liquor stores and convenience outlets that have sold booze illegally. And these stores aren't the only ones being held liable. The Connecticut Supreme Court has ruled that adults holding parties in their homes and serving alcohol to minors can be held liable for injuries resulting from reckless driving. Court decisions such as this one may cause more adults to exercise mature judgment when they host a party for teenagers.

Victims injured in bar fights have not fared as well. The courts seem to recognize that bar patrons should not be surprised if a ruckus ensues after an evening of heavy drinking!

Business Premises—Including Parking Lots

Courts are now holding businesses to a fairly strict standard of security for the parking lots and buildings available for their customers or employees. Many crimes occur in parking lots, and the better the security, the fewer crimes people will have to fear in the future. A South Dakota woman was abducted from a hospital parking garage and murdered. The jury awarded her husband $535,000, and the state's supreme court affirmed the jury verdict. An Atlanta woman raped at the rapid transit company's parking lot at night was awarded $250,000. Customers have also succeeded in bring causes of action against a convenience store (California and Louisiana), a restaurant (Florida and Michigan), a bar (New York), and the parking-lot company itself (Missouri).

Employees have been successful, too. In New Orleans, a woman who worked for a television station was abducted from a drugstore parking lot next door, then raped and robbed. She parked there each workday; in exchange for providing free parking for the TV station employees, the drugstore received free publicity. The court held that the drugstore had a duty to provide safe parking for the woman.

Because of the large traffic and diversity of clientele, malls have been held to an especially high standard of security for parking lots—and even restrooms. A physically handicapped man, sodomized in the men's room of a local shopping mall in Iowa, was given the green light to proceed against the mall.

Intentional acts by employees against customers can also result in liability to the employer. The parents of a four-year-old New Jersey boy sued Walt Disney World, alleging that the boy was molested by a Disney employee while the family visited the theme park. An interesting part of the case is that the parents sued Disney World in New Jersey, their home state, instead of in Florida, where the act occurred. The court ruled that if Disney's heavy television advertising in New Jersey enticed the family to visit the theme park, jurisdiction in New Jersey would be allowed. This ruling is helpful to crime victims—often people with limited financial means—who challenge major companies. The cost of traveling to the company's place of operation could, by itself, be an economic barrier to victims asserting their rights.

In Las Vegas, some out-of-town patrons hit a different kind of jackpot, winning $105,000 in a court action against a casino whose security guards violently assaulted them.

But so-called "premises liability" cases, like so many third-party cases filed by victims of crime, are a challenge to win. The victim must prove that the business owner knew, or should have known, of the dangerous environment and had not taken sufficient steps to protect the public.

Employers
Unsafe workplace conditions used to mean that the equipment was a danger to work around. Now it can mean the threat of violence, either from the public or from other employees. Each year between 800 and 1,400 Americans are murdered at work, and thousands more receive nonfatal injuries because of violence. Violence ranges from a shooting rampage by a disgruntled postal worker in Oklahoma to a fired San Diego employee, shooting his superior at his dismissal hearing.

Usually there is only one remedy: workers' compensation. It covers *any* on-the-job injury, including a crime. (Whether the criminal is a fellow employee, a customer, or an intruder is not relevant.) There are very few exceptions. Here is one: a New Mexico court denied benefits to the widow of a man shot while working alone at his place of employment, a loan office, because there were no witnesses, and no one could prove the murder was work related.

The advantage of workers' compensation is that recovery is almost certain. The disadvantage is that the recovery is usually limited to medical bills, lost wages and, in the case of murder, a small death benefit.

Rarely, recovery is allowed in a civil lawsuit, which generally means a higher award. Here are some examples:

• A pizza-parlor waitress was raped because a fellow employee refused to open the safe for robbers. She may now sue her employer, according to a federal court in Colorado.

• A furniture store employee in Virginia, working alone at night, became the rape victim of a frequent customer. She was permitted to proceed against her employer for providing unsafe working conditions.

• A woman hired as a dancer at a West Coast Navy enlisted club was raped. She was allowed to sue the United States Government. (Some people mistakenly believe that the federal government is immune from tort suits, but the Federal Tort Claims Act permits such suits. In a 1989 case, the Supreme Court held that if the government is negligent, willful acts by another party, or by one of its own employees, will not negate the liability of the United States.)

• The produce manager of a supermarket, assaulted by the store's security guards, was held to have a cause of action against the supermarket chain, and the case was returned by the higher court to the lower court for trial.

• In an interesting twist, two federal cases in Illinois have allowed women raped by their bosses to file claims for *employment sex discrimination*. In one of the cases, the woman reported the rape, but her employer insisted that she continue to work with her supervisor.

• A company retreat turned into a nightmare for a Colorado woman when she was assaulted by fellow employees; the court ruled that the employer, as well as the employees, could be liable.

Usually guests of employees, because they are ineligible for workers' compensation, can sue for damages. A guest at a mortgage-company reception in Alaska was assaulted by another guest, and a higher court ruled that the victim would be allowed to sue the company hosting the event, on the grounds of negligence.

Negligent Employment
When an employee commits a crime against other employees or customers, victims have brought cases charging the company with negligence in employing such an individual. Perhaps the most spectacular example was in New York City, where a nine-year-old girl was raped by a city Parks Department employee who had been hired and given access to children despite a *thirty-five-year* record of sex crimes. The girl and her family won a $2,500,000 judgment.

Other cases of negligent employment include:

• A Texas court awarded $5 million to the family of a teenager who had been raped and murdered by an employee at an employment center for the handicapped. The girl was visiting her blind sister at the time. The employee had earlier served time in Mississippi for abduction and murder.

• A Massachusetts neurosurgeon visited the apartment of a female hospital employee, ostensibly to follow up on medical treatment of a head injury. Instead, he raped her. The court ruled that the hospital where they both worked was liable. The activity fell within the definition of medical malpractice because the assailant appeared in his role as a doctor.

• A pest-control employee entered a woman's house, then proceeded to rape her. It turned out that the employee had been given a polygraph test to measure criminal propensities when hired. However, the test was administered improperly. The jury awarded the woman $125,000 from the exterminating company.

• Religious institutions have been held liable, when they knew of the pedophiliac activities of the clergy and did not stop their access to young people. Such lawsuits, tragically, became increasingly frequent in the early 1990s.

Schools and College Campuses
The story of Howard and Connie Clery illustrates the increasing tendency of courts to hold school and colleges responsible for ignoring security concerns.

Their daughter Jeanne, a freshman at an eastern college, was murdered in her dormitory room by a drunken male student, who entered the hallway through a propped-open entrance that was supposed to be locked. After the murder conviction, the Clerys brought a lawsuit against the college, which settled eventually for a large undisclosed sum.

But the Clerys did not stop there. They began an organization in Philadelphia called Security on Campus, aimed at making America's colleges and universities safer. They fought successfully for laws to require colleges to make their crime statistics public and to make available the nature of their security arrangements. President Bush presented the Clerys with an award for their tireless efforts during National Victims Week, 1990.

Parents have also brought successful suits against primary and secondary schools. The courts approved cases against school districts in Los Angeles, where a female teacher molested a student; in Oakland, where a male teacher molested a student who was visiting the teacher's home on school business; in Massachusetts, where a guidance counselor raped a student; and in Pennsylvania, where a student was injured by a teacher's disciplinary action. A child who was raped after being abducted from a school in the nation's capital won a case against the District of Columbia school system.

Teachers injured by students have had a mixed record of being able to sue the school district. A New York court allowed a teacher who had been assaulted several times by students to proceed against the school system, while a different court in the same state rejected a suit by a teacher raped in the ladies' room. Why the difference? Victims'-rights cases are relatively new, and some courts are still trying to figure out how to operate in this area of the law.

Parental Failure to Supervise Children

Here is a tough area of law. It was only after I became a parent that I understood that kids simply won't do what they are told, no matter what you say or how often you say it!

Still, there are extreme cases in which parents have been required to pay damages. Where a custodial parent (1) knew of the dangerous propensity of the child, (2) should have foreseen that the child would hurt someone, and (3) did nothing to prevent him or her from committing the crime, courts have imposed liability. In South Carolina, a man's mentally ill former wife lived with her parents. The father, who had custody of their two children, permitted visits until the woman bought a gun. He finally agreed to visits when the woman's parents said that they couldn't find the gun and that they would be responsible for the boys' well-being during visits. Tragically, she murdered the boys. The court ruled that their father could maintain a lawsuit against his in-laws.

Hawaii has a law that goes further than those of other states. It provides that parents of minor children shall be liable for damages for torts (including crimes) committed by the latter.

Negligent Oversight of Children
When children are abused in situations where they are in someone's custodial care, courts have found ways to provide compensation.

• A young boy in South Carolina was beaten to death by his mother's boyfriend. The subsequent lawsuit charged that caseworkers had prematurely closed an investigation into the child's abuse. The court allowed a case against the local officials but not against the state.

• A North Carolina case tells an even more gruesome story. A man murdered both his natural child and his stepchild after they had reported him for sexually abusing them. The court ruled that the county could be charged with negligence.

• Children who had been sexually and physically abused in a Cincinnati youth home had a civil-rights claim, ruled a federal judge, noting that the children had been committed involuntarily.

• On the flip side, foster parents in Wisconsin were allowed to sue the county welfare agency for failing to warn them about a dangerous child. Shortly after the child came into their custody, he burned down their barn. The court, recognizing the sacrifices that so many foster parents make to help children, said that the least foster parents deserve is a warning if the child has a prior history of violent behavior.

Negligent Entrustment
The doctrine of negligent entrustment is based on two concepts. First, the victim must have been injured (or killed) by a "dangerous instrumentality," most commonly a weapon or a car. Second, the person who gave the gun or weapon to the lawbreaker must have been negligent in doing so, by realizing that there was a likelihood of illegal or injurious use.

In a New York case, two men, Shim and Bumpus, got into an argument. Shim shouted to his girlfriend to get his gun out of the car; she did so, and Shim shot Bumpus. Bumpus won a case against the girlfriend: she was at fault for getting the gun.

Drunk-driving cases often result in negligent-entrustment cases. All courts, I believe, should be willing to nail car owners who let an intoxicated friend drive their car, but Virginia's Supreme Court recently let such an individual "off the hook."

Negligent entrustment requires both negligence and entrustment. Some courts—wrongly, in my opinion—have permitted cases against car-rental companies or other car owners simply because the driver had an accident. The more enlightened rule is that the owner must have been negligent—such as in knowing that the driver has a record of driving drunk or driving recklessly. With such an airtight rule, we discourage wrongdoers and their negligent accomplices.

Gun Dealers

Federal and state law governs the sale of weapons. All states prohibit the sale to felons, minors, and the mentally ill. Some states require a waiting period or background check. If a gun dealer fails to follow federal or state law and wrongfully sells a gun to someone who is not qualified to buy, the dealer has been held liable for damages for the injuries inflicted by the buyer.

Courts have not, however, held gun manufacturers liable for the weapons they make. There was one exception, Maryland, where the state's highest court held the maker of Saturday-night specials liable, but the state legislature quickly wrote a law overturning that opinion.

Manufacturers of Defective Products

Some products, such as burglar alarms and chemical Mace, are marketed as crime-prevention devices. If they fail to perform, the manufacturer can be held liable.

A woman raped at an Illinois hotel was allowed to sue the manufacturer of a Mace-type self-defense chemical because the substance proved ineffective in stopping the perpetrator. When a burglar alarm failed in New York, the burglars entered, assaulted the occupant, and stole $150,000 worth of valuables. The family had signed a contract with the installers limiting damages, but the court held that the limit would be invalid if the installers were guilty of "gross negligence." The premises of a business in Texas was burned to the ground by burglars after the alarm failed to work. The business sued the telephone company, which had a contract to service the alarm system, on the grounds of deceptive trade practices. The jury returned a verdict for $911,000.

Former and Current Mental Patients

When a mental patient is released and then commits a crime, the first question is whether the victim was the specific object of the perpetrator or was simply picked at random. When the victim is a target whom the patient had identified and threatened, some states, including California, impose a duty on the health provider to warn the potential victim.

In the 1976 case of *Tarasoff* v. *University of California Board of Regents*, the California Supreme Court ruled that when a mental patient indicates intention to harm a specific person and then is released, the counselor and the hospital have a duty to warn the prospective victim. In that case, a young man told his psychiatrist that he intended to kill Tatania Tarasoff, a student, when she returned from a summer study program in Brazil. Amazingly, the man was released, and neither the young woman nor her parents were told of the threat or of his release. Two months later, true to his word, he killed her.

The courts do not agree in cases in which the violent act of a former mental patient is committed against a victim picked at random. The question of whether someone is so inherently dangerous that he or she should remain institutionalized is often a difficult one. Courts in Colorado and Delaware have given victims the right to sue in such a situation, but courts in Michigan and South Carolina have ruled the other way.

The failure of a doctor to commit a dangerous person to a mental hospital resulted in legal action in Wisconsin. A woman whom the physician refused to commit then killed herself intentionally in a car accident. Her daughter, riding in the car beside her, suffered serious injuries and ended up a quadriplegic. The Wisconsin courts gave the daughter the right to sue.

Courts in California and Kentucky have allowed suits by patients injured by other patients. A Connecticut court allowed a suit by a patient against the hospital after she was raped by an employee.

Former Prisoners

Civil liability can also serve as a deterrent. If state parole and corrections officials are held accountable in cases of gross neglect, they may weigh release and furlough procedures more carefully. In Mississippi, a court ruled that a suit brought by a man shot and made a quadriplegic by a parolee could proceed if the facts in the case demonstrated gross negligence on the part of the parole board. Cases against the state for negligent parole or release of a prisoner remain difficult, but the door has been opened, and future courts may follow the Mississippi example.

Victims may sue the state when an *escaped* prisoner causes injury, according to a recent Michigan decision.

Police Failure to Protect the Victim

In cases where the police fail to protect the victim, the general rule is that law-enforcement officers have a duty to the public, not to any individual. So a victim cannot sue an officer of the law unless the victim had a "special relationship" with the officer or the department. An example would be someone whom the police had promised to protect, such as a key witness, or someone whose calls for help were simply ignored.

In Connecticut, Tracey Furman was horribly beaten by her husband after trying repeatedly to get her local police department to keep him away from her. Her successful lawsuit against the city of Torrington resulted in broad changes in Connecticut law—and a dramatic reversal of police attention to battered women.

But in Kansas City, Kansas, a family has not been successful. Here a cousin of the father raped an eight-year-old girl and, when her parents went to the police, they begged for immediate action, pointing out that the cousin was abusive both to them and to a next-door neighbor. The police in neighboring Kansas City, Missouri, where the crime occurred, ignored their constant pleas, calling the man to take a lie-detector test (which he refused), then telephoning him to tell him he was under arrest and should come to the station so the police would not have to serve him in person. Instead, he went to the family's home, killed the little girl, severely burned her little brother, shot the father in the eye, and then took his own life. Despite the officers' failure to come out and arrest the man for the statutory rape, the court held the police officers and the city immune from suit.

A different case in Kansas City, Kansas, had a different result. Here a woman's husband, who assaulted her regularly, was a police officer. Even though she got an order of protection, the police allegedly took no action to ensure her safety. She was allowed to sue the city police department.

In rural Troy, New York, a woman got a court order against her husband, but the sheriff's department did not serve the order

Examples of Third-Party Liability	
Liable Third Party	Circumstance of Liability*
Hotels, motels	Inadequate security
Landlords	Inadequate security
Malls	Inadequate security in parking areas or other common areas
Bars, restaurants	Serving an intoxicant or a person under 21
Liquor stores, convenience stores	Selling to an intoxicant or a person under 21
Parking-lot owners	Inadequate security
Business premises	Inadequate security or violence by employees
Employers	Negligence in hiring or failure to supervise
Schools, colleges	Inadequate security or failure to warn
Providers of children's services	Negligence in hiring or failure to supervise
Parental liability	Knowledge of dangerous propensity of, and custody of, minor child
Negligent entrustment	Giving dangerous instrumentality (gun, car) to reckless person or criminal
Gun dealers	Disregarding law when selling weapon
Crime-prevention devices	Defective product or improper installation
Prisons, parole boards, mental hospitals	Failure to warn a likely victim, or gross negligence in decision to release, or in allowing escape
Health providers	Negligence in hiring, or inadequate security, violence by employees
Law-enforcement officials	Failure to protect
The media	Reckless practices that facilitate the crime.

*Victims must prove (a) that a duty is owed to them by the third party, and (b) negligence by the third party.

upon him. The deputies were notified that he had returned to the house, but did not intervene, and the woman was murdered. The court ruled that the woman's estate could sue the county and prevail, provided that it could prove that the sheriff's department owed a special duty to the woman because of her request.

The Media

These days you may be able to beat city hall, but it seems that you can never beat the all-powerful media. Here are two interesting exceptions:

A woman returned to her Maryland apartment and discovered that her roommate had been murdered. Then, after seeing the killer, she escaped and was able to describe him to the police. Despite a request to protect her identity, the newspaper published her name. The courts allowed her to proceed in a case against the newspaper.

In another case, *Soldier of Fortune* magazine was held liable for reckless acts. The magazine published the advertisement of a hired killer looking for business. He was hired subsequently by a man in Bryan, Texas, to murder his wife, and he carried out his deadly mission. A Texas jury awarded damages of over $4 million to the woman's surviving son and to her mother against the magazine for its irresponsible actions.

A word of caution, similar to that voiced near the start of Chapter 5, is appropriate here: *whether* to proceed to court involves two very different types of factors. One is legalistic: whether you can win, how much you can win, and whether you can collect. The other is subjective: whether civil litigation will help your recovery, whether you wish to commit the time needed for litigation, and whether litigation is consistent with the emotional and spiritual needs of you and your family.

The next section of the book deals with rights and remedies for individual crimes.

Part IV

Crimes: Special Advice for Victims and Their Families

CHAPTER 7

Crimes Against Children

The primary cause of crime in America is also the worst crime in America: child abuse. The fact that prisons are full of child-abuse victims should come as no surprise. Imagine a child terrorized in the one place where the feeling of security should be absolute: the home. If the home, and those who live with the child, create a terrorized state rather than a safe haven, it is not surprising that some adult survivors wreak their vengeance on their own children, or on others in society. Therefore, fighting child abuse must be the top priority of any crime-fighting effort.

Fortunately, many adult survivors of child abuse break the cycle and become stable, law-abiding citizens.

The horror of child abuse is not in the numbers, although even the conservative statistics are terrifying. Whether it is one in forty children, or one in six, who is abused, no one really knows. Child abuse, especially child sexual abuse, is the easiest felony to conceal, and it remains woefully underreported.

Rather, the horror of child abuse is in each individual case: the shocking reality that a person entrusted with the child's care has physically or sexually attacked someone who can neither fight back nor report the crime, and who will probably carry the scars forever, either on the outside or on the inside.

Definition of the Crime

Child abuse occurs when a caretaker takes action that causes injury to the child. Child abuse can be physical, sexual, or emotional. To be considered abuse, the crime must be committed by a person entrusted with the care of the child, such as the parent, step-parent, adult relative, paramour of the parent, baby-sitter, or, in certain situations, day-care provider, teacher, or minister.

If the act is committed by someone other than a caretaker, it is considered a different crime from child abuse, such as felonious assault or sexual assault.

Child neglect is the willful failure to provide for a young child's needs by the caretaker.

Child kidnapping is usually divided into two categories: stranger abductions and family abductions. The first category—what we traditionally think of as kidnapping—is statistically rare but is terrifying because the stranger is likely to harm the child. The second category—family abduction—is the taking of the child by the parent who does not have lawful custody, or a secreting of the child by the custodial parent in violation of a court order permitting visitation by the other parent. Such situations are classified as kidnapping in some states, while others view it as a lesser form of child abduction.

The law gives special protection to children in the area of sexual crimes and morals. *Statutory rape* is sexual intercourse between an adult and a child. It is called "statutory" because it is rape by legal definition, the minor being by law unable to give consent to sexual activity. Whether the child resisted doesn't matter. The age of consent varies: it is fourteen in Arkansas and sixteen in West Virginia. (There is an exception if the adult is close in age to the child. The age difference must be at least two years in Arkansas and four years in West Virginia.)

Child sexual assault includes vaginal or rectal penetration, whether by a penis, a finger, or an inanimate object. Lesser degrees of sexual assault cover other forms of unsolicited feeling or touching. Sexual assault, then, includes rape as well as these other activities. All states have modernized their laws to cover these activities other than rape.

Child molestation is a term for child sexual assault.

Child prostitution refers to bringing children into a sex-for-hire scheme.

Child pornography refers to pictures, films, or written material that emphasizes a child's sexual parts. In some states, violators of the law must participate in the procuring, photographing, or distribution of the pornography in order to be convicted. In other states, knowingly possessing child pornography is itself a crime. Although mere possession of adult pornography is not a crime, child pornography is treated differently because it can be used to entice the child into thinking that such activity is okay.

Contributing to the delinquency of a minor is a lesser offense than the above crimes. It covers enticing a minor into activities that she or he would not otherwise be permitted to do, such as sexual activity, alcohol, or illegal drugs. A minor normally is someone under the age of eighteen, although serving alcoholic beverages to someone under twenty-one is now illegal in all states.

The Aftermath—Living with the Crime

Child abuse and other crimes against children require a response at all levels—by the parents and the extended family, by the community, and by the system of justice.

First and foremost, the child needs professional counseling. The event must be dealt with by the child immediately or at some time in the future. Adult survivors of child abuse often realize that, like all matters of cognitive dissonance (an event that is so totally inconsistent with other aspects of life that it cannot rationally be dealt with), that reality must be integrated into the rest of their life or distanced from it.

If you have neither insurance nor the funds yourself, go to the state victim-compensation board and ask it to pay for counseling for the child. See Chapter 4 on this procedure. Sometimes the board will pay only after the bill is incurred (and all states except New York and Washington have a maximum they will pay). If so, look for a counselor who is willing to wait to get paid.

Second, the family also needs lots of support. Parents may need professional counseling or may want to get involved in a self-help session composed of those who have had a similar trauma in their families.

All kinds of new events may enter the lives of the families of child victims. The media may be helpful, or not—see Chapter 1 on dealing with the media. The closest at hand—family and friends—may be the greatest source of help in your hour of need. Someone in your life may well surprise you with his or her ability to assist you through the first stages. (Of course, the family member—or the whole family—may be the problem. In that case, it is even more important to turn to friends, counselors, and clergy.)

Third, contact the victim-assistance program in your county. The victim-assistance representative, located in either the prosecutor's office, the police department, or a separate agency, is assigned to help victims of crime. The office can be your gatekeeper to services available and to the criminal-justice system. See Chapter 1 for more information.

Fourth, look to victims'-rights groups that specialize in helping child victims and their families. The 1980s witnessed an outpouring of support for victims of child abuse and their families. Existing organizations expanded, and new ones sprang up to help families deal with the tragedy of the crime.

The groups are of many types. Some are local self-help groups. Others are composed of professionals who specialize in counseling and helping victims. Still others are advocacy oriented: they work on improving community response, changing the laws, and reducing crime. The chart on the next page lists some of the national organizations dedicated to helping abused children. To find a group to help you, talk to your victim-assistance representative or contact one of these groups for help. Their addresses and telephone numbers are listed in Directory B.

Dealing with the Justice System

The child victim has special needs that, regrettably, our system of justice has only recently begun to address. The criminal-justice system for child victims, especially victims of sexual crimes, presents excruciating challenges for parents. Some of these problems are being dealt with sympathetically in some American courts. Fortunately, programs to address crimes against children are starting to claim greater societal resources and sensitivity.

Protecting children is a function of both criminal and civil courts in every state. The civil courts deal with issues of custody, removal of a child from a home, and restriction of access to the child by an alleged abuser. The criminal courts investigate and prosecute alleged violators of the law.

People with knowledge of child abuse should report it to the child-welfare agency in their state. Certain people, because of their profession, are *required* to report any child abuse that they suspect. If they don't report what they discover or notice, they can be prosecuted. These people are called "mandatory reporters" and include all health providers, counselors, teachers, and day-care providers. (Even if a doctor or therapist finds out about the child abuse in the context of a physician-patient privilege, he or she must report it.) The mandatory-reporter law now exists in every state.

All reports of child abuse are kept strictly confidential. Most states have procedures that, when the report turns out not to have

---

National Organizations Dedicated to Helping Abused Children

Here are some of the national organizations dedicated to helping abused children. The first three groups have been mentioned several times in this book. The addresses and phone numbers of all these groups are in Directory B.

• The National Committee for the Prevention of Child Abuse, in Chicago, with chapters in every state;

• The National Center for Missing and Exploited Children, in Arlington, Virginia, and its affiliate, the Adam Walsh Foundation, based in Fort Lauderdale, Florida; Columbia, South Carolina; Rochester, New York; and Orange County, California;

• Parents of Murdered Children, in Cincinnati, with chapters in many cities;

• The National Resource Center on Child Sexual Abuse and the National Children's Advocacy Center in Huntsville, Alabama (focusing on advocacy for children and prosecution of criminals);

• The Paul & Lisa Foundation, based in Westbrook, Connecticut (focusing on assisting child prostitutes);

• The Kempe National Center in Denver (an organization that does advocacy, education, research, lobbying, and grantmaking on all aspects of child abuse);

• The National Assault Prevention Center, in Columbus (an organization that teaches children to recognize when their bodies are being violated and how to deal with it);

• Incest Survivors Resource International, in Hicksville, New York (a program for adult survivors of sexual abuse);

• The National Coalition Against Sexual Assault, which has many chapters; among the most outstanding is its Illinois affiliate, whose attorney, Mary Boland, wrote an excellent manual for adult and child sexual-assault victims.

---

merit, the records must be destroyed, in order to protect those innocently accused.

Child victims have often been confronted with retelling their story of abuse over and over—to the social worker, to the police officer, to the prosecutor. Most states now are taking steps to stop this continual reliving of the child's trauma. Increasingly, *multidisciplinary teams* composed of all three categories—social worker, law enforcement, lawyer—are working on the project together. One way is to have just one person ask all the questions in a friendly environment for the child, with the others observing through a one-way mirror, and the adult in the room having an earphone so everyone can ask the interviewer what subjects they want explored.

Today, in all major cities and many smaller communities, there are assistant prosecutors and police officers who specialize in handling crimes against children. They learn how to talk with children instead of interrogating them; they tour the courtroom with them; they make the harshness of a courtroom into a more pleasant environment. This is a welcome step forward from the recent past.

Trials

The American judicial system is modeled after the English courts, which were created eight hundred years ago and changed ever so slowly, maybe every century or two. Not surprisingly, judges and lawyers have been slow to realize the need for fundamental changes in handling testimony by children.

Yet change they must. It is simply not right to traumatize child victims a second time by putting them all alone in a huge witness chair, badgering them with tricky cross-examination, and admonishing them to answer questions "in compliance with the rules of evidence."

Instead, we need to hark back to the mission of the courts: to get at the truth. Any child expert—and any parent, for that matter—will tell you that the courts could do a *better* job getting the truth from a child if they created a compassionate environment.

From the start, the courts must protect the identity of the child, especially the child sexual-assault victim. There is no reason whatsoever for the name of the child to be known, and there are plenty of reasons for it not to be. Much of the media recognizes this privacy interest; some do not. Judges should close the courtroom where needed; in most states, they have that authority.

If you are a parent of a child victim, you should ask the prosecutor to help you keep the child's identity from coming into public view. If the prosecutor is not cooperative, write the judge and the sheriff or police chief for help. Furthermore, if the offender is a family member, it means not revealing the name of the defendant either.

In addition, you should get a court order to keep the alleged abuser separate from the child until the proceeding is over.

In many situations, children deserve their own court advocate. Many courts are willing to appoint such a person trained in helping children. The appointed person is called the "guardian *ad litem*" or the "child advocate." If you would like to learn about such a program, write the National Association for Court-Appointed Special Advocates for Children, 2722 Eastlake Avenue East, Suite 220, Seattle, Washington 98102; the organization has one or more chapters in every state except Wyoming.

Testimony by the child poses one of the stickiest of all legal problems in the area of rights for crime victims. On the one hand, everyone is innocent until proven guilty in a court of law. On the other hand, it may not be conducive to either the child's welfare or even the truth-telling goal of the courts to have the child participate like any other witness. Several alternatives are being tried.

Videotaping the interview: Using a tape of the interview by the multidisciplinary team keeps the child out of the courtroom. The judge and jury see the tape instead of the child. For older children, this approach has not found widespread acceptance by the courts—they want the defendant to be able to confront the accuser and the jury to see everything. For younger children, whose memories fade quickly, judges have been more willing to accept the tape as evidence. They have also been more accepting of having the interviewer describe what the child said and have the interviewer cross-examined, as was done in the famous McMartin preschool case in Los Angeles. This case charged widespread sexual abuse by the owner and her son; the woman was acquitted and the jury deadlocked on the guilt of her adult son.

Closed-circuit testimony: Here the child is interviewed live, in a different room of the courthouse, and the testimony is broadcast into the courtroom. The lawyers, defendant, and judge remain in the courtroom and ask the questions over the monitor. The trauma to the child of seeing the defendant or alleged abuser, and of being before a large crowd, is reduced. Unfortunately, the Supreme Court, in a recent opinion, appeared to throw cold water on this idea, although there still may be a chance to revive and use it.

A helpmate on the stand: Child victims take someone with them to the witness stand. Here the options vary: the adult could take no role other than being there, or could be the one asking the child questions after they are first posed by the lawyers.

The child enters only for cross-examination: My solution would combine these ideas. In cases of sexual assault or other very personalized trauma, I suggest that the children be allowed to give their testimony by closed circuit, without having to face the defendant. Then the child would come into the courtroom for cross-examination. That way the jury hears the testimony without the child being frightened by the presence of the defendant and the large, impersonal courtroom, but the defendant gets his constitutional rights to cross-examine a witness in person.

We have to realize that all persons charged with a crime have a presumption of innocence and the right to a fair trial. A charge of child abuse is perhaps the most serious accusation that can be made against a person. And in fact, in child-custody cases, some fathers have been falsely accused of this crime because of the intensity of the divorce battle.

I am convinced that we can fight child abuse and still preserve our constitutional freedoms.

Financial Recovery

A small but growing number of child-abuse victims are turning to the civil courts and seeking money from the perpetrators. Sometimes such an action is brought by the family, in order to gain needed resources for the probability of years of therapy, and to be compensated for the impact on the parents as well. In other cases, child victims, upon reaching adulthood, are themselves bringing lawsuits. Some adult victims of child abuse bring these cases because of the severe financial hardships they face, given the difficulties of adjusting to adult life; others bring the case as part of the necessary process of emotional recovery.

If successful, such lawsuits often result in large verdicts. Collection is not always easy, but many adult victims feel that the process is worth it.

So child abusers beware! You may face a loss of your assets years into the future.

In some cases, insurance may be available. Homeowners' insurance is the first place the lawyers often look; the results are mixed among the states.

Finally, there is the prospect of going after a liable third party: some person or organization that did not commit the abuse, but whose negligence helped cause it. The most publicized examples are organizations whose mission is to serve, but whose adult leaders abuse children instead. In recent years, parents have succeeded in obtaining damages from national church organizations because of ministers who abuse children, and from youth organizations whose volunteer leaders are child molesters.

Recently in Texas, a young woman sued a minister who raped her repeatedly on church outings, starting when she was thirteen. The jury awarded money both from the minister and from the church, which chose to look the other way when his behavior was brought to its attention. In New England, over fifty adult men who claimed to be survivors of sexual abuse sued an ex-priest and the Catholic diocese and won a large out-of-court settlement. Reportedly, the diocese shuttled the priest from parish to parish after accusations were made, then let him quietly leave the priesthood and move to Minnesota. The silence only let his menacing behavior continue. Recently, the ex-priest, James Porter, was convicted by a Minnesota jury of molesting a female baby sitter.

Dealing with the Criminals

It was the kidnapping and murder of little Adam Walsh that inspired both the movie *Adam's Song* and the creation of the Adam Walsh Foundation, a leading child-advocate group. Adam's father John, who started the group and who has pushed tirelessly for laws protecting children, is now the host of *America's Most Wanted,* a crime-fighting show that invites viewers to help find dangerous criminals still at large.

Sociopaths—criminals with no conscience who murder and terrorize people—and pedophiles—criminals who are fixated on the desire to have sex with male or female children—are the people we fear most for our children. An example of the sociopathic criminal is Ted Bundy, a well-educated, handsome, sweet-talking, Jekyll-and-Hyde monster who, according to his biographer Ann Rule, killed at least 100 women and girls, some as young as twelve. So brilliant was Bundy—a former law student, assistant to the governor of Washington, and a high official in the Seattle Crime Commission—that he was able to live an apparently normal life and cover up his brutal rape-murders for over a decade.

Sadly, some of these criminals who conduct daily terror are children themselves. An example is "Little Man" James of Washington, D.C., who has spent his time since his mid-teen years dealing drugs and shooting strangers whenever "I feel like killing someone." For teenagers—even young teens—who commit violent crimes, I feel we have only one recourse: to treat the teenage criminal as an adult, a step advocated increasingly by prosecutors and social workers alike.

Then there is the pedophile. What I say here cuts against my religious and moral training, but I am increasingly convinced that pedophiles are not curable and should not be allowed to roam freely in our society. While such an abnormality may well have been caused by events out of the control of the pedophile—often because of childhood sexual abuse to themselves—we must stand firm because of the harm they do. Such people must absolutely, totally, and permanently, not be allowed access to children.

The state of Washington now has a law requiring that, upon release, convicted child sex offenders register their home and work addresses with the sheriff. The notice is made public, and neighbors can find out if such a person resides nearby. Those who fail to register are sent back to jail. The Washington law has a second, more controversial part: sex offenders deemed incurable can, after a jury trial, be reincarcerated in a special institution, if their prison term has expired.

Child molesters also have the statute of limitations to hide behind. Because the child victim is not only helpless but often unaware that a crime occurred until he or she has grown up, the time may have run out for criminal prosecution or a civil suit. Courts are increasingly sympathetic to finding ways to proceed. For example, the Commonwealth of Massachusetts prosecuted an ex-priest for molesting boys a quarter of a century earlier, despite a six-year statute of limitations, because the statute stops when someone leaves the state, as he had done. And, in civil cases, the clock does not start to run until the child reaches adulthood, age eighteen.

The Response

If only children could vote, and could vote their interests! Alternatively, we adult Americans should start voting for the children.

Crimes against children need a total response at every level. On the national level, we need programs of education, health care, nutrition, and jobs. Why people over sixty-five get free health care, but people under twelve do not has always baffled me. Increasingly, kids not smart enough to pick rich parents are not having their basic health care needs met.

On both the national and community level, we need to strengthen our law-enforcement efforts. We need to give more support and resources to our men and women on the front lines of the battle against crime. We need to put child abusers behind bars for a long time. We need to have programs that identify to everyone in a community who the released sexual offenders are and where they live and work. We need to have a national priority to put the child-pornography industry out of business, and provide them all room and board in prison for the rest of their lives.

Also on the community level, we need programs of self-help and rebuilding for victims and their families. As with law enforcement, we need to increase the resources we commit to the social workers who work with children and families, and we need to have victim-compensation programs that can fund the counselors who help address their emotional needs.

We must fight the financially lucrative industry that exploits children sexually. We need to bring criminal-racketeering charges; enforcement of this not only results in putting people in jail, but forecloses on all assets, effectively shutting down the enterprise. Frank Barnaba, head of the Paul and Lisa Foundation, has for years spent his weekends walking the streets of New York trying to talk child prostitutes into adopting a different life. We need a hundred Frank Barnabas doing the same in every state in the country.

While the law cannot make parents love their children, we can make parents responsible for them. We've got to do much more to get the deadbeat fathers (and mothers) to pay their billions of dollars of obligations owed to America's children in child support.

We simply must have safe schools. Some inner-city schools are an abomination, with students carrying weapons, ex-students peddling drugs, leaving teachers and students alike in daily fear. Whatever it takes—daily locker checks, metal detectors at the doors, foot patrols in the hallways, expelling each and every violent student—we must do it. Kids must be able to go to school without fear.

We need to teach children prevention techniques in the schools. One of the great ideas in the advertising world was McGruff, the crime-fighting dog and symbol of the National Crime Prevention Council. My daughter—and every kid in America—has known about McGruff since she was about four. McGruff and his organization have focused the attention of children on awareness of crime and participation in "taking a bite out of crime."

Finally, we, as citizens, must resolve that even one abused child in America is too many.

CHAPTER 8

Sexual Crimes

Sexual assault is a crime and should be viewed exclusively as such. But its very nature forces victims and the public alike to view it as not just another crime. Other crimes, however brutal, remain impersonal and can be discussed without the integrity of the victim ever being at issue. Sexual assault, however, is such an intensely personal assault that survivors often question their actions as well as the perpetrator's.

Definition of the Crimes

In the old English law that focused on *rape* (forced sexual intercourse), penetration by a man's sexual organ is required. Recent changes in state laws focus on the broader concept of *sexual assault,* which includes forced vaginal, rectal, or oral sex, or penetration by an object. Some laws increase the severity of the crime, using a term such as *aggravated sexual assault,* if there is also physical injury.

Another category of criminal law punishes the use of force involving sexual activity but without penetration. The terms used in state criminal codes are *sexual battery, attempted sexual assault,* or *second or third degree of sexual assault.*

There are two other ways for rape to occur besides the use or threat of force: when the victim is impaired, and when the victim is under the age of consent. "Impairment" refers to a person who is drunk, physically disabled, held hostage or confined, mentally retarded or insane, or in other situations where choice is not an option. Sexual activity by an adult with an underage person constitutes statutory rape because, as a matter of law, the minor is unable to give consent.

Other criminal laws are aimed solely at *protecting juveniles:* child sexual assault, molestation, incest, child pornography, and contributing to the delinquency of a minor. See the preceding chapter on crimes against children.

Date rape is rape by someone whose identity is already known by the victim (the term "acquaintance rape" is a more accurate one). In the definition of rape, it is of no consequence whether the assailant was a stranger, a neighbor, a date, or a spouse. Only recently have courts begun to recognize rape by other than strangers for what it is.

"Getting It": The Courts Wake Up

Until the very recent past, the criminal-justice system often put the rape victim on trial as much as it put the defendant on trial. The old law required two witnesses; the woman could *never* win if it was her word against his. (No state has such a requirement any longer.) Women's entire sexual history was put before the jury, not only reducing the conviction rate but lowering the number of women reporting rape. (Indeed, as late as the 1950s, some states still had all-male juries.)

During the 1970s, states passed "rape shield" laws, which prevented the defense lawyers from asking questions about the sexual history of the victim. (In date rape or marital rape cases, the sexual history between the accused and the victim is still allowed to be explored.) Why was previous sexual history determined to be irrelevant? Perhaps the unfairness to the rape victim could be best illustrated by a humorous anecdote.

Suppose I was robbed on my way home from work. In due course, the robber is arrested, and I go to trial to testify against the defendant. The cross-examination proceeds as follows:

> Question (by the defense lawyer): "Mr. Brown, you give away money to your church and to charity, don't you?"
>
> Answer (by the victim): "Well, yes, but why does that matter?"
>
> Lawyer: "I'll ask the questions here. And, sir, you gamble a bit, don't you?"

> Victim: "Uh, my dad and I sometimes go to the horse races, yes."
>
> Lawyer: "Furthermore, you've lost money in the stock market, haven't you?"
>
> Victim: "Gee, I, uh..."
>
> Lawyer: "I see, Mr. Brown, that you have a history of giving away your money in a most promiscuous way. So, if my client hadn't demanded that money from you, you probably were going to give it to him anyway, weren't you?"

You know, and I know, that no judge in America would allow a lawyer to ask a robber victim whether he liked to give away his money! The only issue is whether the robber forced the victim to give him the money. The same should be true in rape cases: the issue is whether the defendant used force, or the threat of force, to obtain sex.

General enlightenment seems to have reached the male-dominated system of justice only recently, and even now some men haven't caught on. The myths surrounding rape—that women ask for it by the way they dress, or they say yes but mean no, or that they somehow enjoy rape, are disappearing slowly but are not gone altogether.

Having pointed out the unfairness with which our system of justice has dealt with rape *victims*, I would be remiss in this discussion if I did not point out that the *accusation* of rape has a sordid racist history in this country. As recently as two or three generations ago, black men were lynched if white women simply accused them of rape. An accusation of rape, as much as an accusation of any other crime, does not constitute guilt—indeed, in a study in Howard County, Maryland, more than one accusation in ten was later recanted by the alleged victim or found to be without substance. Guilt remains a matter to be proved in a court of law.

Community Resources

A generation ago, there were virtually no services available for victims of sexual assault. Indignities such as paying for the medical exam, recurrent interviews, and lack of community support were the norm. Today things are different.

First, your county probably has a victim-service program as part of the district attorney's office, the police department, or a separate agency. This program helps victims of sexual assault to orient themselves through the justice system.

Second, almost every community has a sexual-assault crisis center of some kind. Talk to the victim-service representative about what services exist in your community. You and your family probably need counseling, and the crime center will help you get it.

Third, financial help is available. The state victim-compensation board will pay for counseling. Emergency and long-term help for victims is discussed in Part III of this book.

The Criminal-Justice Process

The criminal process is divided into two parts: the filing of charges and the trial. After the reporting of the charges (and as with any crime, the sooner it is reported, the better the victim's credibility), the law-enforcement agency will begin the investigation. If the evidence is sufficient, the case will be presented by the district attorney's office to a grand jury, which makes the decision to indict. In some states, the grand-jury process is not used, and the district attorney files an information, the legal equivalent of an indictment. The pretrial and trial phases of the criminal justice system are discussed in Part II of this book.

If the case goes to trial, it will be no surprise to you that the victim is the chief witness. As with any witness, your credibility (that is, the value of your testimony to the jury) will probably be challenged by the defense lawyer. That can be done in a variety of ways: the lawyer can suggest you made a mistaken identification, or that you consented, or that no sexual act occurred.

The two most common defenses to sexual assault on an adult are alibi ("it wasn't me, it was someone else") and consent ("she was a willing partner"). In stranger rape cases, the alibi defense is the more common; in acquaintance rape, consent is the likely defense.

If criminal-rape cases are difficult for victims to win, date-rape cases are even more so. The highly publicized trials involving William Kennedy Smith in West Palm Beach and Mike Tyson in Indianapolis brought this home to American women in the 1990s.

Going Public: The Nancy Ziegenmeyer Story

Whether to let your name be known publicly is not always a choice for a rape victim; the newspapers may print the name without the consent of the victim or, in a small community, the victim's identity could become known quickly. But, in most cases, the choice to "go public" remains with the victim.

Nancy Ziegenmeyer, a waitress in a small Iowa town, made such a choice. She was in Des Moines, the state capital, to take the test to become a real estate agent, and was attacked in her car in broad daylight. At that time, the state's major newspaper, the *Des Moines Register*, was publishing a series on rapes and, in an editorial, suggested that survivors come forward in order to end the stigma of being a rape victim. She and her husband read the editorial and jointly decided to accept the challenge. Her entire story was written up, she was on numerous talk shows about her decision to go public, and ultimately she was the subject of a made-for-TV movie. At its showing, which I watched with her, she told me she was proud that her decision inspired so many victims to talk about what happened to them. She received countless letters from around the country from sexual-assault victims of all ages and both sexes who were never given the chance to talk about their trauma—with anyone.

Financial Recovery

Be aware there is another option after going through the criminal process: a civil case for damages. Perpetrators of sexual crimes seem to be of no particular socioeconomic status; your attacker could well have financial assets.

A civil case is different from a criminal case. In the latter, guilt beyond a reasonable doubt is required. In the former, guilt by a preponderance of the evidence, or by clear and convincing evidence, is the standard. Thus, the balance of evidence in your favor need only be about 60 percent, not the 90+ percent required in a criminal case. And paying a large sum of money might have the dual effect of changing the behavior of the predator and providing the victim with the compensation to which she or he is entitled under the law.

A civil case for money can also be filed after the criminal case is over, whether or not the defendant is convicted.

Here is another option: if the defendant is convicted, ask the court for an order of restitution, fixing the amount due the victim on the spot. The restitution order becomes part of the sentence and can later be enforced if it is not paid.

Some adult victims of childhood sexual assault see an opportunity for self-healing through a lawsuit. Survivors see the chance not only for financial recovery, but for helping future victims— the perpetrator is socked in the wallet, where it just might hurt the most. Other rape victims have been successful in receiving damages from liable third parties, such as malls, parking lots, and motels that don't provide proper security.

But there are serious disadvantages to filing a lawsuit. Financial recovery is greatest if the emotional harm to the victim is substantial, and permanent. A lawsuit may slow down emotional recovery; it may be difficult to start healing when you have to wait a couple of years to go before a jury and explain how bad off you are. And no lawyer can guarantee a victory in the courtroom.

Living With the Crime

Linda Braswell, a national victims'-rights advocate and the author of the self-help book for sexual assault victims, *Quest for Respect* (Pathfinder Publishing, 1989), lists the five steps for victims to regain control of their lives:

1. Acknowledge the impact on your life and verbalize how the assault changed your life.
2. Make a commitment to yourself to heal and to gather your resources around you.
3. Relive the rape through the telling of your story. (It will hurt.)
4. Turn toward the future—make new decisions about the relationships you want in your life.
5. Let the pain go. The wounds have now healed in a healthy way.

For the adult survivors of childhood sexual assault, there is an added burden. The crime happened to them before the age where they could understand—much less describe—what happened. A long period of confusion must be overcome, and there is no easy way out. For many, the episodes may have been buried in the subconscious—which the brain tends to do in all events of terrible trauma, since it hurts too much to remember them. (That is why people think they blacked out *before* the car or airplane crashed.) In adulthood, if memory returns, counseling is absolutely essential, as is support from those whom people love and trust.

The male sexual-assault victim also faces special problems. In addition to facing the same questions as women—the intensely personal questions involving consent and specificity of what happened to which part of the body—there is the issue that manhood has been equated with strength. Men fear the question of why they couldn't fight off attackers. Furthermore, men have been trained not to discuss their problems in the same way as women, which could make it even harder for them to emerge from the healing process and regain control over their lives.

A Footnote: Sexual Harassment

Two graduates of Yale, the nation's premier law school, provided the backdrop for a 1991 drama in the United States Senate. Professor Anita Hill accused the President's Supreme Court nominee, Judge Clarence Thomas, of a long-time pattern of sexual harassment, a charge he vociferously denied.

The immediate goal of Professor Hill's allies was not met: Judge Thomas was confirmed by the Supreme Court. But a longer-term goal was. The number of sexual harassment complaints by women employees increased dramatically. And women are coming forward to name names. A dozen each accused two powerful United States Senators: Democrat Brock Adams of Washington, who denied the charges but chose to retire rather than run for reelection; and Republican Robert Packwood of Oregon, who admitted the charges were true. The sexual-harassment issue, like rape and child abuse in earlier eras, was no longer hidden away. It reached the nation's consciousness and spurred discussion, debate, and decisions that can help victims.

Sexual harassment is the use by someone of his (or her) superior position, such as a supervisor at work or a lawyer hired for a case, to procure sex or to put the victim in a sexually intimidating or stereotyping situation. It is not forced sex in the traditional sense of using physical force or intimidation. Rather, the victim is forced to accept certain sexualized behavior, or a certain work environment, because of the power of the harasser.

At times, sexual harassment could be considered a misdemeanor (a minor crime), but it is more likely to be classified as a violation of civil law. There would be no criminal charge against the perpetrator, but he could be made to pay damages and lose his job. (It is not always a "he." A female deputy sheriff in Virginia was fired for fondling and other provocative actions toward male deputies.)

Sexual harassment, then, is usually challenged in the civil or administrative courts, rather than the criminal courts. Victims in the workplace may file a complaint with the top official in their company, or with the Equal Employment Opportunity Commission in Washington, D.C., or with their state or city human-rights commission. Victims of sexual harassment by nonemployers, such as a hired professional, may go to the state's licensing board governing that person's occupation.

A better approach than the above channels for some victims has been to file a lawsuit. Victims probably first have to go through company channels (unless the harasser is the chief honcho), but then can file suit. Clear cases of sexual harassment have forced employers to pay damages to victims.

The line defining sexual harassment is not always easy; the language used in this society is much cruder than that of a generation ago and, due to a decline of other institutions, the workplace is often the major place for social relationships to start. But wise employers have started full-scale detection and prevention programs. Otherwise, they risk fighting lawsuits for years. Women are simply no longer going to tolerate behavior that they had to in the past.

CHAPTER 9

Domestic Violence

"**R**ule of thumb"—An expression in the old Anglo-Saxon law which states that a man was allowed to beat his wife with a stick no thicker than his thumb. Only sticks thicker than a man's thumb were outlawed.

Definition of the Crime

Domestic violence occurs between two people in a family setting. The victim is the spouse, lover, or family member of the perpetrator.

Domestic violence is a form of criminal assault and battery. But it is more serious for three reasons:

1. *A second victimization is likely.* With other crimes, the likelihood of the same crime's being repeated by the same assailant to the same victim is small. For domestic-violence victims, it is quite great. With other victims, the crime is over and the focus is on the remedy. For victims of domestic violence, quite often the focus is on how to stop the crime from being repeated.

2. *Domestic violence occurs in a family setting.* It upsets society's most fundamental institution; it creates a special terror for the victim because there may be no place to retreat.

3. *Domestic violence serves as a negative role model for children.* Even if they are not actual victims themselves, they see the behavior as normal. Future generations of boys are more likely to be batterers, future generations of girls to accept their role as victims.

Many changes have taken place in the past two decades in both the public's attitude toward family violence and the response to it

126

by the justice system. Special family courts are much more willing to enact and enforce orders protecting the victims. The response of law enforcement has changed; no longer is there the presumption that the problem is one to be dealt with only within the family. An array of social services has sprung up, the most important being family shelters in communities around America for abused women and their children.

These reforms have come about for a variety of reasons. Women have a better chance now than in the past of leaving their partners and becoming economically independent. Women have entered positions of power previously reserved for men. Voters have elected more responsible officials. Failures to respond to family violence have resulted in lawsuits, such as an award by the city of Torrington, Connecticut, of hundreds of thousands of dollars to Tracey Furman, who was beaten horribly by her husband after she requested help from the police several times.

The Criminal-Justice System

Two types of courts deal with family violence. One is the criminal courts, where the charges are treated the same as any other crime.

There is an alternative—or a supplement—to the criminal courts. In family violence, the civil-law courts (in addition to the criminal-law courts) play a role in deterring behavior. For due cause shown, courts have the power to issue restraining orders on what people must do or must not do. In the area of family violence, these orders are called *protective orders* and are aimed at protecting family members from an abusive or dangerous member. In California, for example, protective orders can be issued for victims of domestic violence to cover the following activities:

1. Restraining the attacker from abusing the spouse (or live-in lover, or boyfriend) or other family member;
2. Directing the attacker to leave the household;
3. Preventing the attacker from entering the household, or the school, business, or place of employment of the potential victim;
4. Awarding custody of—or visitation rights to—minor children;
5. Directing the payment of child support;
6. Directing the payment of debts;

7. Ordering that either or both parties participate in counseling.

What is the value of a protective order? Simply this: any violation is ruled contempt of court and thus can result in immediate arrest and incarceration. Victims don't have to wait for an actual crime to occur, if they have sufficient proof of the perpetrator's propensity to violence toward them.

The Center for Women's Policy Studies has a brochure titled "Legal Help for Battered Women," which costs five dollars. The address is 2000 P St., N.W., Suite 508, Washington, D.C. 20036.

For the worst batterers, though, the criminal courts are probably the only place to go. Consider how our system of justice failed Kristin Lardner, a promising young art student in Boston. Twice in May 1992, Lardner complained to police about a former boyfriend's criminal assaults on her. The man, Michael Cartier, had a history of assaulting women, and was on probation. But statewide records in Massachusetts were not available to the judge, so at the hearing he simply issued a restraining order on Cartier and set him free. The court order was no deterrent; later that same month, Cartier tracked her down and shot her dead.

Almost one-third of female murder victims in America are killed by their husbands or boyfriends.

Law-enforcement officials and the courts have begun to intervene sooner to protect victims. More batterers are being prosecuted and jailed, but solutions remain inconsistent and elusive.

The Battered-Woman Defense

Sometimes the victim strikes back: women are choosing to kill rather than be killed. In such murder cases, courts are allowing defendants to assert the "battered-woman defense": that they feared for their life.

The battered-woman defense is a form of self-defense. In the past, the courts had ruled that self-defense was based on the victim's fear for his or her life *at that point in time*. In recent years, victims of domestic violence have been able to plead the broader defense that they were afraid for their lives in general, although they were not in physical danger at that very moment. Two reasons exist for this broader interpretation. One is that the defense is based on a "syndrome": a pathological state of mind created by the environment. The other is that while a plea of self-defense is rejected if there is room to retreat; for someone already in her home, there may be no safe place to go.

Recent laws in California and Texas provide the opportunity for a pardon or commutation for women who were not able to use this defense in the past. The parole board will determine whether the result might have been different; that is, whether it was a case of self-defense as interpreted today.

The National Clearinghouse for the Defense of Battered Women, 125 South 9th Street, Philadelphia, PA 19107 is a national organization that provides assistance and legal support to women who have acted to protect themselves from life-threatening violence.

The battered-woman defense was perhaps best dramatized in the movie *The Burning Bed,* in which a woman who was subjected to continuing life-threatening abuse finally set her drunken husband's bed afire before she fled with the children. She was ultimately vindicated by the courts.

The battered-woman syndrome also has its limits. Recently prosecutors have held women criminally responsible when their boyfriends or husbands beat their children. In some cases, women have argued that they were battered and therefore couldn't protect their children any more than they could protect themselves. Generally, the courts have had little sympathy with this defense. The Illinois Supreme Court recently ruled—correctly, I believe—that two women who stood by and let their boyfriends beat their infant children to death were also guilty of murder themselves.

In Texas the battered-woman defense has been extended to victims of child abuse who kill their parents if they are able to introduce the abuse as evidence to show either that the crime was committed in self-defense, or that the crime was manslaughter instead of murder. Recently, in Smith County, Texas, a teenager was acquitted of the murder of her father on the grounds of self-defense; he had consistently and brutally assaulted her, physically and sexually. The defense lawyer was Paul Mones of Santa Monica, California, who tries cases across the country for children who are so battered that eventually they strike back. Other states that do not allow the defense for children (but allow it for spouses) are considering changing their laws.

Why do they stay?

Why many battered women stay in the home environment is a complex question. Reasons vary: they have nowhere to go; they have no independent financial means; they have no emotional support from family or community; they have a low level of self-esteem; they witnessed the same domestic violence as children and view it as inevitable; they fear for the safety of their children or their parents if they leave; they believe that if they did the "right thing," the violence would not recur; they fear that the system of justice will deal with the husband more harshly than they would like. These reasons help to explain why—but they don't necessarily excuse all women who accept such treatment as part of their lives.

Financial Recovery

Crime victim-compensation funds are available for victims of domestic violence. But the family-law courts play a major role in this area, too.

The family law courts, through orders to pay child support and divide assets fairly, play a special role to help with the financial problems of victims of domestic violence, as well they should. Too often, victims don't leave the abusive environment because they have no other economic options.

The victim may request transitional alimony, a payment of money for a period until she may reenter the work force. But permanent alimony, unless agreed to in a contract, is virtually a dead concept because the woman as well as the man is expected to work.

In a divorce, the spouses must divide their assets. The division of property is made according to whether the parties live in a civil-law or community-property state. Community-property states (Arizona, California, Idaho, Louisiana, New Mexico, Texas, and Washington) consider all assets acquired during the marriage to be the property of both parties. Civil-law states increasingly have adopted this viewpoint, but tend to allow the parties who maintained separate assets to continue to do so. (Of course, prenuptial agreements can override the general rules.)

In addition to assets that are obvious (land, house, bank accounts), victims should sue for other, less tangible assets: pension plans (courts are now often willing to divide pension payments between the husband and wife, even though the pension had belonged to the husband); and the acquisition of a professional degree or the growth of a family business, where the victim played a major role (courts are divided on giving payment in this area).

Lack of payment for child support—truly a national disgrace—has increasingly drawn the attention of the courts, the media, and state legislators. Help is available from your department of human services or family-law courts in tracking down the deadbeat and making him (or her) pay.

Judges still need some educating. Recently, in the divorce of billionaire Jack Kent Cooke, the owner of the Washington Redskins professional football team, the judge did not require Cooke to set aside money for his baby daughter's college education, even though the sum was equivalent to what Cooke receives from only a minute or two of TV advertising revenue.

What Can Be Done

Many social services exist for victims of family violence. Counseling for all parties is available. Some agencies provide trained mediators to help resolve differences between the parties, although mediation is not recommended in family-violence situations where battering has already occurred.

The most significant development is the emergence of family shelters in small as well as large communities. Available to women victims and their children, the shelters offer temporary residence, transportation to and from work, and other services. Generally, no men except counselors, clergy, and similar professionals, are allowed to know the location of the community's shelter.

Nurses are playing an increasingly valuable role in the front lines of detecting family violence. In a study showing the tragic degree of battering of pregnant women, Professor Judith McFarlane of Texas Women's University found that nurses are increasingly called on to assist such victims. The health-care system in America so closes out poor women that, increasingly, they come to a health-care provider only to deliver a baby. Thus, it is during the pregnancy or delivery that the battering is noticed. Nurses are being trained to detect the signs of battering, to know about such community resources as shelters, and to play a positive role in intervention with these victims.

Doctors, too, are being trained to recognize victims of abuse. The American Medical Association has made its detection and treatment a major priority.

While the number of domestic-violence victims remains a national tragedy, there are hopeful trends. By bringing the issue out in the open and by punishing crimes of violence, we can accomplish two goals: to hold people accountable for the crimes they commit in their homes, and to reduce the likelihood that such behavior will continue on into the next generation.

CHAPTER 10

Murder: Helping the Survivors

> Murder is the ultimate act of depersonalization. It transforms a living person with hopes, dreams, and fears into a corpse, thereby taking away all that is special and unique about that person. The Constitution does not preclude a State from deciding to give some of that back.
>
> —Justice Sandra Day O'Connor, in the United States Supreme Court opinion of *Payne* v. *Tennessee.*

Murder. All religions teach us that it is the ultimate crime. When murder is transformed from the abstractions of movie screens and newspaper headlines to a real family's tragedy, it takes on a dimension that we are unable to understand for years, perhaps for the rest of our lives.

The Criminal-Justice System

In some murders, the culprit is arrested at once. In other murders, he or she is never found. Sometimes, as with many of Ted Bundy's murders, the body can't be found, and whether a murder was committed remains an open question.

The stages of a criminal case are shown on the chart on page 26 in Chapter 2. Because the crime is murder, the stakes are larger at each stage of the process. For example, in a murder case, a judge may be more willing to hear a motion to deny bail to the accused.

Witness assistance and witness protection are important in a murder case. Witnesses can get assistance in understanding the system of justice from a victim/witness coordinator, if the district attorney or sheriff's office has one. Intimidation of witnesses by the accused or anyone associated with him or her is illegal. In a murder case, police are the most likely to give protection to witnesses who ask for it. Protection can include monitoring the phone, police driving past the home at night, and even round-the-clock protection, depending on the circumstances.

After the defendant's arrest, you may want to get involved in the decision as to whether he or she is permitted bail. Because many murders are committed by perpetrators out on bail for a previous murder, your involvement may save someone else's life. Ask the district attorney to fight against release. Gather petitions. Go to the media. Any of these actions could persuade a judge to keep the accused killer in jail until the trial is over.

If bail is granted, the district attorney should make it conditional upon the defendant's having no contact with the victim's family.

An accused murderer can be charged and convicted on any of several levels. Although a number of states have changed the names or definitions, these are the traditional classifications:

First-degree murder is the willful killing with the specific intention to kill, with "malice aforethought": a decision made in advance to kill.

Second-degree murder is also willful killing with the specific intent to do so, but without planning the murder in advance.

First-degree manslaughter is intentional, but without malice.

Second-degree manslaughter is a reckless killing but without an intent to kill.

The Trial and Sentencing

At a trial, the defendant usually raises one of the following four rebuttals, or defenses: (1) he or she didn't commit the crime—the state has arrested the wrong person; (2) he killed the deceased, but in self-defense (which is a legally justified killing); (3) he killed the deceased but did not intend to; or (4) he was insane at the time. If he uses the first defense, he usually has an alibi: that is, evidence of being elsewhere.

A defendant convicted of second-degree manslaughter may go to jail or may receive probation. A conviction of first-degree manslaughter usually means that the defendant will do time. A second-degree murder conviction normally results in a long sentence. A conviction for the first-degree murder frequently means a life sentence, although in most states a life sentence means a defendant can get paroled some years later.

Be aware that many murder cases are pleaded down from a more serious to a less serious charge of homicide (wrongful killing). An important factor here is the length of the sentence, or the range of the sentence for the judge to choose, if the plea is to that lesser level of homicide. The family member should find out the name of the assistant district attorney assigned to the case and talk to him or her early. You should state your attitude toward a plea bargain and also request to be informed of each step in the proceeding. Finally, you should state your desire to attend the entire trial and ask the district attorney's office to help make it possible.

If there is a plea bargain, you should have the opportunity to tell the judge your views, for or against, in writing or in court testimony. You may also wish to convey your views on the length of the sentence.

If the assistant district attorney doesn't seem cooperative, *put your concerns in writing to the elected district attorney*. Politicians fear letters that could be published at election time, so if you ask in writing that your views be considered on a plea bargain, in setting bail, or in sentencing, you are more likely to be listened to.

It's almost too incredible to believe, but family members of the deceased—even parents of a murdered child—have often not been allowed to attend the trial. Some courts decided that the jury would have sympathy for the family and be thereby "prejudiced" to find the defendant guilty. At other times, a defendant's lawyer would put the family member's name on a witness list as a ploy to keep out the family.

Alabama and Wisconsin have laws requiring judges to permit a family member of the murder victim to attend the entire trial. In other states, judges have become more sympathetic to the plights of victims. So the family should raise this issue with the district attorney and insist on their right to attend.

The Statute of Limitations

What if the state can't find the killer? Keep in mind that for murder (and only for murder) there is no statute of limitations. The book on an unsolved murder case is never closed.

One of the most rewarding experiences of my life was to serve as a civil-rights worker in Fayette, Mississippi, for Mayor Charles Evers. Several years earlier, Evers's brother Medgar, the field secretary of the state NAACP, had been assassinated. Abundant evidence pointed to white supremacist Byron de la Beckwith. De la Beckwith was tried twice before all-white juries, and both times the jury hung. (In one of the bleakest days in the history of American justice, the state's governor, Ross Barnett, came into the courtroom to shake de la Beckwith's hand at the conclusion of one of the trials.)

Three decades later, new evidence surfaced, even further fingering de la Beckwith as the triggerman, and a judge ordered a third trial. Now Mississippi is much improved; it no longer shelters racial killings.

Thus murderers can run but, in the words of Joe Louis, "they can't hide."

The Death Penalty

Thirty-six states provide a death penalty for the most heinous murders, while fourteen states never permit it. Over half of the nation's executions have been carried out in three states: Florida, Texas, and Louisiana. Many states that nominally have the death penalty, such as Maryland, Ohio, and Pennsylvania, have not enforced it in several decades.

Why do some states use this ultimate punishment and others do not? Different cultural attitudes seem to prevail in different regions of the country. All the states that prohibit the death penalty are located in the Northeast, the upper Midwest, and the Pacific Northwest, which are considered culturally "liberal" areas. Those which enforce the penalty with some frequency are in the South or Rocky Mountain areas, which are considered culturally "conservative." The states that fall in the middle have enacted death-penalty laws but, owing to divided opinion, either the governor or the courts have acted to halt all executions.

In 1992 the nation's most populous state, California, had its first execution in three decades. After years of legal wrangling, Robert Harris was executed for his gruesome murder of two teenage boys whose car Harris and his brother wanted after a bank robbery. Harris took the boys into the country, executed them despite their pleas (telling one of them to "die like a man"), then ate the boys' hamburgers.

Those who wish to see a killer executed should not get their hopes up; execution is extremely unlikely in *any* state. There are over 40,000 murders each year in the United States, and perhaps two dozen executions. Even if that number is increased tenfold, only 0.6 percent of the killers would be executed.

In addition, the time delay is excruciating. Appeals through the state courts are followed by *habeas corpus* petitions in state and federal courts. Habeas corpus petitions are filed by prisoners who feel they were wrongly convicted; they challenge the state's authority to keep them imprisoned.

It is much more realistic, therefore, to hope that the police find the right person and that he or she is convicted and sentenced to an appropriate prison term. For many years, a sentence of "life" only meant a term of years, perhaps eight or ten. But New Hampshire, for one, now has "truth in sentencing": the sentence given is the sentence served. For example, the state's recently convicted "black widow" killer, a young teacher who had sex with a teenage boy in exchange for his murdering her husband, was sentenced to life and will serve that sentence. Other states have a "life without parole" sentence; only a commutation by the governor can free the inmate.

Sentencing, Appeal, and Parole

If there is a conviction, hopefully the district attorney and the judge will arrange for the survivor to have input in the sentencing. A letter to the court or testimony at the sentencing hearing, or both, are appropriate. Both a letter and testimony are also appropriate before the sentencing of a murderer who has accepted a plea bargain.

While in some states you have the right to testify, in most it is still up to the judge's good graces. Most judges will now permit testimony before sentencing.

Appeals of a finding of guilt are always permitted in murder cases, although in most states the sentence will usually start at once. There is good reason for appellate courts to review convictions: sometimes juries and lower-court judges are wrong. Martin Yant, in *Presumed Guilty—When Innocent People Are Wrongly Convicted* (Prometheus Books, 1991), tells of dozens of such cases.

If the defendant is acquitted by the jury, the state has no right to appeal or to try the defendant again for the crime.

Except for a few defendants who are given a mandatory life sentence, most prisoners come before a parole board sooner or later. A family member of the victim may write the parole board to give his or her views on parole. About half the states also permit surviving family members to testify in person before the board.

One family who exercised this right is the Salernos of San Francisco. Their teenage daughter Theresa, during her first week of college, told her high-school boyfriend, a freshman at the same school, that she wanted to date other men. He shot her in the back as she walked away and, as she lay dying, he went back to his dorm room and watched *Monday Night Football*. The efforts of Harriet Salerno, Theresa's mother, have received national attention as a model for diligence in seeing that a convicted killer actually serves his term.

Parents of Murdered Children and Mothers Against Drunk Driving will help families of murder victims mobilize for a sentencing or parole hearing. They often urge their members to write a judge or a parole board, and then letters pour in from all over the country.

In California, parole hearings are held every year for mass slayer Charles Manson and for Sirhan Sirhan, the assassin of Senator Robert Kennedy. The hearings are a charade because everyone knows that parole will be denied.

But what of those victims who were not actresses or senators? In these situations, the media are uninterested, politicians are quiet, and the murderer frequently is granted early parole. That is why organizing is so important.

Indeed, the situation is often the worst for minority victims and their families. When the victim is black, the killer is likely to receive a lesser sentence, and is virtually certain never to be given the death penalty.

Financial Recovery

In addition to the emotional heartache, death can leave a financial void, but financial recovery can reduce the economic impact of the loss of the family member.

Two groups of professionals are especially well trained to assist with the financial impact of death. Lawyers are one group. If there is a will, go to the lawyer who wrote it and enlist his or her help at once. The second group, funeral directors, attempt to counsel people who have immediate problems.

Chapters 4 to 6 cover financial recovery for all victims.

Several sources of money should be explored:

1. Life insurance policies.
2. Casualty insurance policies.
3. Your state's victim-compensation board. See Directory A for the address and telephone number.
4. Lawsuits. Talk to a lawyer who specializes in plaintiffs law practice to determine whether you can sue (1) the killer or (2) a financially liable third party.
5. Social Security.
6. Employee benefits.
7. Veterans' benefits.

Almost everyone has debts, and the survivor must determine how to deal with them. Sometimes death cancels the obligation on installment loans—be sure to read the fine print. For other debts, explain the situation to the creditor and ask for some time to sort through everything. Don't offer to pay the debts yourself. Unless your name is on the loan, too, it is not your debt. The creditor can be paid out of the estate: the money is taken from the assets of the deceased. If his or her debts are greater than his or her assets, the creditor loses, not you.

Don't ignore all the options for financial recovery.

Dealing with Death: The Survivor's Burden

For family and close friends, a loved one's violent murder creates an immediate feeling of something far more powerful than sadness. Anger and outrage, shock and incredulity, and feelings of total powerlessness are natural reactions.

1. *Get help at once.* Go to your spiritual leader; get emotional counseling; find support groups of others who have experienced a murder in their families; rely on family and friends.

Several national organizations have been formed to help the families of murder victims:

• Parents of Murdered Children provides emotional support and counseling in one of the very worst kinds of murder: the murder of one's child. As a parent, I shudder at the thought of such a tragedy, but it is a burden which thousands of American parents must bear. This Cincinnati-based group, with chapters all over the nation, has helped countless numbers of grief-stricken parents.

• Mothers Against Drunk Driving (MADD) has done an incredible job in just one decade in reforming the laws, reducing drunk-driving deaths, changing attitudes, and seeing that murderers behind the wheel are punished. They have been leaders in helping survivors and injured persons, too.

• Concerns of Police Survivors (COPS), based in Upper Marlboro, Maryland, helps the families of slain police officers.

• Families and Friends of Missing Persons and Violent Crime Victims has published a very sensitive booklet titled "Grief by Homicide." Its address is P.O. Box 27529, Seattle, Washington 98125.

Some groups are started by individuals who channel their tragedy into community activism. Colleen Davis of Whittier, California, an incredibly energetic woman whose teenage son was murdered, has created several local and statewide organizations that fight to make the criminal justice system work for victims. Jack Collins, whose young daughter was murdered in Tennessee, now runs the East Coast office of Citizens for Law and Order and works closely with the Justice Department's Office for Victims of Crime.

2. *Be angry.* An act of terrible evil has happened; and it's devastatingly unfair.

Death strikes in such a random and cruel way. One irony is the sharp contrast between the rights given to those who commit the murders, even after the conviction (appeals, habeas corpus petitions, parole hearings) and the short shrift given victims. A tragicomic cartoon summarizes this difference: a police officer is standing next to a cemetery headstone of a murder victim, reading the victim's rights, starting with "You have the right to remain silent."

3. *Talk about the deceased.* Your family member or close friend walked on this earth, had a major role in your life, and bettered people's lives. For some reason I never understood, many people will not talk about someone who is dead. Because his or her life ended so abruptly and senselessly, it is even more important to resolve what that life meant for you, for other people, and for the society.

It's not the victim's fault that he or she is dead. It's not your fault either. The blame lies with the killer, who intentionally took another life, and not with anyone else.

Statistics about thousands of murder victims do not do justice to the full story. It's said that statistics are people with the tears wiped away. Society is much the worse because wonderful people such as these are no longer with us:

- Alicia McCormick, the program director of the Charleston, West Virginia, YMCA, who was murdered by a convicted criminal on a work-release program;
- Patricia Lexie, a newlywed in Alexandria, Virginia, who was riding with her husband and killed in a random drive-by shooting on a Washington, D.C., interstate highway by a man who had been arrested for another shooting and was out on bail awaiting trial;
- Colleen Shaughnessy, a capable and charismatic aspiring politician in Cleveland, who ran my brother Sherrod's successful campaign for Secretary of State of Ohio. She was killed in her office after she interrupted a burglar;
- Harold T. Doorenbos, a nighttime service attendant in Anaheim, California, who was trying to work himself, his wife, and two children, out of poverty;
- Alexis Welsh, a young advertising-agency executive out walking her dog in New York City, who was killed by a man recently released from a mental institution and recently convicted of attacking another woman in her bedroom with an icepick.

4. *Long-term emotional suffering is a certainty.* Periods of sadness, rage, helplessness, self-pity, and spiritual emptiness all come, and usually, eventually, go. Have faith in yourself, in others, and in God if it is your belief; some people find that they can transform themselves if they keep hope alive.

Many books have been written to help people deal with this saddest of all tragedies. Two I can strongly recommend:

No Time for Goodbyes/Coping with Sorrow, Anger and Injustice After a Tragic Death (Pathfinder Publishing, 1990), by Janice Harris Lord, a top official of MADD. The book discusses how to deal with the violent death of a daughter or son, a brother or sister, a spouse or lover, a parent; plus general advice on spirituality and counseling and on how to rebuild such family occasions as holidays.

When Bad Things Happen to Good People, by Rabbi Harold Kushner (Avon Books, 1991). Rabbi Kushner's only son was born with progeria, the disease of rapid aging. The little boy quickly stopped growing, aged prematurely, and died of old age at thirteen. Relying on the Bible, counseling techniques, and modern-day experiences, Rabbi Kushner offers a compelling account of how to cope with inexplicable tragedies.

Moving Forward

Do not forget the deceased, because your loved one had an impact on you and on the lives of many other people. Now time—perhaps the only thing that moves in only one direction—has begun a new chapter in your life.

When she learned that President Kennedy had been assassinated, the columnist Mary McGrory said to then-ambassador Patrick Moynihan (now the United States Senator from New York), "We'll never laugh again."

Moynihan replied, "Mary, of course we'll laugh again—but we'll never be young again." That statement, I fear, was correct. On November 22, 1963, the United States of America changed from a young nation to a middle-aged nation. There are advantages to maturity, to be sure, but the loss of the innocence of youth is a paradise lost forever.

As John Kennedy's death affected a nation, a death in your family is likely to have a similar effect on you, your family, and your friends. You will laugh again someday. But a transforming event, with a permanent impact, has occurred.

CHAPTER 11

Crimes Against Senior Citizens

Crimes against seniors are no different than crimes against anyone else. But the vulnerability of many seniors to violence, and the fact that white-collar scam artists tend to target them, means that this area of crime is often analyzed separately.

To be a senior citizen and a victim of crime is to experience a "double sorrow," in the words of Marlene Young and John Stein, who run the National Organization for Victim Assistance. Older Americans are more likely to be hurt when they are victimized. They are especially traumatized if the direct victim of a violent crime is their child or grandchild. And, even more than the rest of us, they feel powerless to stop crime.

While seniors are the most common targets of white-collar crime and similar crimes of theft, they are less likely to be victims of violent crime. Is it because they are less likely to be attacked? Not at all. Polls make clear what we already instinctively know: *seniors are staying indoors, behind lock and key: That* is the reason they are less likely to be crime victims. And what a sad commentary that is!

When I was growing up in Mansfield, Ohio, we never locked our house or car doors. Now my parents, living by themselves in the same house, always do. I daresay that pattern is repeated in every neighborhood in America. A Harris poll of senior citizens found that they fear crime even more than poor health or financial problems.

The leading crime-fighting group for senior citizens is also the nation's largest organization: The American Association of Retired Persons. AARP's criminal-justice section has long been active in both crime-prevention and legal-reform efforts.

Definition of the Crime

Three types of crime are addressed in this chapter: violent crime, white-collar crime, and elder abuse.

Violent Crime

By lobbying their state legislatures, senior citizens have secured laws making them a less inviting target for street hoods. So far, sixteen states have increased the criminal penalties for violent crimes against senior citizens:

A *longer sentence:* Eight states—Arizona, California, Colorado, Connecticut, Illinois, Indiana, New Mexico, and Texas—either increase the length of the sentence if the victim is a senior citizen or reclassify the crime as a more severe one. (Illinois also increases the sentence for sexual assaults on disabled people.)

Mandatory minimums: Six states—Delaware, Hawaii, Oklahoma, Massachusetts, Pennsylvania, and West Viriginia—require that those who commit violent crimes against seniors serve time. Probation is not an option.

Both: Two states—Florida and Rhode Island—have both a mandatory minimum *and* a reclassification of the crime into a more serious category.

Seniors are also fighting back with crime-prevention efforts, organizing Neighborhood Watch and similar groups in their neighborhoods. The Columbus-based National Assault Prevention Center has published a booklet on crime-prevention strategies titled "Preventing Assaults Against Older Adults."

White-Collar Crime

Consumer fraud is more common against senior citizens. Some criminal syndicates target seniors as their prey. Charles Keating, the convicted savings-and-loan racketeer, set up a scheme to persuade thousands of senior citizens to switch their savings from government-guaranteed investments to risky, uninsured bonds in his fraudulent enterprises. Only seniors were targeted by Keating's bank employees.

Some states have set up watchdog programs to help seniors. Attorney General Hubert H. Humphrey III of Minnesota has created a special unit to fight consumer fraud against the elderly. Minnesota has increased civil penalties for consumer frauds against seniors, and Indiana has increased penalties for fraud against seniors in home-improvement scams.

If you are a senior who is a victim of consumer fraud, contact your state attorney general, who may have a toll-free number in your state. Other places to look are your city consumer-protection agency (if there is one), your state securities commissioner (for stock and investment frauds), the United States Postal Service (for fraud through the mails), and the Federal Trade Commission (for any consumer fraud).

Find an agency that will not only pursue the criminal, but one which will help you recover your money. If you can't, consult a lawyer.

Elder Abuse

Elder abuse, like child abuse, occurs when someone in a special relationship, such as a family member or an institution, commits a criminal offense against a senior citizen. There are three categories of abuse: physical, psychological, and material (such as theft of funds).

Like child abuse, elder abuse is a problem that most societies really prefer to ignore. The recognition of elder abuse as a major problem has occurred because of the disintegration of so many families, the growth in the number of senior citizens (almost all of whom vote), and a growing sensitivity to other family-abuse situations. Thus, in the late 1970s, states started to recognize elder abuse as a major problem.

By 1987 all fifty states had laws prohibiting elder abuse. All have a special unit established for adult protective services in either their Department of Human Services or their Commission on Aging.

However, no real uniformity exists among the laws on (1) the age at which someone starts to be protected, and (2) which acts violate the law. While all laws cover infliction of physical pain, only a bare majority cover willful infliction of mental anguish. Most states—but not all—cover criminal neglect. Only one-third cover unreasonable confinement.

Slightly over a majority of the states include disabled adults of any age under their adult protective services.

Over thirty states have enacted criminal laws requiring health providers, social workers, and the like to report what they know of elder abuse. The law is patterned after the child-abuse "mandatory-reporter" laws. The impact of a mandatory-reporter law for elder abuse appears to be positive: a study of the Rhode Island law concluded that a substantial increase in the amount of reporting occurred.

Two other categories of laws aim to stop elder abuse:

Guardianship laws, although reformed in recent years, still often lack significant safeguards for wards to make sure that their rights and assets are protected; and

Nursing home law reforms. Now every state has an "ombudsperson," someone to whom the resident's family can complain to and who must check out the problem at once.

Two national organizations focus solely on elder abuse. One is the National Committee for the Prevention of Elder Abuse, the University of Massachusetts Center on Aging, 55 Lake Avenue North, Worcester, Massachusetts 01655. The other is the Clearinghouse on Abuse and Neglect of the Elderly, the University of Delaware College on Human Resources, Newark, Delaware 19716.

Dealing With the Justice System

For seniors and their families, the challenge is the same as that faced by other victims of crime: to prevent a second victimization in the criminal courts!

You will find, as do other victims, that you may well have to fight to participate in the process to get your views heard by the court in the setting of bail, in a prospective plea bargain, in the sentencing, and in the parole. Demand to be notified of changes in court dates; for seniors, especially, repeated trips to court can be quite difficult. Demand to be present throughout the trial, and demand that the district attorney oppose any motion to exclude you.

In time, I believe, those who run our criminal-justice system will realize that justice is enhanced from start to finish by including the victim in the process.

Financial Recovery

With crime victim–compensation boards in place in every state and the District of Columbia, victims of violent crime now have somewhere to go for at least partial recovery. All states cover medical bills and funeral expenses not otherwise covered (up to a maximum), and some have been especially sensitive to seniors' needs. Pennsylvania covers stolen Social Security checks; many states cover broken eyeglasses.

In general, however, economic and property losses are not covered by victim-compensation boards, and seniors must pursue other remedies. I believe that three approaches are especially effective. Pursue all three, not just one exclusively:

1. See whether a government agency will get your money back. Try the state attorney general's office, a local consumer-affairs office, and/or the state securities commissioner.

2. Consult a lawyer. As surely as experienced hunters know where to find the ducks, capable lawyers know how to find out whether there is money for their clients.

3. Ask the judge for a restitution order as part of the sentencing. Then the convicted criminal is under a court order to pay you. But keep in mind that a restitution order grants you the right to the money, but not the money itself. You may still have a fight to attach the criminal's assets.

CHAPTER 12

Physical Assaults

"Who is left to weep for Logan? No, not one."
Chief Logan

The Logan Elm, situated near Chillicothe, Ohio, is the site of a speech given by a great Native American leader, Chief Logan of the Mingo tribe. Returning home from hunting one day in 1774, Logan, who had treated the white man well, discovered that his entire family had been massacred by settlers. So now, as he noted in this famous address, there was no one to weep for him.

I think that many victims of brutal physical assaults also feel that no one is weeping for them. Victims of physical assaults often face a lifetime of pain or permanent injury. Although they can obtain crime-victim compensation money (up to a minimum that may well not cover their actual bills), they do not have the same government-sponsored programs, community service agencies, and self-help groups that victims of other (equally horrible) crimes seem to have.

Definition of the Crime

A *physical assault* is an informal term for an act of violence committed against another person. Under the old Anglo-Saxon legal definitions, the term *assault* refers to any action that puts another in bodily fear, whether or not any contact is made. The term *battery* covers actual physical contact. Thus, technically, there can be an assault without a battery (such as a menacing step taken toward another), and a battery without an assault (such as a sucker punch, where the victim had no time to become afraid). Commonly, when someone is struck by a physical blow or a weapon, there is both an assault and a battery.

The old terms "assault" and "battery" still hold, but assault has been combined with other words to define harmful physical contact. Most states have defined felonies of *malicious assault* (striking another with the intent to cause great bodily harm) and/ or *assault with intent to kill* (intentionally inflicting harm hoping to kill the victim). Battery by itself, simply harming someone with felonious intent, is usually defined as a misdemeanor.

The Criminal Justice System

Crime takes a terrible toll for those who survive physical assault:

- A Kentucky man comes to Washington, D.C. to sell Christmas trees and is shot, robbed, and left for dead. Unconscious for weeks, he remains incapacitated and unable to provide for his children.
- A music teacher in Morgantown, West Virginia, is shot by a hitchhiker whom he befriended. After twelve weeks in intensive care, he goes home, still bedridden.
- An immigrant from El Salvador, working at Wendy's and sending home several hundred dollars a month to his wife, children, and mother, is shot during an attempted robbery and remains in a long-term coma.

If you are a victim of a violent physical assault, you need *help,* you need *money,* and you need *fairness from the criminal system.*

Victims need to assert their rights. For victims of violent assaults, I'm afraid that it's harder to succeed than with many other crimes. The media pay less attention, there is no rally of constituent groups, and prosecutors and judges rarely see a political percentage in making your case a priority. Still, fight on, because you can succeed!

Tell your victim/witness advocate of your desire to have your views known at each stage of the proceeding. If you don't get cooperation from the police or the assistant district attorney, write the police chief or the district attorney. You deserve to have input on bail (because the person who hurt you may want to hurt you or others again), at a plea bargain, at sentencing, and parole.

Unfortunately, the sentences for those who commit physical assaults are often quite short. Tougher legislation is needed. California reexamined its sentencing for those who commit violent crimes other than murder and rape only after one of the most horrible crimes on record. A man kidnapped a young woman, took her into the desert, and chopped off both her arms, leaving her for dead. Miraculously, she survived. His sentence was remarkably short and, when he obtained parole, as required by law, no community in the state would allow him to live there. His "parole" is being served on the grounds of—but outside—a jail; technically, he is a "free man." Unable to change any criminal law retroactively, the California General Assembly responded with tougher laws to deal with such dangerous sociopaths in the future.

Diane Crandall, a graphics-design graduate student in Erie, Pennsylvania, was attacked savagely while she slept by an assailant who had lain in wait at her apartment. The perpetrator, a white female business executive, was able to plead "impaired capacity" and was thus given a short sentence. (How many black male assailants in a woman's apartment could assert an impaired-capacity defense and not be laughed out of court?) Crandall fought back, not only to see that the criminal received a prison sentence, but also by joining the National Organization for Victim Assistance and designing an informative brochure to advise victims of their rights.

While attorney general of West Virginia, I sought to toughen the sentencing for violent crime while changing the sentences for nonviolent crime to alternatives that were less costly to the state, but more costly to the lawbreaker. As mentioned before, I didn't have much luck.

Despite creating a sentencing-reform commission composed of representatives of all sectors of the system of justice and the public, I couldn't get the state legislature to move. Why? The state bar opposed the bill, because the lawyers wanted to be able to wheel and deal with the prosecutors and negotiate the best plea bargains possible. The prosecutors opposed the bill, because they saw political value in negotiating deals with defense lawyers, who would remember them in their reelection campaigns. Some women's groups opposed the bill, on the grounds that sentences for brutal physical assaults were being categorized similarly to rape. The state ACLU opposed the bill, saying that no sentences should be increased. So, year after year, the special interest groups defeated a bill that probably 98 percent of the public supported.

Financial Recovery

State crime-victim compensation boards expend most of their money each year on physical-assault victims. They pay for medical bills not otherwise covered, and for lost wages. The bad news is that almost every state has a cap (maximum payout), and for badly injured victims that cap is reached all too quickly. The cap varies from $1000 (Georgia) to $50,000 (California). The Uniform Commission of State Laws, a blue-ribbon bar group, has recommended that the cap be at least $25,000 in every state.

You can do other things to go after money: get a restitution order at the time of sentencing, sue the assailant, or sue a liable third party. Each of these remedies is explored fully in Part III.

Restitution is a court order at the time of sentencing for the perpetrator to repay the victim. Restitution is the simplest strategy, but the court may not order it, or the award may be too low. Or the court may not find the perpetrator guilty.

Thus, you may want to sue the assailant in civil court. A criminal conviction is evidence in a civil court, but no finding of guilt is required to win a civil case. The two court systems are quite different. A defendant may not be guilty beyond a reasonable doubt in criminal court, but may be liable under the 51 percent or 60 percent standard applied in civil court.

Or you may be able to sue a "third party," some person or company that was negligent in not properly providing for your security. Third parties are being increasingly held liable in civil court. Malls, parking-lot owners, hotels, and apartment owners that do not provide adequate security on their premises to their customers are paying damages to injured victims. So are tavern owners who served people who were already intoxicated, and who then went out and caused a wreck due to their drunk driving.

But such cases don't just happen. Injured victims must initiate action themselves against liable third parties; no government agency will bring such an action for you.

Injured victims in a civil action are entitled to recover for:

- Medical and counseling bills;
- Lost wages;

- Costs of rehabilitation and recovery;
- An award for permanent injury; and
- An award for pain and suffering endured.

(If you recover, you may have to reimburse the crime-victim compensation board or your insurance company to the extent that there has been a double payment for the same bills.)

Living With the Crime

An increasing number of organizations are focusing on injured victims. Seriously injured victims can suffer head injuries, paralysis, or other damage to their nervous systems:

- Head injuries are quite common for victims and carry the risk of being permanent. Organizations working in this area include the National Head Injury Foundation in Southborough, Massachusetts (800-444-NHIF); the Brain Trauma Foundation in New York (212-753-5003); and the Think First Foundation, part of the American Association of Neurological Surgeons, Chicago (708-692-2740).

- Paralysis victims, either paraplegics (those unable to walk) and quadriplegics (those paralyzed from the neck down) can contact the Miami Project of Cure Paralysis (800-STAND-UP); the Paralyzed Veteran of America, Washington, D.C. (202-872-1300); and the American Paralysis Association, Springfield, New Jersey (800-225-0292).

- Victims who need physical rehabilitation should contact their state division of rehabilitation and recovery. It may be a separate department or part of the Department of Human Services or the Department of Labor.

- Find out about a self-help group for victims in your community. Believe me, in your community there are many crime victims suffering permanent injury or a lifetime of physical or emotional pain.

A poster of the Mothers Against Drunk Driving shows a picture of a young man in a wheelchair, with the caption "Don't call me lucky." No, the victim of a drunk driver who is paralyzed for life is not "lucky to be alive," as some thoughtless people tell him. Nor is a woman attacked and beaten on the streets "lucky you weren't raped," as she may be told.

Someday, efforts such as those by MADD, by Diane Crandall, and by the West Virginia Sentencing Commission will succeed. Victims of violent crime have started a revolution in our system of justice, and the forces of the status quo will either have to get out of the way or get knocked over.

As a victim of physical assault, assert your rights and don't listen to those who say you were lucky. Only those who aren't victims are lucky, and there are fewer of them every day.

CHAPTER 13

Drunk Driving

> "Dear Ann Landers: I am twenty-nine years old. When I was four, my grandfather was killed in a car accident, struck by a drunk driver. My only memory of him is the funeral. When I was ten, my brother was killed while coming home after serving in Vietnam. He was within a few miles of home when the car he was riding in swerved to avoid a car driven by a drunk driver. Yesterday we buried my father, who was killed in a head-on collision while going to work. That driver was also drunk. Dad was fifty-seven. He had never touched alcohol. Please, dear readers of Ann Landers column, I'm begging you to think about my family before you get behind the wheel of your car. Haven't we been through enough?" (signed) Wapakoneta, Ohio.
>
> —Column of June 23, 1990

Twice in the past generation, American boys fought for freedom in small corners of Asia, and both times the toll was gruesome. About 100,000 Americans were killed in action in the Vietnam and Korean wars combined. Yet, in the 1980s alone, about twice as many Americans were killed by drunk drivers.

Death or injury caused by a drunk driver is not merely a car "accident." The tragedy was set in motion—and therefore caused by—someone drinking too much and then, without any regard for others, getting behind the wheel.

Definition of the Crime

Driving while intoxicated, or driving while under the influence of alcohol, is defined in most states as operating a motor vehicle while having a blood alcohol content of 0.10 percent. Victim advocates are working for laws to lower the threshold to 0.08 percent, and California has done so.

Drunk driving is different from many other crimes in that the perpetrator does not have the same kind of intent. He or she did not intend to kill or injure that particular victim. But the behavior is still criminal in nature; it is like waving a loaded gun at a crowd and pulling the trigger.

The Criminal Justice System

There are *three* proceedings for drunk-driving victims to be concerned with. They are (1) the administrative case, which determines whether the driver can keep his or her driver's license; (2) the criminal case, which determines the innocence or guilt of the driver, and, if the latter, the sentence; and (3) the civil case, which permits victims to recover money for their losses.

The administrative case: In most states, a separate hearing is held to suspend the defendant's driving license. These cases are conducted by administrative courts, a third type of judicial proceeding different from both criminal and civil courts. The presiding official is usually an official of the state's department of motor vehicles and is often not a judge or a lawyer. The purpose of the hearing is limited to whether the driver's license will be suspended.

The criminal case: The laws and the courts used to be quite soft on drunk drivers. Even now, with tougher laws, sentences are much shorter for death caused by drunk driving than for death caused most other ways; typically, the sentence is a year or two, and probation remains quite common. On very rare occasions, a drunk driver has been charged with murder instead of vehicular homicide.

Resources to help you navigate through the system include the victim-service representative, probably located in the district attorney's office or the police department, or a local chapter of

Mothers Against Drunk Driving (MADD). Part II explains the stages of the criminal-justice process: the investigation, the filing of charges, the plea bargain or guilty plea (if any), the trial, the sentencing, and parole.

Mothers Against Drunk Driving has been active in victim advocacy in particular cases. For example, MADD may write a letter to the prosecutor about the plea bargain, or to the judge about the sentence. Whether elected judges and prosecutors listen to MADD out of respect or fear doesn't matter: they seem to listen! Part II explains the criminal-justice process.

To find out about your local Mothers Against Drunk Driving chapter, contact MADD's national office: P.O. Box 541688, Dallas, Texas 75354 (800-GET-MADD). Another excellent grass-roots organization dedicated to fighting drunk driving and with numerous chapters is Remove Intoxicated Drivers (RID), based in Schenectady, New York (518-393-4357). It, too, helps victims in individual cases and does national advocacy. A national group active in many of our high schools is Students Against Driving Drunk, based in Marlboro, Massachusetts (508-481-3568).

The Civil Case: Discussion of the civil case follows.

Financial Recovery

Victims of drunk driving have a better opportunity for financial recovery than any other group of victims. The reason can be stated in one word: insurance.

There aren't many millionaires around, but the majority of drivers carry insurance. If the other driver is at fault, even if only 51 percent at fault, the first source for recovery is his or her insurance policy. If the victim has any injuries at all, it is better to hire a lawyer. Insurance companies will almost always settle for a higher figure if they negotiate with a good lawyer. Why is that? The insurance companies say lawyers rip off the system by threatening costly lawsuits; the lawyers say the insurance companies take advantage of helpless victims without counsel and always offer too little. Both arguments have merit.

Most communities have lots of lawyers, but you should not settle for just any lawyer. Retain one with trial experience, one you trust when you interview lawyers, and one who specializes in representing the "little guy" in civil cases. Tips on hiring a lawyer are listed on pages 86–88.

In addition to the drunk driver's insurance, several other sources may be available:

The car owner's insurance policy—If the driver was not the owner of the car and was driving with the owner's permission, in some states the owner may be held liable for the drunk driver's behavior.

The victim's car-insurance policy—Most people carry uninsured-motorist coverage. If the drunk driver does not have insurance, or if the accident is hit-and-run, uninsured-motorist coverage applies. Another useful area of insurance is "underinsured motorist," which applies if the drunk driver has insurance, but the insurance isn't enough to cover all the losses of the victim.

The tavern or club—More and more victims are suing the taverns that served the drunk driver "one for the road." If someone is already intoxicated, he or she may not legally be served. Fortunately, responsible taverns are being much more careful about whom they will serve. Unfortunately, there are still many irresponsible taverns who don't pay attention to the problem. Lawsuits in this area are called "dram-shop" cases.

Adults who serve minors—If the drunk driver is under twenty-one (in every state the legal drinking age is now twenty-one), then any adult who sold or served the liquor can be liable. The Connecticut Supreme Court ruled in 1988 that an adult who serves alcohol to minors can be held liable for injuries caused by them. So victims may sue not only stores that sell alcohol to teenagers, but also adults who serve young people alcoholic beverages at a party in their home.

Crime-victim compensation boards—Some states, fearing large judgments, initially excluded victims of drunk driving from coverage, but those exclusions no longer exist. However, because of ceilings for each victim and the high cost of injuries associated with drunk driving, you are best advised to try all the other options in addition to this one.

Living with the Crime

As with other crimes, victims need help with emotional recovery as well as physical and financial recovery.

Some victims who survive a crash with a drunk driver are called "lucky." No one intends to be thoughtless, but it is the wrong thing to say. Someone who is badly hurt or emotionally scarred is definitely not lucky. Sympathy and offers of support are a much more meaningful response to a drunk-driving victim (or any other victim).

Physical recovery depends on the nature and extent of the injuries, but help can be found in many places. Information and help are available from the state's department of vocational rehabilitation, the local hospital, and the state physical-therapy association on recovery from debilitating injuries.

Counseling for victims and their families is extremely important. In addition to professional therapists and mental-health centers, victims should look to a local self-help group, composed of victims with similar experiences.

Advice on finding the right counselor is indicated on pages 6–7.

The horror of drunk drivers killing innocent people continues. The week you read this book, 400 people will die on American highways in alcohol-related crashes. Is there a way for this country to escape such madness?

You bet! Drunk-driving deaths are going down in this country, and the most important reason is the victims'-rights movement. And if victims rights succeeds with fighting drunk driving, then we can make it succeed in the area of crime fighting, too. Here's why:

1. *We are beginning to win the war against drunk driving.* Thousands of victims of drunk driving have died needlessly. But without a change of our attitudes, our laws, and our law enforcement in the early 1980s, things would have been much worse: 25,000 of us are alive and walking around because of the grass-roots movement that forced change in this country.

Americans drive 20 percent more miles now than in 1982, and the number of automobile deaths is up 5 percent. But the number of drunk-driving deaths is *down* 5 to 10 percent, and as a *percentage* of highway deaths it is down 12 percent.

The percentage of drunk teenagers who caused highway deaths went down twice as much as the overall rate. The message got through to our young people much better than it did to their elders.

Drunk-driving deaths never fell in the 1960s and 1970s. We all knew then what we know now about drunk driving. So what happened in the 1980s that was different?

First, and most important, we started to punish criminals. In the 1970s, sympathy reigned for the law violator; people caught driving drunk were told to take an education class, even if they killed another human being.

In the 1980s, most states started a new policy: *you drive drunk, you go to jail.* Human behavior changed quickly: many people who wouldn't have minded taking an education class saw the light when they realized they could go to jail. There was another message for bartenders and taverns: *you serve a drunk, and he has an accident, then you get sued.* Once a direct threat to the pocketbook started, many restaurants and bars also saw the light, encouraging "designated drivers" and refusing service to the intoxicated.

Everyone should want to provide treatment to alcohol-impaired people. I do, too—so long as they don't get behind the wheel. I want to help the emotionally disturbed person who waves a gun at a crowd of children, too, but before I get him to treatment, I want to take away the gun.

One rule needs to apply to all: *if you drink and drive, you go to jail.* It should not apply only to second- and third-time offenders. It's so hard to catch the drunk drivers that the rule should apply from the first offense.

A second rule should go with it: *if you drink and drive, you won't be driving anywhere for a long, long while.* The license should be taken away at once. Some states like Maryland do this now.

2. *The reason we are winning the war against drunk driving is the success of the victims'-rights movement in America.*

We owe a great deal to Mothers Against Drunk Driving, which has spearheaded the victims'-rights movement in the area of drunk driving. The group was founded by Candy Lightner of Sacramento, California, whose teenage daughter was killed by a drunk driver.

A similar loss was suffered by Flicka Graves of Beckley, West Virginia, whose lovely daughter Kelli, the school valedictorian, was killed by a drunk driver on her high school graduation night. The killer was immediately released on bail and resumed driving; Ms. Graves and her son used to see him driving around town. On the day of the pleas and sentencing, she showed up in court, only to be told that the judge, prosecutor, and defense lawyer were ahead of schedule that day, so they did the sentencing early! Soon thereafter, Ms. Graves started the MADD chapter in West Virginia.

The actions of an aroused citizenry worked. In the early 1980s, thousands of people went to jail and lost their licenses because they drove drunk. Many interrelated events spurred more changes: the police arrested many more drunk drivers, often 50 percent more. The media talked about the issue. Student chapters were organized. Taxicab companies offered free rides home. Victims went to court to make sure the judges and prosecutors took the whole matter seriously. Comedians took drunk driving out of their routines. A major transformation occurred in America.

To say that drunk-driving deaths are down in no way lessens the burden for today's victims: the battle is far from won. In many ways, the battle is much tougher now. We have removed that so-called "social drinker" from the road, but the hard-core drunk drivers remain: those who are out-of-control alcoholics or those who have no concern for their fellow man. One study found that fully half of those arrested for drunk driving have had one or more previous convictions.

3. *Since fighting for victims' rights can reduce deaths from drunk driving, our movement can reduce other crimes, too.*

It would be wonderful if all victims'-rights groups could have the impact that MADD has. I know it's possible. Grass-roots movements force politicians to respond quickly and make the media pay attention. They inspire new public attitudes and make the change permanent. Indeed, MADD founder, Lightner, has recently expanded her horizons, starting a broad-based group called Americans Against Crime.

The successes in the drunk-driving battle tell us both that victims'-rights movements can help reduce crime and that it is difficult to reduce crime *without* citizen involvement.

CHAPTER 14

Hate Crimes

> Those who are bigots do not stop at classes, at races, or again, at gays and lesbians. Those who hate you, hate me. Those who hate, hate everybody. Hate is contagious.... No one has the right *not* to allow you to acquire the dignity, the respect, and the self-respect to which we are all entitled.
> —Elie Wiesel, Jewish writer and Holocaust survivor

Definition of the Crime

H*ate crimes* are crimes committed against others based on their race, religion, national origin, or sexual orientation.

Hate crimes are not new. Our goal should be to make sure that they exist only in the history books.

The greatness of America is that we have brought together people from all over this planet and utilized their talents, cultural diversity, and sheer willingness to succeed. To be a Swede, or a Nigerian, or an Egyptian, or a Chinese, is to suggest a certain racial and geographic ancestry. But to be an American is to suggest nothing at all about where someone's family is from; the "homeland" is the here and now.

But the legacies of our country are not all positive: they include killing Native Americans and sending the rest to live on desolate reservations; enslaving African-Americans for 200 years, followed by 100 years of segregation; making life generally tough for each wave of immigrants as they arrived—Irish, Germans, Italians, Greeks, Poles, Jews, Hispanics, Asians.

Unfortunately, it is unclear whether we are moving in the right direction: Arab-Americans being targets during the Persian Gulf War, gay bashing by skinheads, white officers attacking motorist Rodney King in Los Angeles, blacks attacking whites during the subsequent Los Angeles riots, blatant anti-Semitism by those who call themselves "Christians," intimidation of Korean immigrants, and attacks against women (many psychologists consider rape a hate crime)—all of which demonstrate how far we have to go.

The Criminal-Justice System

Because hate crimes are aimed not only at an individual but at an entire group, they need special recognition in the law. Now, in most states, they have it. Some states have specific criminal laws aimed at hate crimes. Other states add to the severity of the sentence when the crime is motivated by hatred aimed at a particular group. All such laws include hatred based on race, religion, or national origin, but only some include protection based on sexual orientation; hopefully, all laws will soon include this latter category as well. Call your state, county, or city human-rights commission for information on your state's laws. If you don't have such a commission, call the local district attorney's office or the state attorney general.

The United States Department of Justice is active in fighting hate crimes. First, the department files suits based on the theory that a person has been deprived of his or her civil rights. Second, it began recently to collect statistics on hate crimes and incidents, so we can continue to monitor the severity of the problem. If you have any evidence of a hate crime, call the Department of Justice's Hate Crimes Reporting Line (800-627-6872).

Many national groups work closely with law enforcement to assist victims of hate crimes. Here are some of the key groups, with their headquarter city in parenthesis:

- For hate crimes generally, the National Institute Against Prejudice and Violence (Baltimore);
- For hate crimes based on race, the National Association for the Advancement of Colored People (Baltimore), the

NAACP Inc. Fund (New York), the National Congress of American Indians (Washington);
- For hate crimes based on religion, the Anti-Defamation League of B'nai Brith (New York);
- For hate crimes based on national origin, the Arab American Anti-Discrimination Committee (Washington) and the National Council of La Raza (Washington);
- For hate crimes based on sexual orientation, the National Gay and Lesbian Task Force (Washington).

Violence against gays has perhaps been the last area to garner the attention of the public. A recent study by the National Gay and Lesbian Task Force found that crimes committed solely because the victim is gay are widespread. One solution is to sensitize the law-enforcement community which, a generation ago, began to meet the challenge of better law enforcement in racial-minority communities.

Many law-enforcement agencies have redoubled their efforts to combat hate crime. The National Organization for Black Law Enforcement Officials, based in Baltimore and Washington, has published a booklet entitled *Hate Crime: A Police Perspective.*

A hate crime must, first of all, be a crime. Hateful expressions of speech or opinions, though distasteful, are constitutional. The Supreme Court ruled in 1992 that a St. Paul, Minnesota ordinance that prohibited cross burning is unconstitutional because it infringes on free speech. Yes, America is a free country for everyone, even for those who want to deny freedom to others.

Financial Recovery

The best place to hit the leaders of these hate groups is in their pocketbooks. The champion of making these merchants of hate pay for the crimes they mastermind is Morris Dees, a folksy lawyer from Montgomery, Alabama, who heads KlanWatch and the Southern Poverty Law Center. After several Klansmen lynched (yes, lynched) a young Alabama man about a decade ago, Dees sued the Klan on behalf of the dead man's mother, Beulah Donald. The *all-white* Alabama jury awarded Mrs. Donald $7 million.

Victims of hate crimes have the same financial remedies available as victims of other crimes of violence, such as victim-compensation boards and restitution. See Part III.

Responding to Hate Crimes and Hate Groups

Around the country, the response to hate crime is both encouraging and creative. Consider these examples:

- Faced with a settlement of the neo-Nazi group Aryan Nation, Mayor Roy Stone and the residents of Coeur d'Alene, Idaho, embarked on a ten-year aggressive but nonviolent campaign to make them feel unwelcome; most of the racists finally gave up and left.
- When the Ku Klux Klan asked to participate in the annual Potato Festival in Summersville, West Virginia, Mayor Steve LeRose surprised the Klan by saying, "Sure, here's your permit. You will have place number 22 in the parade route." The Klan, seeking a confrontation and publicity, withdrew its parade-permit application.
- When misguided zealots brought a ballot initiative to Oregon in 1992 that would have legalized discrimination against gays, the voters decisively voted it down.
- When the demagogue politician David Duke and his followers fought the integration of churches in Forsythe County, Georgia, civil-rights leaders, joined by the U:S. Justice Department and Georgia political and civic leaders, held a huge vigil in the town to demonstrate that they would not be intimidated.

When these hate groups rail against racial quotas, people should remind them that for generations in America, we had a rigid quota system: the less qualified white got the job over the more qualified black 100 percent of the time!

In the long run, love will triumph over hate—it's the short run we have to keep worrying about. When I had the opportunity to be a civil-rights worker in Fayette, Mississippi two decades ago, I saw Mayor Charles Evers, previously the head of the state NAACP, invite a large Southern discount chain to locate a store in his town. A few years before, Evers had led a picket of the chain for its hiring practices. The regional manager accepted. What a great sight it was to see those two former antagonists digging the first shovelful of earth to build the new store, bringing jobs and commerce to that community.

CHAPTER 15

White-Collar Crime

> The law—it punishes the man who steals the goose from off the green, but lets go free the man who steals the green from under the goose.
>
> —An old saying

Definition of the Crime

White-collar crime is nonviolent economic crime, in which money is stolen through false pretense, consumer fraud, or conspiracy. It costs Americans over $200 billion each year, several times more than the financial impact of all violent crime combined. Yet, whether by design or circumstance, we continue to fall enormously short in exacting punishment or recovering our losses.

The Criminal-Justice System

The federal government has several criminal statutes that apply to those engaging in white-collar crime. The major laws cover (1) *mail fraud,* criminal acts committed through the mails; (2) *tax fraud,* willfully hiding income from the IRS; (3) *extortion,* forcing a victim to pay money or provide services; (4) *racketeering,* a pattern of criminal activity; (5) *securities fraud,* stock manipulations and similar acts; and (6) *antitrust conspiracy,* an agreement to fix the price of a product.

State governments have enacted criminal laws covering a wide range of *consumer frauds:* deceptive acts and practices that lead to consumers giving money to the criminal. States also have enacted some or all of the above six categories of laws that the federal government has: all states, for example, outlaw securities fraud. Check with your local district attorney or state attorney general's consumer-protection office if you have a problem.

Opportunities to bring cases in civil court may be more important than in the criminal courts, due to the often large amount of financial losses involved. Virtually all of the above criminal laws have a *civil component:* the right to charge a violation and obtain reparation rather than a criminal conviction. The civil side is quite important: the level of proof required to win is much less in civil court, and the focus is on which side has the preponderance of the evidence, not on protecting a defendant's constitutional rights.

Financial Recovery

Financial recovery for victims of white-collar crime has its own peculiar roadblocks:

1. *The money may be gone.* The white-collar criminal may have squandered the money through a high-flying life-style, the way banker Charles Keating lived off senior citizens' life savings.

2. *The money may be hard to find.* It may be in a Swiss bank account or disbursed to relatives. Or it may have filtered into the netherworld of organized crime, which has its own ways of seeing that cash is never found by the IRS or anyone else. Or the defendant may be in bankruptcy.

3. *State crime-victim compensation boards do not help victims of nonviolent crime.* I am not criticizing them—they were not set up to do so, and have only so much money. We need other mechanisms to provide help for victims of economic crime.

4. *Victims are less likely to come forward.* To acknowledge being a victim of a white-collar criminal is, in the eyes of some people, to admit to naïveté or stupidity in financial matters or, even worse, to being associated with a fraud. Even when courts notify victims of a scam and ask them to come forward to be eligible for restitution, many people fear that doing so would place them in the public eye.

Having said all this is not to disparage the remedies we *do* have. Let's start with the *three remedies available to all victims:*

1. *Restitution:* The first option is restitution, a court order at the time of sentencing. This order can get the victims their money back, or at least provide a partial remedy. Talk to the victim representative; in a federal case, contact the local United States Attorney's office.

2. *Suing the perpetrator:* Civil lawsuits often result in verdicts of millions of dollars. These cases may be filed by a federal, state, or city government agency, by a private attorney in a class-action case, or by a private attorney whom you hire. Some lawyers specialize in white-collar-crime cases and base their fee entirely on a percentage of the recovery. (So, if you don't collect, neither do they.)

Even bankruptcy by the wrongdoer does not necessarily mean you are shut out. There may be *some* money, so go to the victim representative at your United States Attorney's office and ask him or her how to file a claim before the bankruptcy judge.

The federal government sued Michael Milken, whose manipulations lost tens of thousands of American workers their jobs, and recovered hundreds of millions of dollars. Yet, even after parting with such money, Milken remains a half-billionaire. Would you trade two years in federal prison for having $500,000,000 in your bank account? The question is at least worth pondering.

3. *Suing liable third parties:* Let me praise something the government is doing now. To retrieve money stolen by savings-and-loan swindlers, it is suing the lawyers and accountants who worked for them. Hooray! These CPAs made millions by examining the books of the S&Ls, then assuring the public and the government that everything was okay when they knew—or should have known—otherwise. The lawyers had knowledge of illegal activity, yet stonewalled the government and let these frauds continue to be perpetrated on the public for may more years. Lawyers are permitted to defend clients against fraud but, under the code of ethics, may not assist a client in perpetrating it.

J. P. Morgan, the leading robber baron at the turn of the last century, once discussed why he chose Elihu Root as his lawyer. "The others tell me what I can't do. Mr. Root figures out a way for me to do what I want to do." The savings and loan's law firms, as confederates for the S&L con artists, were following in this path, and it's time that they paid for it.

Now let's cover the remedies that are especially available to victims of white-collar crime. They fall into two categories: the government's helping you recover your money, and private parties helping you recover it.

Assistance from the Government
These state and federal agencies help victims of economic crime; their addresses are listed in Directory B:

• The Federal Trade Commission, the federal watchdog group for consumer protection;
• The United States Postal Service, whose investigators prosecute mail fraud;
• Your state attorney general's office, which has a division devoted to consumer protection. (Of course I am biased, but this would be the first place I would go);
• Your state securities commissioner, who can act to stop phony investment schemes;
• Your local district attorney, or a city consumer-protection agency.
• The Better Business Bureau in your community. The BBB is not really part of government—it is funded by local businesses—but it has become so established in its relationship with government that I place it here between government and private remedies.

Assistance from Private Parties
It's important to view fraud from the perspective of average businesspeople:

• They are honest and know that the scam artists are competing unfairly;
• They know that these frauds hurt the reputation of their business or profession;
• They may be victims, too—businesses are often easy targets of scam artists.

Not surprisingly, then, business and professional groups have set up systems to fight fraud in their own industry and to provide remedies for defrauded consumers. In short, *some groups provide money for you if a member cheats you out of your money*. Consider the following:

• Bar association trust funds have been set up in many states. Lawyers have taxed themselves so that citizens of those states who are cheated by a lawyer can apply to that fund for recovery.

• In my state of West Virginia, and in other states, the funeral directors have set up a fund to cover those who prepaid funeral expenses, and then discovered that the funeral director was no longer in business to provide the service.

• The stock exchanges provide arbitration when stockbrokers rip off their clients. Admittedly, one of the goals of Wall Street is to keep citizens out of court, but the arbitration system has been an inexpensive way for many citizens to retrieve their money.

True, you may say, some of these groups sound like foxes guarding the chicken coop. But give these groups their due: their members are trying to help you with the bad apples that exist in every profession. So check with your state attorney general's office of consumer protection (there is probably a toll-free line) whether remedies like these are available in your state for the business or profession in which you were defrauded.

A Word on Insurance

One of the major victims of crime in this society is our nation's insurance companies. We seem to have a national sport of getting the most from insurance companies, and a substantial part of this effort is direct fraud.

And it doesn't take a rocket scientist to figure out whose premiums pay for this fraud.

The insurance industry is fighting back on behalf of themselves and us, too. It has created several organizations, among them the Insurance Crime Prevention Institute, a group that works for changes in laws, law enforcement, and court procedures, and for initiatives in the private sector that can strengthen our battle against crime.

What to Avoid

I spent much of my time as a state attorney general educating our citizens about avoiding consumer frauds and helping them obtain redress against such con jobs. Yet it seemed that the more effort we made on education, the more clever the scam artists got. And the more aggressive we became in enforcement, the quicker they were to pick up and take their assets to another state.

An outstanding book on fighting economic crime is *White-Collar Crime 101 Prevention Handbook* by Jane Kusic. Kusic runs a victims'-rights organization called White-Collar 101 in Vienna, Virginia.

Here are some good suggestions for avoiding scams:

- *If it sounds too good to be true, it probably is.* Santa Claus never gives anything to grown-ups.
- *Know whom you are dealing with.* Get references before any service is performed. Get a *written* description of the company and the offer. If you are investing a lot of money, pay for a background check. Likewise, if you are investing, get the information that the company has disclosed to the state securities commissioner, e.g., prospectuses.
- *Know the remedy before you buy.* If you already know what you will do if something goes wrong, you are ready. If it is a product, get and keep the warranty. Find out where the company's local office, if any, exists and confirm its presence.
- *Take your time.* Those bills with Hamilton's, Franklin's and Grant's pictures on them will be good tomorrow, too. The company that doesn't want you to take time to learn about it and its investment or buying opportunity isn't the right company for you.
- *Know your own weaknesses.* The scam artist is looking for them. Some of us are more likely to believe a particular story line, some others a different one. After a devastating flood in West Virginia, I put emergency rules into effect to protect consumers in the affected area as they were rebuilding their homes. Natural disasters weaken people psychologically and physically, and put urgency into their purchases. We didn't want people to make rash decisions and invest their savings in an unsafe structure or otherwise get ripped off by unscrupulous contractors.

The final word on economic crime is the same as that for other victims: assert your rights. Go to those in government who are there to help, such as the victim advocate, the Federal Trade Commission, and the state attorney general's office of consumer protection. Talk to a private attorney about the options for litigation. Help to publicize the existence of scams in your community. You'll make it more likely that victims in future years will have a road map to follow.

CHAPTER 16

Burglary and Robbery

Your home has been burglarized—you have been robbed while walking home from work—your car has been stolen. Millions of Americans face this problem every year. The question now is, "What to do next?"

While writing this book, a funny thing happened to me. I took the train from Washington to New York, got off, and was directed to a taxi by a nice-looking young man. I naïvely believed he was there to help me. In the few seconds it took to get into the cab, I had my wallet stolen by him and his associate. I found the nearest police station, and two detectives returned with me to Grand Central Station to look for the robbers, but to no avail. So I got some firsthand experience as a victim while I was working on a book to help victims of crime!

Definition of the Crime

Robbery refers to the taking of property from a person in their immediate presence, against their will, accomplished by means of force or threat.

Burglary refers to the entering of a habitation or any building not open to the public—or remaining concealed in such a building after entering legally—with the intent to commit a felony or theft. (Interestingly, in the old English law, burglary applied only to entering homes at nighttime. But now burglary generally applies to entering at any time of day, and to buildings not open to the public as well as homes. The definition I gave you is a summary of the Texas law on burglary; your state's law is probably similar.)

Larceny or *theft* refers to the fraudulent taking and carrying away of property. "Larceny" generally applies to any act of stealing that is not burglary or robbery; "theft" is the more popular term.

Embezzlement refers to the stealing of funds properly in the control or custody of someone holding the money for another, but who then unlawfully converts it to his own use.

Carjacking is a new term for someone who steals a car from someone who is in or next to the car; there is now strong sentiment to define the act as a separate crime by state legislatures and Congress.

The punishment should fit the crime. Many burglars are career criminals, and you are doing a great favor to your community by helping to get them off the street. The line separating burglary or robbery from violent crimes is a very thin one. In fact, robbery is classified as a crime of violence in FBI statistics.

For first-time offenders, justice may best be tempered by mercy. The kid who steals can go in two directions with his life, and I'd like to see a system of justice that encourages him to straighten out his life. Sending teenagers and young people to the penitentiary for robbing a gas station may hurt society in the long run because it could turn an unwanted or abused child into a criminal.

I am impressed with a program called the U.S. Association for Victim–Offender Mediation. Originally begun by the Mennonite Church of Canada, it brings victims and offenders together with a third party. Far from letting the offender go scot-free, the program includes punishment but discourages incarceration. The offender—often a young person—is supposed to compensate the victim, even if it takes several years, or otherwise work out a solution with the victim. For more information, contact the group at 254 S. Morgan Blvd, Valparaiso, Indiana, 46383 (219-462-1127).

Tips on participating in the criminal-justice system are given in Part II.

Retrieving Your Property

Your first goal is retrieving your property. Stolen cars are quite easy to identify, consumer goods and antiques not so, unless they have been marked with an identification number.

Your problems may not be over when the police find the property. Sometimes the district attorney must keep the property as evidence in the trial. While some evidence is so important to a case that it must be kept until after the trial, in most courts a picture of the stolen object is sufficient to count as evidence. I have talked to prosecutors who continue to miss the point that when they keep the property for evidence, the owner still doesn't have it!

If your property is not recovered, your insurance company is the logical recourse. Check all policies (homeowners, car, etc.), and be aggressive in dealing with recalcitrant claims agents.

The banks and credit-card companies cannot make you pay for their losses when someone steals your wallet and illegally uses your checkbook, travelers checks, or credit cards. Credit card companies have a $50 limit on what they can charge for transactional losses. But you must report the theft and cooperate fully with the bank or card company.

Crime-victim compensation boards do not give people money for stolen property; their purpose is to help people who were physically assaulted. There are a few innovative exceptions, however: Colorado's board gives money to victims to repair broken locks and otherwise make their homes safe again, and some states give money for a new pair of eyeglasses.

Living with the Crime

Theft is about more than money. Consider the following:

1. *Burglary can lead directly to violence.* A woman in my neighborhood came home at lunchtime and surprised a burglar who beat her to death. The story is a common one, which is why, in the next section on crime prevention, you are advised to leave your home if you have any reason to believe that a burglar is in the house.

Robbery likewise can lead to murder. Bill Ullrich, the general counsel of the Indiana board of health, was robbed, then kidnapped, and spent two hours listening to his captors argue about whether to kill him to remove him as a witness. Fortunately, in this case, he was released.

2. *Burglary and robbery often cause major emotional damage.* It can ruin the family's equilibrium, making it hard for things to return to normal. Consider a single woman whose home was burglarized. Will she ever feel safe coming home again? What about a senior citizen who is robbed on the street where he lives?

3. *Belongings have a material value; you are now poorer, deprived of things you earned.* And belongings have a sentimental value; some things are simply not replaceable.

4. *Fear is contagious.* Each crime affects the victim's family, friends, and neighborhood, and persuades people to stay indoors. Ray Marvin, the former executive director of the National Association of Attorneys General, points out that today in America's cities it is the law-abiding people who are locked up every night (out of fear of going out), while the criminal element is in control of the streets, instead of the other way around.

So you may need the same type of emotional recovery period that victims of other crimes need. Get the help you need from the victim-assistance representative, from counselors, and from self-help groups.

Part V

Crime Prevention: Don't Be Victimized Again

CHAPTER 17

Security for You and Your Family

If anyone wants to tell the world about crime prevention, it is crime victims. Most victims'-rights groups are started by those who experienced the impact of crime firsthand, either as a victim or as the family member of a victim. Victims have encouraged me to talk not only about rights for victims, but about crime prevention.

I have met so many victims who are unselfish about their fate. Instead of saying, "It's too late, I'm already a victim," they say, "I don't want others to go through what I have." So it is only appropriate to conclude a book on victims' rights by covering crime prevention.

Chapter 17 discusses personal security for you and your family, both in and outside the home. Chapter 18 moves away from personal crime prevention to community solutions and national strategies for combating crime.

Security in the Home

Crime prevention starts in the home. Security in the home necessitates strategies in several areas:

- Keeping intruders out.
- Not being deceived into letting the wrong people in.
- Having a plan in case unwanted people actually do get into the home.

Unfortunately, the totally burglarproof home has not yet been invented. However, you can make your home such an unappealing house for burglars that they are less likely to take the risk. (The next chapter covers how to make your entire neighborhood equally unappealing to the criminal element.) Here are some tips:

1. *Buy deadbolt locks for the doors.* The average burglar takes 60 seconds to break in. If your devices delay entry by, say 90 seconds, that's fine—it may suffice.

2. *Make an inventory of your doors.* Have a peephole and use it. The door frame should be checked before new locks are added. Hollow-core doors should be replaced with solid wood or metal: a solid wood door could be improved by a metal sleeve, and a wood-paneled door could be replaced or reinforced by a metal plate or decorative grillwork. Glass in the door within 40 inches of the inside turn latch requires attention; reinforce it with a double-cylinder deadbolt lock. Double doors are particularly difficult to secure; extension flush bolts may offer the best protection.

3. *Reinforce all windows.* Drills and pins are cheap and effective. Don't forget those on upper floors: many second-story windows are easily accessible.

4. *Pay attention to garage doors.* Locking the door in the first place is a good first step. Garage door locks installed by manufacturers are often too flimsy. Install a case-hardened hasp, or padlock, or both.

5. *Padlock basement entranceways.*

6. *Get special devices so that sliding-glass doors cannot be opened from outside.* Make sure the window cannot be lifted out of its track or forced open.

7. *Dogs can be a great deterrent.* Many career criminals say that they automatically avoid houses with barking dogs.

8. *Searchlights on the outside of the house are a deterrent.* Don't give the burglar room to run around in the dark. Also, make sure that the light doesn't just shine out and away from the house so that burglars could hide against the house in the shadows under the light.

9. *High fences are* not *a good idea.* Once the burglar gets over the fence, he or she can never be seen by a neighbor. Low fences are best.

10. *Bushes should be trimmed, lest they also provide a hiding place.*

11. Decals on the house that say "Protected by ——— security

agency" are a good idea. While sophisticated thieves may know better, the rookies may be afraid to take the risk.

12. Burglar alarms are a wise investment, if you can afford them. Except for those homes in rural areas, the noise would scare away most would-be burglars.

13. *Have lights that go on and off at night.* A professional agency can set them so they operate in sequence, with the bedroom lights going off last, as would be the case if someone were there.

14. *For women, put a first initial and last name on the mailbox.* There is no reason to telegraph that a woman or women are occupants of a residence.

15. *Change the locks when you move into a new residence.*

Many guides to crimeproofing your home are available. One I especially like is the "Home Security Survey" published by the Virginia Beach, Virginia, Police Department.

That covers the structural side. Let's turn to the behavioral side of protecting your home. I have fifteen tips in this area, too:

1. *When you are gone, keep a light on.* (If you can afford it, or can rig it up yourself, use the automatic-light system in tip 13, above.) Also, keep a radio or TV on when you are gone. It will keep burglars guessing whether someone is home.

2. *Know the emergency phone number(s) in your community.* Fortunately, more and more cities are now moving to the 911 system, a number that every child over age five should know how and when to use.

3. *Have a phone in the bedroom within reach of your bed.* Also be able to lock your bedroom door; give a relative or trusted friend a duplicate key.

4. *For goodness' sake, if you have guns, keep them locked away.* Every year, kids are killing kids, and the numbers are increasing. As adults, we know that children like to play games with pretend guns. We also know that teenagers will fight. Let them fight with their fists, not their parents' guns. *Please* don't let your home become the site of accidental bloodshed between family or friends.

5. *Know who is at the door before you open it.* A window, peephole, or latch would accomplish this preliminary task.

6. *Know who you are letting in.* Do not let someone in who asks to use the phone in an emergency—instead, *you* make the call for them. Check the ID of any utility representative or repairperson.

7. *Get references from your baby-sitter and check them carefully.* Ideally, use someone whom your friends use and recommend. The chances of a sadistic sitter are infinitesimal, but the horror stories are real.

8. *Do not reveal personal information on the phone.* Do not admit that no adult male lives in a house: "No, my husband/father is not in now."

9. *Do not telegraph your absence on a telephone-answering machine.* I did once—and had a lecture waiting on my machine from my older brother that I should never admit to being out of town! Simply say "We [even if you live alone] can't get to the phone now—please leave a message."

10. *When you leave town, have someone get your newspaper and mail daily.* If you have a friend who is willing, have him or her move your car each day; open the drapes for part of the day, then close them later; and turn lights on and off. Ideally, it would be nice to have someone stay at your home during a long absence.

11. *Your neighbors on either side should be told that you are leaving and asked to report suspicious activity to the police.* (Be sure to tell them who will be there legitimately to get the mail, etc.) This advice presupposes that you have gotten to know your neighbors, which unfortunately is less and less true in this mobile society.

12. *If you return home and believe a burglar is in the house, leave!* Cemeteries are full of heroes. Let the police go in and find out whether someone is there.

13. *If you discover a burglar, cooperate.* Property can be replaced— you cannot be.

14. *Put valuables in a safe-deposit box at the bank.*

15. *Inventory your property.* Make a list of everything of value and its serial number, if it has one. Photograph valuable items, then photograph each room. This preparation will be invaluable in your insurance theft (or fire) claim, and will help the police recover your property.

See the book list in Directory D for more information on home security.

Personal Security Outside the Home

Personal security takes on a different challenge when you are away from home. It is not possible to have the same preparation for the unexpected as in your home, due to the unfamiliarity of the surroundings, the likelihood of no nearby telephone, and the lack of physical barriers that your home provides. While, as in the home, there are no foolproof techniques to avoid being preyed on by criminals, proper precautions can improve everyone's chances.

Crime-Prevention Techniques While Walking

1. *Stick with a crowd.* Loners are by far the most likely crime victims.

2. *If you have a choice of one-way streets, walk on the one facing the traffic.* Then someone walking toward you isn't sure whether a car—hence a witness—is heading your way.

3. *Dogs are a great deterrent.* If you have a dog, take him along on a leash.

4. *If accosted, turn over your money and, if requested, your jewelry, too.* Most criminals are seeking only your property; for those, it is best not to upset their plans.

5. *Don't carry much money.* But do carry some, so you have something to give.

6. *Don't carry a purse with a long strap; it's a target that is far too inviting.* If you carry a purse at all, carry it close to the body.

7. *Intoxicated people are sitting ducks: for robbery, for rape, for scams, you name it.* If you have drunk too much and you are not in the company of trusted friends, take a cab—don't try to "walk it off" alone.

8. *Carry a noisemaking device.* I recommend something that you can activate with your hand and that makes an unusual sound. A freon horn, popularized by Ellie Wegener and her citizens' group in Philadelphia, meets both criteria. If you have to blow something, you may be attacked so quickly that you can't do so. If your sound is only a loud whistle, people nearby may think someone is looking for their dog.

9. *Learn self-defense.* There should certainly be some good courses in your town.

Crime-Prevention Techniques While in Your Car

1. A new term entered the American vocabulary in the past couple of years: *carjacking,* the attempt to steal a car while the driver is in it. *If the threat of assault or robbery is imminent, stay in your car.* But do not resist an armed suspect—give the carjacker your

car keys and your car. For your sake, and your family's, no car is worth fighting for. Make it clear that you do not want to go with him or them, and that they may have your car to drive off as they please.

2. *Keep your doors locked while you drive.* It is safer if there is an accident, it helps keep children inside, and it also discourages crime. Many property crimes, car thefts, and crimes of violence occur when a criminal approaches a car stopped at an intersection.

3. *When leaving your car, always lock the doors, even if there are no valuables inside.* Not only are you more likely to stop a theft of the car itself, but you will deter a thief's getting into the car and lying in wait for you to return. Before entering your car, see if anyone is inside.

4. Car alarms and security devices can be helpful. A lesser alternative is a sticker on the car that *says* that the car has a security device, at least as a deterrent for the less-sophisticated crook. Here is another idea: after a rash of car thefts in Queens, New York, residents put signs on their cars requesting that police officers stop the car if it was being driven between 1:00 and 5:00 in the morning!

5. *If the car is broken down, go for help* only *if it is easily accessible.* Otherwise, put a white rag on the driver's side door. If another driver asks to help, *do not get out of the car*—instead, roll down the window a few inches to talk. Ask that driver to call the police or a repair company.

6. *If you think you are being followed, drive quickly to a police or fire station.* A good second choice is to a public, well-lit store. Pull right up to the station or store; don't park out in the lot. Do not drive home; it tips off criminals to where you live.

7. *If your car is hit and you feel uncomfortable getting out, motion the other driver to follow you to the nearest police station, where you will report the accident.*

8. *Whether parking in a lot or on the street, park near the other cars.* Stay away from isolated places. Stay away from corners where a quick exit from your car is difficult.

9. *At night, or if your car will be there until after dark, park under a light, whenever possible.*

10. *Keep your car keys separate from your house keys.*

11. *Determine where you are going before you get out of the car, so you look like you know where you are going.* Notice the layout, including

the location of telephones, stairwells, and exits. When you return, if accosted, you will be better able to make a getaway or otherwise get help. Have your key ready when you get back to your car.

Other Crime-Prevention Techniques

1. Before leaving on a vacation, sit down with your children and make plans about what to do if someone gets lost. Give a telephone number to call to the older ones, and describe how to find and talk to a safe person, such as a police officer, for the younger ones.

2. *Don't carry lots of cash.* Carry valuables on your body, such as in a hip pack, not in a purse or pocket.

3. *In buses, sit near the driver.* On subways and trains, sit near other people.

4. *In hotels* always *lock, and double-lock, the doors.* Do not let in anyone whom you have not already talked with by phone. If a bellman comes without invitation, call the front desk first to ask whether he was sent.

5. *Check the elevator before entering and always feel free to wait for the next one if you don't like the looks of who is inside.* If accosted while on the elevator, push all buttons, including the alarm.

6. When traveling on business, find out as much as possible about the hotel, parking, and travel directions before you leave.

7. *Safety in the workplace means more than freedom from industrial accidents.* Homicides, rapes, and other violent crimes at the job site are increasing. Indeed, for women, homicide is the largest cause of death on the job! (For men, it is still industrial accidents.)

Special Cases: Protecting Our Children, Guarding Against Rape, Stopping White-Collar Crime

Protecting Our Children

Physical and sexual violence against children is not only the most unforgivable crime, but is almost certainly the number-one *cause* of crime. As the twig is bent, so goes the tree.

This is what we can teach our children about crime prevention:

1. *Never admit anyone into the house whom the child does not know well, even if the stranger pretends to know the child.*

2. *Always keep the doors locked, even if you are home.*

3. *Never tell anyone who phones that there are no adults in the house.*

Simply say, "My mommy/daddy isn't able to come to the phone now."

4. *As early as possible, the child should be taught to dial zero or 911 in an emergency.* For parents and older children, a list with the following information should be available next to *each* phone:

POLICE	**"O"** or **911**
FIRE	**"O"** or **911**
AMBULANCE	**"O"** or **911**

Doctor   _____

Parents' work numbers: _____

                                _____

Close relative: _____

Close friend: _____

School(s):   _____

                                _____

                                _____

Poison-control center: _____

5. *Make sure your child's school has a policy that only people on your approved list can pick up the child.* Additions can be made only with a letter you send to the school, or a system of verification that entails phoning the parent. If the school doesn't have such a policy, make sure that it understands and agrees that this will be the policy for *your* child.

6. *If there is no adult in the house, your child should telephone you when getting home.*

7. *Children should know what to do when they are lost, whether it is out shopping a mile from home, or on vacation a thousand miles away.* They should be taught to find a uniformed officer to help solve their problem. In a store, clerks are also safe people. Your children need to know the phone number and address of where they are staying.

8. *When on vacation, have a backup person—a friend or relative who is likely to be at home—for everyone to call in an emergency so that your family can reconnect with each other.*

9. *Children should not enter their homes if a window is broken or there is any other sign that a stranger is inside.* Instead, they should go to a trusted neighbor and explain what they saw.

10. *Teach your children that a stranger is someone they don't know—even if that person acts as if they know him or her.* They should be taught to run away from anyone who approaches them or offers them anything.

11. *A good technique for a child grabbed by a man is to shout, "You're not my dad" and try to get away.* Such a denial alerts passersby that more than a disciplinary action is going on.

12. *Other self-defense tips for children are available from the National Assault Prevention Center and the National Crime Prevention Council (the McGruff people).* See Directory B for the address and telephone number.

13. *Obtain references before hiring a baby-sitter.*

14. *If your children are baby-sitters, allow them to work only for people you know, or for whom you can get references.*

15. *When your child babysits, the same rules of safety apply as at home—when the phone rings, when someone comes to the door, etc.*

16. *Keep current photographs of your children.* Take pictures of birthmarks or other distinguishing features, and have their fingerprints taken (which generally will be done free by the police or a civic group).

17. *Teach your children to tell you about any adult or teenager who did something that made them uncomfortable, who offered them a gift or food, or who asked them to keep a secret.*

Guarding Against Sexual Assault

1. *Reread the advice in this chapter dealing with safety in the home, in the car, and while walking.* All these tips are aimed at avoiding both physical and sexual violence.

2. *It is a sad commentary on society that women must be more careful than men when they are alone or with a single male.* But it is also a reality—don't forget it. (And let's not kid ourselves either: men can and are victims of rape by other men; it's just that such events are much less common, and less reported, too.)

3. *Walk with confidence and the sense you know exactly where you are going.* Rapists and muggers are more likely to attack someone who appears distracted, preoccupied, or vulnerable.

4. *When expecting to walk distances, wear clothes and shoes that permit freedom of movement.*

5. *Don't be afraid to scream, to set off a noisemaking device, or to run.*

6. *Take self-defense classes.*

7. *Emotional appeals about children, or appeals to the would-be rapist's self-interests, such as a story that you have a contagious venereal disease, sometimes work.*

8. *Rape by an acquaintance (known more commonly, though less accurately, as "date rape") is drawing increasing public scrutiny, as well it should.* Tips to reduce the chances of acquaintance rape include:

• Stay with a group until you know someone well; indeed, it's best to meet in a public place.

• Make clear what are the limits of acceptable behavior.

• Don't forget that alcohol both impairs judgment and reduces physical strength.

• Be willing to walk away. Threaten to leave only once, then do it.

• Fight back, unless the man is armed or you otherwise feel that you would be injured more seriously if you do. Ira Lipman, an expert on crime prevention, suggests in his book, *How to Protect Yourself from Crime* (Contemporary Books, 1989), using a knee to the groin if attacked from the front, an elbow to the stomach if attacked from behind, and a stomp on the instep in either case. Keys and umbrellas can be useful weapons.

Use common sense. Why trust someone who has not yet earned your trust?

Stopping White-Collar Crime

1. *If something sounds too good to be true, it probably is.* Every consumer watchdog, from Jane Bryant Quinn to Jane Kusic, starts with that advice.

2. *Know your remedy before you spend your money.* Ask yourself, "What would I do if this product/service/investment doesn't work out?" Chapter 17 discusses remedies, and Directory B lists state and federal agencies that deal with consumer complaints. The best bet is often your state attorney general's office, which may have a toll-free number.

3. *Don't be in a hurry to spend your money.* People who offer you opportunities that "can't wait" are usually people who can't wait to leave town with your money.

4. *When you are solicited over the phone, do not give your credit-card number or other personal data.* If you are comfortable buying over the phone, call the seller back so that you can verify its office location.

5. *Before having a service or repair done, get references and a written estimate.*

6. *Scrutinize hospital and other health-care bills.* All studies show that they are frequently rife with overbilling errors.

7. *Before investing in the stock market or in any business opportunity, get the information in writing.* Find out the licensing or credentials of the salesperson. Assume that any reluctance to disclose means that information is being hidden from you. If the investment is any large sum at all (a "large sum" is whatever *you* consider to be a large sum), get the advice of a CPA, lawyer, or other professional who has no stake in the success of the venture.

CHAPTER 18

Neighborhood, Community, and National Crime-Prevention Strategies

Neighborhood Strategies for Fighting Crime

In the summer heat in Philadelphia in 1776, delegates convened to vote on Thomas Jefferson's Declaration of Independence. With King George's army stationed just miles away in New York, the delegates were about to take a step considered an act of treason against the Crown. Wise old Ben Franklin urged unanimous action, admonishing the group that they must "hang together, or surely we will all hang separately."

Two hundred years later, Philadelphians faced a different threat to their safety. Instead of the Redcoats, the threat this time came from within: the criminal element terrorizing neighborhoods all over the city. Ellie Wegener, a Philadelphia homemaker and civic activist, followed Dr. Franklin's sagacious advice. After three rapes in her neighborhood in one week, she and her husband Bill, a Lutheran minister, initiated a neighborhood-based, community-wide approach to fighting crime by launching one of the first citizen-based crime-prevention programs in the nation.

Wegener's program, eventually known as the Citizens Local Alliance for a Safer Philadelphia (CLASP), was based on grass-roots involvement, with people showing criminals that they were unwelcome in the neighborhood. First, each participating block elected its own leader. Second, each block conducted neighborhood foot patrols on two-hour shifts each night. Third, neighbors got to know each other, conducted outdoor events, and otherwise showed criminals that they were taking the streets back. Fourth, citizens lobbied City Hall for structural improvements, such as more lighting. Fifth, the alliance conducted educational campaigns on personal safety. Neighborhoods consisting of all races and income levels joined in; in all, 3,000 blocks started their own organizations. Soon it became clear that participation not only lowered the crime rate but also raised property values, as local realtors would tell buyers which blocks were in the program. The alliance had its own trademark: foot patrols carrying freon horns that made an unpleasant, highly recognizable sound to indicate danger.

Most important, the effort in Philadelphia inspired people to reassert control over their neighborhoods. Politicians were suspicious initially; Philadelphia's Mayor Frank Rizzo told the citizenry to limit their activities to telling the police what they saw or heard. Eventually, however, politicians all over town lined up to support—and take credit for— the effort.

A decade later in Philadelphia, as drugs became both the chief cause and effect of violence, Dr. Herman Wrice, decided to do full-time battle against the scourge of his city. Wrice and his Philadelphia Anti-Drug Coalition went to drug-infested street corners and conducted all-night or even several-day vigils, effectively driving away the criminals. Wrice's attack procedure, with its single-minded focus on drugs, has been imitated in cities across the country.

Examples of citizen action against crime prevention abound. In Tulsa, Oklahoma, Drew Diamond, the city's former police chief, had seen Neighborhood Watch programs fail because, after being started by the police, they never developed grass-roots involvement. He made sure that Tulsa's Neighborhood Watch programs grew from concern with crime prevention to focus on other community needs as well.

Neighborhood Watch programs exist all over America today. They work best when they have a positive emphasis—this is our neighborhood and exists for our enjoyment—rather than the narrower focus on preventing crime. Neighborhood Watch programs encourage citizen foot patrols, the reporting of suspicious activity, and neighbors sharing information about what is going on. Citizens are encouraged to enjoy the outdoors as part of the effort to keep the "unwelcome mat" out for criminals.

For Neighborhood Watch, then, both words are important. As well as watching out for crime, citizens are taking back their neighborhoods. President Ronald Reagan pointed out that neighborhoods keep crime down by being the place where "the real spirit of a community can develop."

Citizen involvement in effective law enforcement has a long history. The term "raise a hue and cry" came from the Middle Ages in England, when people would attempt to corner the lawbreaker, then start shouting until the sheriff arrived.

The twentieth century may be remembered for being the era of the experts. By mid-century, involvement by ordinary people in solving anything was discouraged; doctors automatically anesthetized women in order to deliver their babies, everyone had to have a lawyer to pursue a legal claim, and only cops and robbers ever entered police stations. By the end of the century, however, we have realized the error of turning all decisions over to the experts. We have found that doctors and hospitals are no substitute for good health habits. We have started small-claims courts for citizens to address grievances without lawyers. And we have involved our communities in crime fighting.

Law-enforcement and court officials are now seeing the advantage of involving victims. When the city of Tampa, along with its mayor and police department, started its successful program to root out drugs (QUAD), its cornerstone was citizen involvement.

Some community actions against crime should win Oscars for their creative solutions to fighting crime. In Washington, D.C., citizens upset by the spread of prostitution into their neighborhood, and frustrated by the failure of the court to control it, set up cameras, replete with large signs, advising potential customers that they were being filmed (and who knows what television station would want to show such a film!). Unable to do business, the prostitutes moved out of the neighborhood.

In Berkeley, California, seventy-five irate neighbors sued the landlord who owned a drug-infested apartment building, claiming that the drug activities were a public nuisance. The neighbors won, receiving $5,000 each and a court order that required the landlord to evict the drug dealers.

Two men in Michigan, at wits' end about the availability of drugs to children in their community, burned down a crack house in their neighborhood. The jury promptly acquitted them of arson. Such an approach is not recommended here, but the community response, as demonstrated in the jury verdict, is not surprising.

Grass-roots action against crime works. The most successful programs work closely with the police, who have long recognized that they cannot go it alone.

Chief Reuben Greenberg of Charleston, South Carolina, is one such cop. The no-nonsense approach of this police chief has drawn accolades all over the country. With strong support from the entire community, Greenberg and his force have reduced crime substantially in this historic city. There is one message—and one message only—for drug dealers and hoods in Charleston: you go to jail.

A program with an outstanding success rate is Crime Stoppers. First begun in Albuquerque, New Mexico, Crime Stoppers asks people to provide tips for catching criminals. The program succeeds because it guarantees anonymity and provides rewards. (If the tip results in an arrest, the reward money is left at a designated bank, and the tipster picks it up at the drive-in window using a secret number provided by the police on a secure telephone line.) The reward money is donated by civic groups, and the police have a separate line for its Crime Stoppers operation.

Crime Prevention in Minority Communities

Nowhere is crime prevention needed more than in our minority communities. Young African Americans and Hispanics are much more likely to be victims than the rest of us, and, increasingly, it is the communities' political leaders who are calling for the toughest action against crime.

The sad commentary of crime in minority neighborhoods is illustrated by the tragedies that befell Jose Roman in the Bronx, New York City's poorest borough. Roman's young son was murdered by a punk named Jose Dominges. Dominges bailed himself out and quickly committed two actions that, in a white suburb, would almost certainly have resulted in immediate parole revocation. First, when he saw Roman, he opened his coat, showing a concealed weapon. Roman told the assistant district attorney, who reportedly said that there was "nothing we can do about it." Then Dominges attempted a drive-by shooting of Roman's other son. He missed but wounded three bystanders. Dominges was arrested a second time, and released on only $2,500 bail!

Dominges remained free. His trial was delayed month after month. Roman kept going to pretrial hearings. Finally, at the *tenth* pretrial hearing, as Dominges walked toward the courthouse, he spotted Roman and reached for his pocket. Assuming that Dominges was going for his concealed weapon, Roman pulled a gun he had bought to protect himself and fired. Dominges (who had no gun that time) was wounded, but recovered quickly.

Unlike with Dominges, the district attorney acted quickly against Roman, trying him *before* Dominges was tried. (I suppose lawyers consider crime outside the courthouse more important than crime elsewhere in the community.) The jury acquitted Roman on attempted murder, and voted 11 to 1 for acquittal on the assault charge.

Finally, two years after killing Roman's son, Dominges was convicted, but only of manslaughter. He is in prison as this book was being written, but who knows—he may be out on parole by the time you read this page.

Crime Prevention on Campuses

Michael Clay Smith knows American universities as well as anyone. Now a professor at Southern Mississippi State University and a specialist in education law, Smith has degrees in both law and divinity. In fact, he has the unique distinction of having been a priest and the county prosecutor at the same time. Later, when he was chief deputy attorney general of West Virginia, I used to kid him that he must have gotten *very* few confessions from parishioners!

Several years ago, a freshman at West Virginia University was allegedly gang-raped by several members of the elite basketball team. Despite substantial evidence, the case simply faded away. Smith investigated WVU, then did his own survey of the national university scene. The result was so stark that Smith accused American universities of a cover-up of crime, both by discouraging its reporting and hiding the overall crime rates.

American universities first denied Smith's charges, but soon admitted them. Some horrifying murders and rapes, plus million-dollar jury verdicts for lack of security, forced them to face reality. They did not object when the major campus crime-fighting group, Security on Campus, lobbied Congress to require disclosure of their crime rates to prospective students, and they started programs to deal with crime. Now security and foot patrols are common at all major universities and at most small colleges as well.

Professor Smith and his wife Margaret have written a book on how to stay safe on campuses: *Wide Awake—A Guide to Safe Campus Living in the 90s* (Peterson's Guides, 1990).

National Organizations

Leading the charge among volunteer organizations is the National Crime Prevention Council. The symbol of the group is McGruff, the dog in the trenchcoat who has encouraged young and old alike to "take a bite out of crime." The Washington-based group also heads the Crime Prevention Coalition.

Two leading organizations deal with child abuse, our primary crime problem: the National Committee against Child Abuse, based in Chicago, with chapters in all fifty states; and the National Center for Missing and Exploited Children, based in Arlington, Virginia.

Many local crime-fighting organizations have sprung up all over America. The Stephanie Roper Committee in Maryland, VOCAL in Alabama, and Citizens for Justice/Crime Victims United in Oregon are all examples of citizens pooling their energies to demand changes from their government.

Taking Back the Streets

When law-abiding people must stay home behind bars and criminals control the streets, we have it backward. One example of this mixed-up situation is the legislative effort to close stores at night, on the grounds that it decreases crime. Instead, we should get criminals off the street so that people can shop at a time convenient to them.

A few years ago, I had the chance to visit the Holy Land, and walked the streets of Jerusalem alone late one night. All around me were people from every race, culture, and continent, people who belong to all three major Western religions, and every denomination and faction within those religions. Jerusalem teems with people who have fought and continue to fight each other since King David founded the city. Yet I felt safe, or at least a lot safer than walking at night in a large American city.

With action at the neighborhood and community levels, we can take back our streets—but we need help on the national level to do it. As the second half of this chapter explains, we need leadership to deal with drugs, guns, and child abuse, and to provide opportunities for America's young people.

National Strategies

Despite the crime wave, our nation still lacks a national crime-prevention strategy. Why? Part of the answer is politics. Instead of rolling up their sleeves to solve problems, both political parties in Congress have indulged in an effort to paint themselves as tough on crime and the other side as favoring the criminal element. Not surprisingly, then, all we get is do-nothing sloganeering. Republicans would have the voters believe that the crime problem would disappear with heavy use of the death penalty and the impeachment of softhearted judges. Democrats counter with a bigger-government argument: give prosecutors bigger staffs, even though bigger staffs won't make them more sensitive to victims' rights; and pass out more money all around. Both parties should know better—and probably *do* know better.

While crime fighting must remain essentially local, with strong law enforcement and an aroused citizenry, a national strategy can make a huge difference.

To fight crime effectively on the national level, we must focus on four major areas: child abuse, drugs, guns, and a national message. For each, there must be a national strategy that involves government, business, law enforcement, the nonprofit sector, and the public.

1. Child abuse

Time and again, we find that violent criminals were themselves victimized at a young age. How do we break this vicious cycle?

First, we must prosecute. There was a time—indeed, it is a period stretching back many generations—that allowed parents to do anything they wanted to do to their kids. Such parents, and others in the household, need to know that child abuse, when detected, will result in prosecution.

Prosecution of sex and violent crimes against children requires special skills. District attorneys need to have assistants specializing in this area. They need to work closely with social workers, who are often the key to getting the child out of a threatening environment. Rules of evidence should permit children to testify in a way that does not retraumatize them.

Second, we must confront the reality of repeat offenders. In the case of pedophiles, there is a serious question whether they can *ever* be cured. As a society, we must find a way, consistent with the United States Constitution, to isolate these people from children.

Long prison sentences for repeat offenders are an obvious answer; but, even then, what is to be done when those sentences end? Several alternatives should be considered. One, the most obvious, is to prevent people convicted of child sexual abuse from ever having jobs with access to children, such as in day-care centers or schools. A possible federal role would be to keep a directory of such people on a national basis and, working with the states, make sure no school, day-care center, or other high-risk employer, hires any of them. Such a law was drafted at the instance of celebrity Oprah Winfrey, who went public to reveal that she was a victim of child sexual abuse by her uncle. Without federal participation, such people could drift from state to state and not be detected when they apply for high-risk jobs.

An approach worth watching is being taken in the state of Washington, in the aftermath of a horrible sex crime. A repeat child molester, while in prison, outlined to fellow inmates the tortures he intended to inflict on children after his release, even drawing a picture of a van and listing the items with which he would stock it (broomsticks, barbed wire, razor blades, etc.). His fellow inmates were so horrified that they turned the drawing in to prison officials. The man's prison term expired—officials of course were powerless to keep him after that period—and he moved to a Tacoma neighborhood. Soon thereafter, he attacked a seven-year-old boy riding his bicycle, strangling and mutilating him, amputating his penis, and leaving him for dead. The child survived. The offender was again sent to prison, but the entire state was outraged that he had ever been released in the first place. The child's mother, Helen Harlow, started a group of crime fighters called the Tennis Shoe Brigade and demanded action from the Washington state legislature. The result was a law, passed in 1991, that requires all sex offenders, upon their release from jail, to register their residence with the county sheriff within twenty-four hours. If they don't, they can be sent back to jail for one to four months and will continue to be sent back if they continue to fail to register. Any citizen can get a list of the offenders from the local law-enforcement agency.

The Washington law has another aspect, something never done before in America, to my knowledge. It permits the permanent incarceration of the most deviant offenders: those whom the law can prove to be "sexual predators." After a sex offender's prison term expires, the district attorney can have a jury trial, where two issues must be proved: does he have a mental abnormality or personality disorder that makes him a sexual predator, and is he likely to commit the offense again? A jury decision against the offender commits him involuntarily to a treatment center for an indefinite period, perhaps a life term. Both provisions of this law—the registration of *all* offenders, and the institutionalization of *some* of them—will certainly be tested in higher courts. The success of the program, and the results in the courts, bear close scrutiny by those of us in the other forty-nine states.

Third, we must break the back of the child-pornography industry. Anyone who doesn't know the difference between adult sex films and child pornography doesn't know the difference between sex among consenting adults and rape. Child pornography—its production, its distribution, and its possession—must be rooted out. Start by finding out who subscribes to such literature through the mail and who belongs to child porn–promoting groups, such as the North American Man-Boy Love Association.

Although mere possession of adult pornography is not a crime, possession of child pornography should be, as it now is in West Virginia. Such literature is used as a tool to show the child that sex with adults is "okay." Those who publish graphic magazines and those who produce sex films with children should go to jail, and the key should be dropped down the nearest manhole. The Justice Department should go after the North American Man-Boy Love Association as a racketeering criminal enterprise and bust it.

Fourth, we must give more support to the people and the institutions that deal with children: our day-care providers, our teachers, our social workers, our nurses, our Scout leaders, our Big Brothers and Big Sisters, and so forth. With so many single-parent families, and working mothers, these child-care workers have become the real heroes of today. Those who meet our children's educational, social, and physical needs should be given more pay, more respect, and more helping hands.

2. Drug abuse

The first step to combating drug abuse is education. The money and weaponry behind the international drug cartels are so great that the surest way to defeat them is to reduce demand. If no one wants these drugs, they will go the way of the horse and buggy. Am I dreaming? Yes, but I have reason to be.

Let's look at two episodes of history. Near the end of the last century, the Chinese had become, courtesy of British smugglers, a nation of opium smokers. Millions of adult men had become addicts and spent their days in the opium dens. When the Chinese overthrew the Manchu dynasty and declared a republic in 1911, they had a change of heart as well, and opium usage declined precipitously. A similar episode happened in this country at about the same time. Cocaine usage in the United States was quite high at the turn of the century; indeed, a leading soft drink acquired its name from the substance. In the second decade of this century, people simply stopped using cocaine. Congress also helped, passing laws to take addictive drugs out of medicines and foods. Cocaine did not, in a major way, raise its ugly head in the American culture for another sixty years.

We need a similar transformation of people's hearts and minds now.

But we need more than education and a change of public attitudes. We need to prosecute. We need to seal our borders to cut off supply, and we need to prosecute suppliers to the full extent of the law. Furthermore, our schools need to be, as we declared them in West Virginia, "drug-free zones."

Treatment of addicts seems to be falling by the wayside in these hard times. We cannot let this happen. Many drug users can return to being productive citizens if we give them the treatment they so badly need.

Finally, we must fight the most dangerous drug in America. If you think that the drug problem is only about those that are illegal, think again. The most abused drug in this country, by young and old alike, is alcohol. Since alcohol is legal, a different strategy is needed. Again, the solution starts with education. Among the young, alcohol use is zooming. Why is that? Just turn on your TV during a sports game, and the answer will be apparent. These advertisements tell our young people that the only way to be cool, the only way to impress people of the opposite sex, and even the route to athletic prowess (!) is through the bottle (or, if you will, the can).

When cigarette ads were barred from the airwaves twenty-five years ago, the results were not apparent overnight. But the long-term effect is now clear: substantially fewer Americans now smoke. It's time to send a message about alcohol abuse by banning beer ads.

A second step in fighting alcohol abuse is to make people responsible for their acts. If adults serve alcohol to minors, they should be held liable, such as for any ensuing car accident. Bartenders already face such liability for serving the young, or for serving adults too much. And every person caught driving while under the influence of alcohol, even if there is no accident, should serve time—even if it is only a day.

Why did drinking and driving become less frequent in the 1980s? Here's my theory, which I also discussed in Chapter 13. People found out that if they were driving while intoxicated, they would go to *jail*. They would not get a lecture on alcoholism, they would not pay a fine—no, they would suffer the indignity of doing jail time.

3. Guns

We simply must get guns out of the hands of the wrong people. In particular, we must work to keep guns out of the hands of children and the criminal element.

Guns in our schools are increasingly commonplace. We are always going to have fights among young people. These fights used to end with a bloody nose or a sore stomach. Now we are ending up with dead kids, children killing children. Whatever it takes to keep weapons out of the schools—metal detectors, locker checks, suspensions for violators—we must do it.

Furthermore, parents who can't keep guns out of the hands of their children shouldn't have guns in the home. Far too often, we read of young children using guns that they thought were playthings, or of older children who are not taught proper gun safety, causing the most awful tragedies. We need laws to make these adults liable for their criminal negligence, as Florida and other states have done.

A background check of gun buyers is essential. It is the best way to apprehend felons and drug dealers. Gun dealers who don't comply with such requirements should be prosecuted.

Homicides are now the leading cause of death among young black males. If as many suburban white kids were dying from gunfights, you'd see immediate action in Washington. Because these are inner-city kids, Congress works on other problems it considers more pressing (generally, where political action committees ask for something), fiddling around while the inner cities are depleted of their young men.

That's one reason I started the Victims' Rights Political Action

Committee. We want America's victims to know who our friends in Washington and the state capitals are.

A National Policy: Help Our Kids / Help Our Victims

Now for the positive side of crime fighting. We need a clear national message: we are on the side of law-abiding citizens. We support our police. We support safe neighborhoods. We support our young people.

Our young people should be shown what a great country this is and be given the opportunity to join in the productive main-stream. It's not enough to tell kids to say no to drugs. We need to give every one of them good schools, crime-free schools, and the opportunity to get the training they need. As President Clinton has said, the government should give every student who needs it a loan to go to college, a loan that can be repaid with money or with public service.

We need a responsible national media, both the news industry and the movie industry. They need to stop glorifying crime; there is nothing great about it. While they're at it, they need to stop glorifying alcohol and drugs. Positive advertisements have an effect, and the National Ad Council should keep up its fine work with messages against drugs and similar themes.

In the words of former attorney general Richard Thornburgh, we need a "national anticrime coalition," one that recognizes the seriousness of violent crime, unites victims, and acts aggressively and is unified to stop it.

Part VI

Justice

CHAPTER 19

Making the Criminal Justice System Work for Victims

In Biblical parables, Jesus used to criticize the scribes (teachers of the law) and the Pharisees (the religious leadership) for their lack of compassion. To be sure, they knew the law, but the law had become too focused on nitpicking. Justice, the goal of the law, was being ignored.

There is a lesson here for our day. It's time for those involved in the system of justice to step back and look at the big picture. Are we following the law without meting out justice, as the scribes and Pharisees were doing?

We do not need to tear down what we have built, nor do we need to repeal any part of our Constitution, the great document that gives every accused his day in court. But unless we have rights for victims, too, there can never be justice. Victims, too, deserve their day in court.

If we give rights to victims—in our courtrooms and, yes, in our federal and state Constitutions—we will accomplish a number of important goals.

- First, more victims will be able to rebuild their lives. They will be helped financially as well as emotionally.
- Second, we will catch more criminals. Involvement of victims surely improves the effectiveness of law enforcement.
- Third, we will lower the crime rate. The more violent criminals we catch, put away, and keep away, the fewer repeat offenders will be out in circulation.

- Finally, we will have laws that focus on *justice for all.*
  America's system of justice, up until recently, excluded
  victims from the process. We can restore the balance and
  protect victims' rights.

Victims' rights means *victim participation* in our system of justice,
compensation for victims for their losses, and *services* for victims to
help them with their emotional and physical traumas.

In most places in America today, none of the above is being
handed to victims on a silver platter. Victims need to assert their
rights—and victims are doing just that in communities from
Maine to Hawaii.

Victims are fighting back against the criminal and against
crime, and for themselves and their families. Victims are bringing
justice to our courts and communities. They are moving forward
from being *victims* to becoming *survivors* of crime.

As a state attorney general, I saw what was wrong with our
system of justice. I didn't like it then, and I still don't. I hope this
book's road map leads to justice for you—and for all future
victims.

DIRECTORIES

DIRECTORY A

State Crime Victim Compensation Boards

National Association of Crime Victim Compensation Boards
P.O. Box 16003
Alexandria, VA 22302
(703) 370-2996

Alabama

Crime Victims Compensation
   Commission
P.O. Box 1548
Montgomery, AL 36102-1548
(205) 242-4007

Alaska

Violent Crimes Compensation
   Board
P.O. Box N
Juneau, AK 99811
(907) 465-3040

Arizona

Criminal Justice Commission
1501 West Washington, Suite 207
Phoenix, AZ 85007
(602) 542-1928

Arkansas

Office of the Attorney General
323 Center Street, Suite 601
Little Rock, AR 72201
(501) 682-1323

California

Victims of Crime Program
P.O. Box 3036
Sacramento, CA 95812-3036
(916) 323-6251

Colorado

Division of Criminal Justice
700 Kipling Street, Suite 3000
Denver, CO 80215
(303) 239-4442

Connecticut

Commission on Victim Services
1155 Silas Deane Highway
Wethersfield, CT 06109
(203) 529-3089

Delaware

Violent Crimes Compensation
   Board
1500 East Newport Pike, Suite 10
Wilmington, DE 19804
(302) 995-8383

District of Columbia

Crime Victims Compensation
  Program
Department of Employment
  Services
1200 Upshur Street, N.W.
Washington, DC 20011
(202) 576-7090

Florida

Division of Victim Services
Office of the Attorney General
2012 Capital Circle, S.E.
104 Hartman
Tallahassee, FL 32399-0650
(904) 488-0848

Georgia

Criminal Justice Coordinating
  Council
10 Park Place South, Suite 200
Atlanta, GA 30303
(404) 559-4949

Hawaii

Criminal Injuries Compensation
  Commission
335 Merchant Street, Suite 244
Honolulu, HI 96813-2907
(808) 587-1143

Idaho

Victim Compensation Program
Idaho Industrial Commission
317 Main Street
Boise, ID 83720
(208) 334-6000

Illinois

Crime Victims Division
Office of the Attorney General
100 West Randolph, 13th Floor
Chicago, IL 60601
(312) 814-2581

Indiana

Violent Crimes Compensation
  Division
402 West Washington Street, Room
  W-196
Indianapolis, IN 46204
(317) 232-3809

Iowa

Crime Victim Assistance Programs
Department of Justice
Old Historical Building
Des Moines, IA 50319
(515) 281-5044

Kansas

Crime Victims Reparations Board
700 S.W. Jackson, Suite 400
Topeka, KS 66603-3741
(913) 296-2359

Kentucky

Crime Victims Compensation Board
115 Myrtle Avenue
Frankfort, KY 40601
(502) 564-2290

Louisiana

Crime Victims Reparations Board
Commission on Law Enforcement
1885 Wooddale Boulevard,
  Suite 708
Baton Rouge, LA 70806
(504) 925-4437

Maine

Crime Victim Compensation
  Program
Office of the Attorney General
State House Station #6
Augusta, ME 04333
(207) 626-8510

Maryland

Criminal Injuries Compensation
  Board
6776 Reistertown Road, Suite 313
Baltimore, MD 21215-2340
(410) 764-4214

Massachusetts

Victims Compensation and
  Assistance
Office of the Attorney General
One Ashburton Place
Boston, MA 02108
(617) 727-2200, ext. 2875

Michigan

Crime Victims Compensation Board
P.O. Box 30026
Lansing, MI 48909
(517) 373-7373

Minnesota

Crime Victims Reparations Board
N. 465 Griggs-Midway Building
1821 University Avenue
St. Paul, MN 55104
(612) 642-0395

Mississippi

Crime Victim Compensation
  Program
P.O. Box 267
Jackson, MS 39205
(800) 829-6766

Missouri

Crime Victims Compensation Unit
Department of Labor and
  Industrial Relations
P.O. Box 58
Jefferson City, MO 65102
(314) 526-6006

Montana

Crime Victims Unit
Board of Crime Control
303 North Roberts, 4th Floor
Helena, MT 59620-1408
(406) 444-3653

Nebraska

Commission on Law Enforcement
P.O. Box 94946
Lincoln, NE 68509
(402) 471-2828

Nevada

Victims of Crime Program
2770 Maryland Parkway, Suite 416
Las Vegas, NV 89109
(702) 486-7259

New Hampshire

Department of Justice
State House Annex
Concord, NH 03301-6397
(603) 271-1284

New Jersey

Violent Crimes Compensation
  Board
60 Park Place, Suite 10
Newark, NJ 07102
(201) 648-2107

New Mexico

Crime Victims Reparation
  Commission
8100 Mountain Road, N.E., Suite
  106
Albuquerque, NM 87110-7822
(505) 841-9432

New York

Crime Victims Board
845 Central Avenue
Albany, NY 12206
(518) 457-8001

North Carolina

Victim and Justice Services
Department of Crime Control and
  Public Safety
P.O. Box 27687
Raleigh, NC 27611-7687
(919) 733-7974

North Dakota

Crime Victims Reparations
4007 North State Street
Bismarck, ND 58501
(701) 224-3770

Ohio

Crime Victim Services
Office of the Attorney General
30 East Broad Street, 26th Floor
Columbus, OH 43266-0410
(614) 466-5610

Oklahoma

Crime Victims Compensation Board
2200 Classen Boulevard, Suite 1800
Oklahoma City, OK 73106-5811
(405) 521-2330

Oregon

Crime Victims Program
Department of Justice
100 Justice Building
Salem, OR 97310
(503) 378-5348

Pennsylvania

Crime Victims Compensation Board
333 Market Street
Harrisburg, PA 17101
(717) 783-5153

Rhode Island

Judicial Planning Section,
  Supreme Court
250 Benefit Street
Providence, RI 02903
(401) 277-2500

South Carolina

State Office of Victim Services
P.O. Box 210009
Columbia, SC 29221-0009
(803) 737-8100

South Dakota

Crime Victims' Compensation
  Commission
Department of Corrections
523 East Capitol
Pierre, SD 57501
(605) 773-3478

Tennessee

Division of Claims
  Administration
Andrew Jackson Building,
  11th Floor
Nashville, TN 37219
(615) 741-2734

Texas

Crime Victims Compensation
  Division
Office of the Attorney General
P.O. Box 12548, Capitol Station
Austin, TX 78711-2548
(512) 462-6400

Utah

Office of Crime Victim
  Reparations
350 East 500 South, Suite 200
Salt Lake City, UT 84111
(801) 533-4000

Vermont

Crime Victim Compensation
  Program
P.O. Box 991
Montpelier, VT 05601
(802) 828-3374

Virgin Islands

Criminal Victims Compensation
   Commission
Barbel Plaza South
Charlotte Amalie
St. Thomas, VI 00802
(809) 774-1166

Virginia

Crime Victims Compensation
P.O. Box 5423
Richmond, VA 23220
(804) 367-8686

Washington

Department of Labor and
   Industries
P.O. Box 44520
Olympia, WA 98504-4520
(206) 956-5340

West Virginia

Court of Claims
Room 6, Building 1
State Capitol
Charleston, WV 24305
(304) 348-3471

Wisconsin

Office of Crime Victim Services
Office of the Attorney General
P.O. Box 7951
Madison, WI 53707-7951
(608) 266-6470

Wyoming

Crime Victims Compensation
   Commission
1700 Westland
Cheyenne, WY 82001
(307) 635-4050

DIRECTORY B

National Victims' Rights Organizations

The following is a list of agencies and organizations that assist victims and survivors on a national level. This directory was compiled through the assistance of the National Victim Center, with assistance from Mothers Against Drunk Driving and Parents of Murdered Children.

American Red Cross
National Headquarters
431 18th Street, N.W.
Washington, DC 20006
(202) 737-8300

Mothers Against Drunk Driving
   (MADD)
National Office
511 East John Carpenter Freeway,
   Suite 700
Irving, TX 75062
(800) GET-MADD

National Association of Crime
   Victim Compensation Boards
P.O. Box 16003
Alexandria, VA 22302
(703) 370-2996

National Crime Prevention Council
1700 K Street, N.W., 2nd Floor
Washington, DC 20008
(202) 466-6272
(800) WE-PREVENT

National Organization for Victim
   Assistance
1757 Park Road, N.W.
Washington, DC 20010-2101
(202) 232-NOVA
(800) 879-NOVA

National School Safety Center
Pepperdine University
4165 Thousand Oaks Boulevard,
   Suite 290
Westlake Village, CA 91362
(805) 373-9977

National Self-Help Clearinghouse
25 West 43rd Street, Room 620
New York, NY 10036
(212) 642-2944

National Victim Center
2111 Wilson Boulevard, Suite 300
Arlington, VA 22201
(703) 276-2880

National Victim Center
309 West 7th Street, Suite 705
Fort Worth, TX 76102
(817) 877-3355
(800) FYI-CALL

Children's Support Groups

ACTION
806 Connecticut Avenue, N.W.,
  Room M1007
Washington, DC 20525
(202) 634-9410

The Association of Junior Leagues
825 Third Avenue
New York, NY 10022
(212) 355-4380

Big Brothers of America/Big Sisters
  of America
230 North 13th Street
Philadelphia, PA 19107
(215) 567-2748

Boy Scouts of America
1325 Walnut Hill Lane
Irving, TX 75062
(214) 659-2000

Boys Clubs of America
711 First Avenue
New York, NY 10017
(212) 557-7755

Camp Fire, Inc.
4600 Madison Avenue
Kansas City, MO 64112
(816) 756-1950

Family Research Center
University of New Hampshire
128 Horton Social Science Center
Durham, NH 03824
(603) 862-1234

General Federation of Women's
  Clubs
1734 N Street, N.W.
Washington, DC 20036
(202) 347-3168

Girl Scouts of the USA
830 Third Avenue, 14th Floor
New York, NY 10022
(212) 940-7500

Girls Clubs of America
205 Lexington Avenue, 2nd Floor
New York, NY 10016
(212) 689-3700

Junior Optimist Clubs and Octagon
  Clubs
4494 Lindell Boulevard
St. Louis, MO 63108
(314) 371-6000

Kiwanis International
3636 Woodview Terrace
Indianapolis, IN 46268
(317) 875-8755

Lions Clubs International
300 22nd Street
Oak Brook, IL 60570
(312) 986-1700

National Assembly of National
  Voluntary Health and Social
  Welfare Organizations
1319 F Street, N.W., Suite 601
Washington, DC 20005
(202) 347-2080

National Council of Jewish Women
15 East 26th Street
New York, NY 10010
(212) 532-1740

National Organization for Victim
  Assistance (NOVA)
1757 Park Road, N.W.
Washington, DC 20010-2101
(202) 232-NOVA

National Parent Teacher Association
700 North Rush Street
Chicago, IL 60611-2571
(312) 787-0977

Phi Alpha Delta Public Service
  Center
7315 Wisconsin Avenue, Suite 325
  East
Bethesda, MD 20814
(301) 961-8985

Rotary International
1600 Ridge Avenue
Evanston, IL 60201
(312) 328-0100

U.S. Jaycees
P.O. Box 7
4 West 21st Street
Tulsa, OK 74102
(918) 584-2481

YMCA National Headquarters
755 West North Avenue
Chicago, IL 60610
(312) 280-3400

YWCA National Headquarters
726 Broadway
New York, NY 10003
(212) 614-2700

Child Victims

Adam Walsh Child Resource Center
7812 Westminster Boulevard
Westminster, CA 92668
(714) 898-4802

Adam Walsh Child Resource Center
3111 South Dixie Highway, Suite 244
West Palm Beach, FL 33407-3223
(407) 833-9080

American Association for Protecting
  Children
63 Inverness Drive East
Englewood, CO 80112
(800) 227-5242

American Bar Association
Center on Children & the Law
1800 M Street, N.W., Suite 200-S
Washington, DC 20036
(202) 331-2200

American Bar Association
Criminal Justice Section
Victim/Witness Project
1800 M Street, N.W.
Washington, DC 20036
(202) 331-2260

American Humane Association
63 Inverness Drive East
Englewood, CO 80112
(303) 792-9900

American Professional Society on
  the Abuse of Children
332 South Michigan Avenue,
  Suite 1600
Chicago, IL 60604
(312) 554-0166

Boys Clubs of America
711 First Avenue
New York, NY 10017
(212) 557-7755

The Center for Child Protection
and Family Support
714 G Street, S.E.
Washington, DC 20003
(202) 544-3144

Child Find of America, Inc.
7 Innis Avenue, P.O. Box 277
New Paltz, NY 12561
(914) 255-1848
(800) I-AM-LOST
(800) A-WAY-OUT

Childhelp USA
6463 Independence Avenue
Woodland Hills, CA 91367
(800) 4-A-CHILD
(818) 347-7280

Children's Defense Fund
122 C Street, N.W., Suite 400
Washington, DC 20001
(202) 628-8787

Children's Rights of America, Inc.
12551 Indian Rocks Road, Suite 11
Largo, FL 33544
(813) 593-0090

Child Welfare League of America
440 First Street, N.W., Suite 310
Washington, DC 20001-2085
(202) 638-2952

Clearinghouse on Child Abuse &
Neglect Information
P.O. Box 1182
Washington, DC 20013
(703) 385-7565

Cocaine Hotline
Fair Oaks Hospital
19 Prospect Street
Summit, NJ 07901
(800) COCAINE

Family Life Information Exchange
Project Share
P.O. Box 2309
Rockville, MD 20852
(301) 907-8198
(301) 231-9539

Family Service Association
Covenant House
346 West 17th Street
New York, NY 10011
Teen Crisis Hotline
(800) 999-9999

4-H Program/Extension Service
U.S. Department of Agriculture
Room 3860, South Building
Washington, DC 20250
(202) 447-5833

C. Henry Kempe National Center
for the Prevention and Treatment
of Child Abuse and Neglect
1205 Oneida Street
Denver, CO 80220
(303) 321-3963

National Assault Prevention Center
P.O. Box 02005
Columbus, OH 43202
(614) 291-2540

National CASA Association
2722 East Lake Avenue East,
Suite 220
Seattle, WA 98102
(206) 328-8588

National Center for Missing &
Exploited Children
2101 Wilson Boulevard, Suite 550
Arlington, VA 22201
(703) 235-3900
(800) 843-5678

National Center for Prosecution of
Child Abuse
American Prosecutors Research
Institute
1033 North Fairfax Street, Suite 200
Alexandria, VA 22314
(703) 739-0321

National Children's Advocacy
Center
106 Lincoln Street
Huntsville, AL 35801
(205) 533-5437

National Coalition Against
Domestic Violence
P.O. Box 34103
Washington, DC 20005
(202) 638-6388

National Coalition Against
Pornography
800 Compton Road, Suite 9224
Cincinnati, OH 45231
(513) 521-6227

National Committee for Prevention
of Child Abuse
332 South Michigan Avenue,
Suite 1600
Chicago, IL 60604
(312) 663-3520

National Council of Juvenile and
Family Court Judges
P.O. Box 8970
Reno, NV 89507
(702) 784-6012

National Families in Action
2296 Henderson Mill Road,
Suite 300
Atlanta, GA 30345
(404) 934-6364

National Institute on Drug Abuse
(NIDA)
U.S. Department of Health and
Human Services
5600 Fishers Lane
Rockville, MD 20857
(800) 638-2045

National Institute on Drug Abuse
(NIDA) Hotline
5600 Fishers Lane
Rockville, MD 20857
(800) 662-HELP

National Network of Runaway and
Youth Services
905 6th Street, N.W., Suite 411
Washington, DC 20024
(202) 488-0739

National Resource Center on Child
Sexual Abuse
107 Lincoln Street
Huntsville, AL 35801
(205) 534-6868
(800) 543-7006

National Runaway Switchboard
2210 North Halsted
Chicago, IL 60614
(312) 929-5854
(800) 621-4000
(800) 972-6004 (in Illinois)

National School Boards Association
1680 Duke Street
Alexandria, VA 22314
(703) 838-6722

Operation Lookout
National Center for Missing Youth
P.O. Box 231
Mountlake Terrace, WA 98043
(206) 771-7335
(800) 782-SEEK

Parents' Resource Institute for Drug
  Education (PRIDE)
Georgia State University
University Plaza
Atlanta, GA 30303
(800) 241-9746

Paul & Lisa Foundation
P.O. Box 348
Westbrook, CT 06498
(203) 399-5338

Runaway Hotline
P.O. Box 12428
Austin, TX 78711
(713) 524-3821
(800) 231-6946
(800) 392-3352 (in Texas)

Students Against Driving Drunk
  (SADD)
P.O. Box 800
Marlboro, MA 01752
(508) 481-3568

Vanished Children Alliance
1408 Parkmoor Avenue, Suite 400
San Jose, CA 95126
(408) 971-4822
(800) 826-4743

Corrections: Community and Institutional

American Correctional Association
  (ACA)
8025 Laurel Lakes Court
Laurel, MD 20707-5075
(301) 206-5100
(800) ACA-JOIN

American Probation and Parole
  Association
c/o The Council of State
  Governments
Iron Works Pike, P.O. Box 11910
Lexington, KY 40578-1910
(606) 231-1914

Crime Prevention

Just Say No Foundation
1777 North California Boulevard,
  Suite 200
Walnut Creek, CA 94596
(415) 939-6666
(800) 258-2766

McGruff's Computer
National Crime Prevention Council
733 15th Street, N.W.
Washington, DC 20005
(202) 737-4603

National Child Safety Council
P.O. Box 1368
Jackson, MI 49204
(517) 764-6070

National Crime Prevention Council
1700 K Street, N.W., 2nd Floor
Washington, DC 20006
(202) 466-NCPC (6272)
(800) WE-PREVENT

National Federation of Parents for
  Drug-Free Youth
8730 Georgia Avenue, Suite 200
Silver Spring, MD 20910
(301) 585-KIDS

National Institute for Citizen
  Education in the Law
25 E Street, N.W., Suite 400
Washington, DC 20001
(202) 662-9620

Cults

American Family Foundation
P.O. Box 2265
Bonita Springs, FL 33959
(813) 495-3136

Cult Awareness Network
2421 West Pratt Boulevard, Suite
    1173
Chicago, IL 60645
(312) 267-7777

Domestic Violence

Clearinghouse on Family Violence
    Information
P.O. Box 1182
Washington, DC 20013
(703) 385-7565

Family Violence Research and
    Treatment Program
University of Texas
2900 University Boulevard
Tyler, TX 75701-6699
(214) 566-7060

Michigan Coalition Against
    Domestic Violence
P.O. Box 463100
Mount Clemens, MI 48046
(313) 954-1180
(800) 333-7233

National Center on Women and
    Family Law
799 Broadway, Room 402
New York, NY 10003
(212) 674-8200

National Clearinghouse for the
    Defense of Battered Women
125 South 9th Street, Suite 302
Philadelphia, PA 19107
(215) 351-0010

National Clearinghouse on Marital
    and Date Rape
2325 Oak Street
Berkeley, CA 94708
(415) 524-1582

National Coalition Against
    Domestic Violence
P.O. Box 34103
Washington, DC 20043-4103
(202) 638-6388

National Council of Juvenile and
    Family Court Judges
P.O. Box 8970
Reno, NV 89507
(702) 784-6012

National Council on Child Abuse
    and Family Violence
10 Universal City Plaza,
    Suite 1027
Universal City, CA 91608
(800) 222-2000

Task Force on Families in Crisis
Suite 306, Coleman Building
3716 Hillsborough Road
P.O. Box 120495
Nashville, TN 37212
(615) 383-4480
(615) 383-4575

Drunk Driving

Alliance Against Intoxicated
 Motorists (AAIM)
870 East Higgins Road, Suite 131
Schaumburg, IL 60173
(708) 240-0027

Mothers Against Drunk Driving
 (MADD)
National Office
511 East John Carpenter Freeway,
 Suite 700
Irving, TX 75062
(800) GET-MADD

RID-USA (Remove Intoxicated
 Drivers)
P.O. Box 520
Schenectady, NY 12301
(518) 393-4357

Students Against Driving Drunk
 (SADD)
P.O. Box 800
Marlboro, MA 01752
(508) 481-3568

Elder Abuse/Neglect

American Association of Retired
 Persons (AARP)
601 E Street, N.W.
Washington, DC 20049
(202) 434-2277

Clearinghouse on Abuse and
 Neglect of the Elderly
College of Resources
University of Delaware
Newark, DE 19716
(302) 292-3525

Clearinghouse on Family Violence
 Information
P.O. Box 1182
Washington, DC 20013
(703) 385-7565

National Aging Resource Center on
 Elder Abuse
c/o APWA
810 First Street, N.E.
Washington, DC 20002-4267
(202) 682-0100

National Committee for the
 Prevention of Elder Abuse
c/o University of Massachusetts
 Medical Center
55 Lake Avenue North
Worcester, MA 01655
(508) 856-0011

Federal Government Agencies

DARE
Bureau of Justice Assistance
Office of Justice Programs
633 Indiana Avenue, N.W.
Washington, DC 20531
(202) 272-6838

Department of Human Services
Child and Family Services
609 H Street, N.E.
Washington, DC 20002
(202) 727-0995

Executive Office for U.S. Attorneys
LECC/Victim-Witness Staff
Room 1612, Main Justice Building
10th and Pennsylvania, N.W.
Washington, DC 20530
(202) 514-3982

Federal Law Enforcement Training
Center
Glynco, GA 31524
(912) 267-2100

Juvenile Justice Clearinghouse/
NCJRS
Box 6000
Rockville, MD 20850
(301) 251-5500
(800) 638-8736

National Center on Child Abuse
and Neglect
P.O. Box 1182
Washington, DC 20013
(202) 245-0813

National Criminal Justice Reference
Service
Box 6000
Rockville, MD 20850
(301) 251-5500
(800) 851-3420

National Institute of Justice
Clearinghouse
Box 6000
Rockville, MD 20850
(800) 732-3277

National Institute of Mental Health
Department of Health and Human
Services
Park Lawn Building, Room 15, CO5
5600 Fishers Lane
Rockville, MD 20857
(301) 443-4513

National Victims Resource Center
1600 Research Boulevard
Rockville, MD 20850
(800) 627-6872

Office of Juvenile Justice and
Delinquency Prevention (OJJDP)
633 Indiana Avenue, N.W.,
Room 742
Washington, DC 20531
(202) 307-0751

Office for Victims of Crime (OVC)
U.S. Department of Justice
633 Indiana Avenue, N.W.,
Room 1342
Washington, DC 20024
(202) 307-0774
(800) 627-6872

Hate Crime

Anti-Defamation League of B'nai
B'rith
823 United Nations Plaza
New York, NY 10017
(212) 490-2525

Center for Democratic Renewal
P.O. Box 50469
Atlanta, GA 30302
(404) 221-0025

Human Rights Resource Center
615 B Street
San Rafael, CA 94901
(415) 453-0404

National Association for the
Advancement of Colored People
4805 Mount Hope Drive
Baltimore, MD
(410) 358-8900

National Gay and Lesbian Task
  Force
1734 14th Street, N.W.
Washington, DC 20009
(202) 332-6483

National Institute Against Prejudice
  & Violence
31 South Green Street
Baltimore, MD 21201
(301) 328-5170

Southern Poverty Law Center
P.O. Box 548
Montgomery, AL 36101
(205) 264-0286

Incest Survivors

The Chesapeake Institute, Inc.
11141 Georgia Avenue, Suite 310
Wheaton, MD 20902
(301) 949-5000

Incest Survivors Resource Network
  International
P.O. Box 7375
Las Cruces, NM 88006
(505) 521-4260

Survivors of Incest Anonymous, Inc.
World Service Office
P.O. Box 21817
Baltimore, MD 21222
(301) 282-3400

Law Enforcement

Concerns of Police Survivors, Inc.
9423-A
Marlboro, MD 20772
(301) 599-0445

International Association of Chiefs
  of Police
1110 North Glebe, Suite 200
Arlington, VA 22201
(800) 843-4227

International Conference of Police
  Chaplains
Route 5, Box 310, #82
Livingston, TX 77351
(409) 327-2332

Law Enforcement Television
  Network
1303 Marsh Lane
Carrollton, TX 75006
(214) 416-4100

National Association of Attorneys
  General
444 North Capitol Street, N.W.,
  Suite 403
Washington, DC 20001
(202) 628-0435

National District Attorneys
  Association
1033 North Fairfax Street,
  Suite 200
Alexandria, VA 22314
(703) 549-9222

National Law Enforcement Council
888 16th Street, N.W., Suite 600
Washington, DC 20006
(202) 835-8020

National Organization of Black Law
  Enforcement Executives
908 Pennsylvania Avenue, S.E.
Washington, DC 20003
(202) 546-8811

National Sheriffs Association
1450 Duke Street
Alexandria, VA 22314
(703) 836-7827
(800) 424-7827

Police Foundation
1001 22nd Street, N.W., Suite 200
Washington, DC 20037
(202) 833-1460

Legal Services

California Center on Victimology
1221 22nd Street
San Diego, CA 92102
(619) 235-4459

Coalition of Victims' Attorneys &
  Consultants (COVAC)
2111 Wilson Boulevard, Suite 300
Arlington, VA 22201
(703) 276-2880

Trial Lawyers for Public Justice
1625 Massachusetts Avenue, N.W.,
  Suite 100
Washington, DC 20036
(202) 797-8600

Native Americans

American Indian Law Center
P.O. Box 4456, Station A
Albuquerque, NM 87196
(505) 277-5462

National Indian Justice Center
McNear Building
74th Street, Suite 28
Petaluma, CA 94952
(707) 762-8113

Other

American Prosecutors Research
  Institute
1033 North Fairfax Street, Suite 200
Alexandria, VA 22314
(703) 549-4253

American Social Health Association
P.O. Box 13827
Research Triangle Park, NC 27709
(919) 361-8400
(800) 227-8922
(800) 342-AIDS

Committee to Halt Useless College
  Killings (CHUCK)
P.O. Box 188
Sayville, NY 11782
(516) 567-1130

Crime Victims Research and
  Treatment Center
Medical University
171 Ashley Avenue
Charleston, SC 29425
(803) 792-2945

Crisis Management Group, Inc.
99 Russell Avenue
Watertown, MA 02102
(800) 444-7262

General Federation of Women's
Clubs
1734 North Street, N.W.
Washington, DC 20036-2990
(202) 347-3168

Justice Fellowship/Neighbors
Who Care
P.O. Box 17500
Washington, DC 20041-0500
(703) 834-3650

National Association of Social
Workers (NASW)
750 First Street, N.E., Suite 700
Washington, DC 20002
(202) 408-8600

National Association of Town Watch
P.O. Box 303
7 Wynnewood Road, Suite 215
Wynnewood, PA 19096
(215) 649-7055

National Families in Action
2296 Henderson Mill Road,
Suite 300
Atlanta, GA 30345
(404) 934-6364

U.S. Association for Victim-
Offender Mediation
254 South Morgan Boulevard
Valparaiso, IN 46383
(219) 462-1127

Sexual Assault

National Assault Prevention Center
P.O. Box 02005
Columbus, OH 43202
(614) 291-2540

National Center for Women Policy
Studies
2000 P Street, N.W., Suite 508
Washington, DC 20036
(202) 872-1770

National Clearinghouse on Marital
and Date Rape
2325 Oak Street
Berkeley, CA 94708
(415) 524-1582

National Network for Victims of
Sexual Assault
955 South Columbus Street, Suite
502
Arlington, VA 22204
(703) 671-0691

Spiritual

The Spiritual Dimension
in Victim Services
P.O. Box 163304
Sacramento, CA 95816
(916) 446-7202

Support to Parents

Al-Anon/ALATEEN
Family Group World Service
  Headquarters
P.O. Box 862
Midtown Station
New York, NY 10018
(212) 302-7240

Children of Alcoholics Foundation
200 Park Avenue, 31st Floor
New York, NY 10166
(212) 949-1404

Families in Action
3845 North Druid Hills Road,
  Suite 300
Decatur, GA 30033
(404) 325-5799

A Way Out
Child Find of America
7 Innis Avenue
New Paltz, NY 12561
(914) 255-1848

Mothers Against Drunk Driving
  (MADD)
National Office
511 East John Carpenter Freeway,
  Suite 700
Irving, TX 75062
(800) GET-MADD

National Association for Children of
  Alcoholics
31706 Coast Highway, Suite 201
South Laguna, CA 92677-3044
(714) 499-3889

National Education Association
1201 16th Street, N.W.
Washington, DC 20036
(202) 833-4000

National Federation of Parents for
  Drug-Free Youth
8730 Georgia Avenue, Suite 200
Silver Spring, MD 20910
(301) 585-KIDS

National Organization for Victim
  Assistance
1757 Park Road, N.W.
Washington, DC 20010-2101
(202) 232-NOVA

Parents Anonymous
6733 South Sepulveda Boulevard,
  Suite 270
Los Angeles, CA 90045
(213) 410-9732
(800) 421-0353
(800) 352-0386 (in California)

Parents Music Resource Center
1500 Arlington Boulevard,
  Suite 300
Arlington, VA 22209
(703) 527-9466

Parents Resource Institute for Drug
  Education (PRIDE)
100 Edgewood Avenue, Suite 1002
Atlanta, GA 30303
(404) 658-2548
(800) 241-9746

Parents United, Inc.
P.O. Box 952
San Jose, CA 95102
(408) 280-5055

Toughlove
P.O. Box 1069
Doylestown, PA 18901
(215) 348-7090

Survivors of Homicide Victims

Children of Murdered Parents
P.O. Box 9317
Whittier, CA 90608
(310) 699-8427

The Compassionate Friends, Inc.
P.O. Box 3696
Oak Brook, IL 60522-3696
(708) 990-0010

Parents of Murdered Children
100 East 8th Street
Cincinnati, OH 45202
(513) 721-5683

Training Information Referral Research for Professionals

Human Rights Resource Center
615 B Street
San Rafael, CA 94901
(415) 453-0404

National Drug Prosecution Center
1033 North Fairfax Street, Suite 200
Alexandria, VA 22314
(703) 549-6798

National Criminal Justice
    Association
444 North Capitol Street, N.W.
    Suite 608
Washington, DC 20001
(202) 347-4900

National School Safety Center
4165 Thousand Oaks Boulevard,
    Suite 290
Westlake Village, CA 91362
(805) 373-9977

Victims With Disabilities

The Arc
P.O. Box 1047
Arlington, TX 76004
(817) 261-6003

National Assault Prevention Center
P.O. Box 02005
Columbus, OH 43202
(614) 291-2540

White-Collar-Crime Victims

Public Citizen
2000 P Street, N.W.
Washington, DC 20036
(202) 833-3000

Trial Lawyers for Public Justice
1625 Massachusetts Avenue, N.W.,
    Suite 100
Washington, DC 20036
(202) 797-8600

White-Collar Crime 101
8300 Boone Boulevard, Suite 500
Vienna, VA 22182
(703) 848-9248

Your District Attorney or County
    Prosecuting Attorney

Your State Attorney General—
    Consumer Protection Division

Your State Insurance Commission

Your State Securities Commission

State-by-State Listing of Victims' Rights Services

The following is an abridged list of victims'-rights services in each state. A complete list is available from the National Organization for Victim Assistance (NOVA), 1757 Park Road, N.W., Washington, DC. 20010; contact NOVA for price and availability.

This list focuses on direct service providers and advocacy organizations. In general, govermental agencies are not included. If you need help from the government, contact the victim/witness program in your county, your local district attorney, or the state attorney general. If you don't know which district attorney or county prosecutor is responsible for your case, contact the attorney general or the state association of district attorneys; the location of each state group can be obtained by contacting the National District Attorneys Association in Alexandria, Virginia (703) 549-9222.

State Directory
Victim Services

Alabama

East Alabama Task Force on
Battered Women
P.O. Box 1104
Auburn, AL 36831-1104
(205) 887-9330

Crisis Center of Jefferson County
3600 8th Avenue South
Birmingham, AL 35222
(205) 323-7782

National Resource Center on Child
Sexual Abuse
106 Lincoln Street
Huntsville, AL 35801
(205) 533-5437

Mobile Rape Crisis Center
2400 Gordon Smith Drive
Mobile, AL 36617
(205) 473-RAPE

Portraits International (Missing
  Children Resource)
1119 Dauphin Street
Mobile, AL 36604
(205) 479-6050

Alabama Coalition Against
  Domestic Violence
P.O. Box 4762
Montgomery, AL 36101
(205) 767-3076

Alabama Network of Victim
  Services
P.O. Box 1772
Montgomery, AL 36104
(205) 242-4007

Kiwanis Domestic Abuse Shelter
P.O. Box 4752
Montgomery, AL 36101
(205) 263-0063

MADD State Office
P.O. Box 230834
Montgomery, AL 36123
(205) 277-7722

Parents of Murdered Children
3714 Dresden Court
Montgomery, AL 36111
(205) 284-2721

Victims of Crime and Leniency
P.O. Box 4449
Montgomery, AL 36103
(205) 262-7197
(800) 239-3219

RID Coordinator
702 24th Avenue East
Tuscaloosa, AL 35404
(205) 553-5270

Alaska

Abused Women's Aid in Crisis
100 South 13th Avenue
Anchorage, AK 99501
(907) 279-9581

Alaska Youth Advocates
  (Missing Children Resource)
3745 Community Park, LP #202
Anchorage, AK 99508-3466
(907) 274-6541

Victims for Justice
619 East 5th Avenue
Anchorage, AK 99501
(907) 278-0977

Arctic Women in Crisis
P.O. Box 69
Barrow, AK 99723
(907) 852-2942

Fairbanks Chapter of SLAM
  (Stronger Laws Against
  Molestation)
P.O. Box 84367
Fairbanks, AK 93703
(907) 456-2250

Alaska Network on Domestic
  Violence & Sexual Assault
130 Seward Street, #501
Juneau, AK 99801
(907) 586-3650

Arizona

Arizona Coalition Against
  Domestic Violence
301 West Hatcher
Phoenix, AZ 85021
(602) 495-5429

Center Against Sexual Assault
6629 Clarendon Avenue
Phoenix, AZ 85003
(602) 956-1163

Community Mediation Program
301 East Bethany Home Road
Phoenix, AZ 85254
(602) 210-2567

Parents of Murdered Children
Valley of the Sun Chapter
2115 West Royal Palm Road
Phoenix, AZ 85021
(602) 995-2083

Crime Victim Foundation
2901 North 78th Street, #100
Scottsdale, AZ 85251
(602) 949-9711

Center for Victims of Family
  Violence
P.O. Box 3425
Tucson, AZ 85722
(602) 623-3246

Las Familias, Parents United
3618 East Pima Street
Tucson, AZ 85716-3321
(602) 327-7122

Tucson Centers for Women and
  Children
P.O. Box 40878
Tucson, AZ 85717
(602) 795-4266

Parents of Murdered Children
1099 Hereford Avenue
Yuma, AZ 85364
(602) 782-0915

Arkansas

Project for Victims of Family
  Violence
P.O. Box 2915
Fayetteville, AR 72701
(501) 442-9811

Justice for Crime Victims of
  America, Inc.
P.O. Box 3906
Fort Smith, AR 72913
(501) 783-7993

Arkansas Coalition Against
  Violence to Women and Children
P.O. Box 807
Harrison, AR 72601
(501) 741-6167

Advocates for Battered Women
P.O. Box 1954
Little Rock, AR 72203
(501) 376-3221
(501) 376-3219 crisis

MADD State Office
203 Center Street
Little Rock, AR 72201
(501) 376-6100

Parents of Murdered Children
#3 NW Court
Little Rock, AR 72212
(501) 225-5720

Parents United
P.O. Box 1437
Little Rock, AR 72203
(501) 371-2217

Volunteers in Courts
509 National Building
Pine Bluff, AR 71601
(501) 535-6770

RID Coordinator
Route 1, Box 260
Scranton, AR 72863
(501) 938-7146

Criminal Justice Ministries
United Methodist Church
9901 Brockington
Sherwood, AR 72120

California

Concerns of Police Survivors
288 South Leandro Street
Anaheim, CA 92807
(714) 998-1724

National Clearinghouse on Marital
and Date Rape
2325 Oak Street
Berkeley, CA 94708
(415) 524-1582

California Center for Family
Survivors of Homicide
P.O. Box 256
Beverly Hills, CA 90210
(818) 363-8550

California State Coalition of Rape
Crisis Centers
P.O. Box 423
Chico, CA 95927
(916) 891-1331

YWCA of Los Angeles
(Sexual Assault Center)
509 East Compton Boulevard
Compton, CA 90221
(213) 636-1429

California Federation of Women's
Clubs
Crime Prevention Division
11487 Forty-Niner Circle
Gold River, CA 95670
(916) 638-7133

Childhelp USA
P.O. Box 630
Hollywood, CA 90028
(800) 422-4453

Children of the Night
1800 North Highland, Suite 128
Hollywood, CA 90028
(213) 461-3160

MADD State Office
P.O. Box 188
Lancaster, CA 93584
(805) 945-6233

Find the Children
11811 West Olympic Boulevard
Los Angeles, CA 90064
(213) 477-6721

Los Angeles Commission on
Assaults Against Women
543 North Fairfax Avenue
Los Angeles, CA 90036
(213) 655-4235

National Council on Child Abuse
and Family Violence
633 West Century Boulevard
Los Angeles, CA 90045
(818) 914-2814

Parents Anonymous National
Office
6733 South Sepulveda Boulevard
Los Angeles, CA 90045
(213) 410-9732

Victims of Crime Law Center
12001 Pico Boulevard
Los Angeles, CA 90064
(213) 575-0100

Vanished Children's Alliance
P.O. Box 2052
Los Gatos, CA 95031
(408) 354-3200

Child Assault Prevention Training
Center of California
51 Jack London Square
Oakland, CA 94607
(415) 893-0413

Citizens for Law and Order
P.O. Box 13308
Oakland, CA 94661
(510) 531-4664

Teen Age Grief, Inc.
P.O. Box 4935
Panorama City, CA 91412-4935
(805) 252-5596

National Indian Justice Center
McNear Building
74th Street, Suite 28
Petaluma, CA 94952
(707) 762-8113

California Foundation for the
  Protection of Children
1708 Florin Road
Sacramento, CA 95822
(916) 429-7435

The Spiritual Dimension
  in Victim Services
P.O. Box 163304
Sacramento, CA 95816
(916) 446-7202

Victims of Crime Resource Center
McGeorge School of Law
3200 5th Avenue
Sacramento, CA 95817
(916) 739-7061

California Center on Victimology
1221 22nd Street
San Diego, CA 92102
(619) 235-4459

Home Run: A National Search
  for Missing Children
4575 Ruffner Street
San Diego, CA 92111
(619) 292-5683

Child Adolescent Sexual Abuse
  Resource Center, San Francisco
  General Hospital
995 Potrero Avenue
San Francisco, CA 94110
(415) 821-8386

Community United Against
  Violence
(Gay & Lesbian Resource)
514 Castro Street
San Francisco, CA 94114
(415) 864-3112

Kevin Collins Foundation
  for Missing Children
P.O. Box 590473
San Francisco, CA 94159
(415) 771-8477

National Center of Youth Law
114 Sansome Street, Suite 9000
San Francisco, CA 94104
(415) 543-3307

Parents of Murdered Children
State Coordinator
3250 Hedda Court
San Jose, CA 95127
(408) 258-8123

Vanished Children's Alliance
1407 Parkmoor Avenue
San Jose, CA 95126
(408) 971-4822

Victims of Crime Resource Center
P.O. Box 14259
San Luis Obispo, CA 93408
(800) 842-8467

Victims for Victims, Orange County
3941-B South Bristol
Santa Ana, CA 92704
(714) 979-5001

Victims of Child Abuse Legislation
1212 North Broadway, Suite 133
Santa Ana, CA 92701
(714) 558-0200

Southern California Coalition
  Against Domestic Violence
P.O. Box 5036
Santa Monica, CA 90405
(213) 392-9874

Justice for Murder Victims
P.O. Box 5601
South San Francisco, CA 94083
(415) 564-7327

Justice for Victims of Homicide
3179 Winterbrook Court
Thousand Oaks, CA 91360

VOICES—Victims of Incest
  Can Emerge Successfully
P.O. Box 1722
Tustin, CA 92681
(714) 832-9625

Adam Walsh Child Resource Center
7812 Westminster Boulevard
Westminster, CA 92668
(714) 898-4802

Coalition for Victims Equal Rights
8102 South Michigan Avenue
Whittier, CA 90602
(213) 696-8374

Colorado
Center for the Prevention of
    Domestic Violence
P.O. Box 2662
Colorado Springs, CO 80901
(719) 633-1462

MADD State Office
P.O. Box 26149
Colorado Springs, CO 80936
(719) 522-0292

American Association for
    Protecting Children
American Humane Association
9725 East Hamden Avenue
Denver, CO 80231
(303) 792-9900

American Association of
    Suicidology
2459 South Ash Street
Denver, CO 80222
(303) 692-0985

Colorado Coalition Against
    Sexual Assault
P.O. Box 18663
Denver, CO 80218
(303) 333-3311

Colorado Direct Assistance to
    Women in Need
P.O. Box 18212
Denver, CO 80218
(303) 322-7010

Colorado Domestic Violence
    Coalition
P.O. Box 18902
Denver, CO 80218
(303) 394-2810

Denver Victims Service Center
P.O. Box 18975
Denver, CO 80218
(303) 860-0660

Domestic Violence Initiative
    for Women with Disabilities
P.O. Box 300535
Denver, CO 80203
(303) 839-5510

Men Assisting, Leading,
    Educating
(Incest Survivors Resource)
P.O. Box 380181
Denver, CO 80238
(303) 320-4365

National Center for Prevention
    and Treatment of Child Abuse
    and Neglect
1205 Oneida
Denver, CO 80221
(303) 321-3963

Volunteers of America
2636 Larimer Street
Denver, CO 80205
(303) 294-0111

Victim Outreach Information
P.O. Box 10739
Golden, CO 80401
(303) 980-1112

Parents of Murdered Children
State Coordinator
228 La Paz Place
Longmont, CO 80501
(303) 772-6004

Justice for Surviving Victims
146 Mesa Circle, Box 1503
Salida, CO 81201
(719) 539-4924

Connecticut

Bridgeport YWCA
Shelter Services and
   Rape Crisis Service
753 Fairfield Avenue
Bridgeport, CT 06604
(203) 334-6154

Association for Death Education
   and Counseling
638 Prospect Avenue
Hartford, CT 06105
(203) 232-4825

Commission on Victim Services
175 Main Street
Hartford, CT 06106
(203) 566-4156
(800) 822-VICT

Connecticut Coalition Against
   Domestic Violence
22 Maple Avenue
Hartford, CT 06114
(203) 524-5890

Services for Families of
   Homicide Victims
175 Main Street
Hartford, CT 06106
(203) 566-4156

Connecticut Self Help & Mutual
   Support
19 Howe Street
New Haven, CT 06511
(203) 789-7645

Council on Children in Crisis
900 Grand Avenue
New Haven, CT 06515
(203) 624-2600

MADD State Office
677 State Street
New Haven, CT 06511
(203) 773-5066

Women's Center of Southeastern
   Connecticut, Inc.
120 Broad Street
New London, CT 06320
(203) 447-0366

Parents of Murdered Children
79 Franklin Street
Vernon, CT 06066
(203) 871-6776

RID
50 Arnoldsdale Road
West Hartford, CT 06119
(203) 232-4987

SLAM
27 George Street
West Haven, CT 06516
(203) 934-3821

Delaware

Victim Services Center
P.O. Box 430
Dover, DE 19903
(302) 739-3711

Statewide Victim Center
13 S.W. Front Street
Milford, DE 19963
(302) 422-1562

CANE—Clearinghouse on Abuse
   & Neglect of the Elderly
University of Delaware
Newark, DE 19716
(302) 451-2940

RID/VOID Coordinator
128 Stature Drive
Sherwood Forest
Newark, DE 19713
(302) 737-3335

CHILD, INC.
Central YMCA
11th and Washington Streets
Wilmington, DE 19801
(302) 655-3311

Parents of Murdered Children
130 Maple Hill Road
Wilmington, DE 19804
(302) 994-8510

District of Columbia

American Association for
   Marriage and Family Therapy
1717 K Street, N.W., Suite 407
Washington, DC 20006
(202) 429-1825

American Bar Association
Center on Children and the Law
1800 M Street, N.W.
Washington, DC 20036
(202) 331-2200

American Red Cross
2025 E Street, N.W.
Washington, DC 20006
(202) 737-8300

Anti-Violence Project
National Gay & Lesbian Task Force
1517 U Street, N.W.
Washington, DC 20009
(202) 332-6483

Associated Catholic Charities
1133 15th Street, N.W.
Washington, DC 20005
(202) 659-9371

The Carol Gray Committee
6816 32nd Street, N.W.
Washington, DC 20015
(202) 244-8024

Center for Child Protection
   and Family Support
714 G Street, S.E.
Washington, DC 20003
(202) 544-3144

Child Abuse Coalition
733 15th Street, N.W., Suite 930
Washington, DC 20005
(202) 347-3666

Children's Defense Fund
122 C Street, N.W., Suite 310
Washington, DC 20001
(202) 628-8787
(800) 424-0602

Childhelp USA
5225 Wisconsin Avenue, N.W.,
   #603
Washington, DC 20015
(202) 537-5193

Child Welfare League of America
440 First Street, N.W.
Washington, DC 20001-2085
(202) 638-2952

Criminal Justice Services
American Association of Retired
   Persons
601 E Street, N.W.
Washington, DC 20049
(202) 434-2277

D.C. Coalition Against
   Domestic Violence
P.O. Box 76069
Washington, DC 20013
(202) 857-0216

D.C. Crime Victim Assistance
First and I Streets, S.W.
Washington, DC 20024
(202) VICTIMS

D.C. Office on Emergency
   Shelter and Support Services
25 M Street, S.W., 3rd Floor
Washington, DC 20024
(202) 727-2030

D.C. Rape Crisis Center
P.O. Box 21005
Washington, DC 20009
(202) 232-0202

House of Ruth
501 H Street, N.W.
Washington, DC 20002
(202) 547-6173 office

National Association for the Deaf
Legal Defense Fund
Gallaudet University
800 Florida Avenue, N.E.
Washington, DC 20002
(202) 651-5375 (V/TTY)

National Organization for
  Victim Assistance (NOVA)
1757 Park Road, N.W.
Washington, DC 20010
(202) 232-6682

Samaritan Ministry
1525 Newton Street, N.W.
Washington, DC 20010
(202) 797-0360

Trial Lawyers for Public Justice
1625 Massachusetts Avenue, N.W.
Washington, DC 20036
(202) 797-8600

Florida

People Against Crime Together
P.O. Box 702
Boynton Beach, FL 33435
(407) 732-9200

The Center for Crime Victims
  and Survivors, Inc.
P.O. Box 6201
Clearwater, FL 33518
(813) 535-1114

Florida Refuge Information
  Network
c/o Women in Distress
P.O. Box 676
Ft. Lauderdale, FL 33302
(305) 761-1133

Sexual & Physical Abuse
  Resource Center
P.O. Box 23769, Suite 93
Gainesville, FL 32604
(904) 377-8255

Justice for Surviving Victims
322 Kent Street
Groveland, FL 32736
(904) 429-4200

Children's Home Society of
  Florida
P.O. Box 5616
Jacksonville, FL 32247
(904) 396-2641

Childkeepers International
P.O. Box 6456
Lake Worth, FL 33466
(305) 586-6695

Children's Rights of America
12551 Indian Rocks Road
Largo, FL 33544
(813) 584-0888

Child Protection Team
1150 Southwest 14th Street, #2
Miami, FL 33130
(305) 547-6916

Jewish Family Services
1790 S.W. 27th Avenue
Miami, FL 33145
(305) 445-0555

Miami Bridge, Inc.
1149 N.W. 11th Street
Miami, FL 33136
(305) 324-8953

Parents of Murdered Children
State Coordinator
10600 S.W. 83rd Avenue
Miami, FL 33157
(305) 547-5359

Family Survivors Program
American Police Hall of Fame
1100 N.E. 125th Street
North Miami, FL 33161
(305) 891-1700

Spouse Abuse, Inc.
Florida Refuge Information
  Network
P.O. Box 536276
Orlando, FL 32853
(407) 886-2856

We Care, Inc.
(Incest/Abuse Resource)
112 Pasadena Place
Orlando, FL 32803
(407) 425-2624

Valuing Our Children and Laws
1769 66th Street North
St. Petersburg, FL 33710
(813) 960-1226

Coordinator for Victims Rights
Office of the Governor
The Capitol
Tallahassee, FL 32399
(904) 488-3494

Florida Citizens Against Crime
P.O. Box 10504
Tallahassee, FL 32302-2504
(904) 681-9781

MADD State Office
223 East Virginia
Tallahassee, FL 32301
(904) 681-0061

Missing Children Information
  Clearinghouse
P.O. Box 1489
Tallahassee, FL 32303
(904) 488-5221
(800) 342-0821 (in Florida)

Hillsborough County Crisis Center
2214 East Henry Avenue
Tampa, FL 33610
(813) 238-8411

Missing Children Help Center
410 Ware Boulevard
Tampa, FL 33619
(813) 623-KIDS
(800) USA-KIDS (in Florida)

Suicide Survivors Support Group
2214 East Henry
Tampa, FL 33610
(813) 238-8411

Adam Walsh Child Resource Center
319 Clematis Street, #409
West Palm Beach, FL 33401
(407) 833-9080

The Children's Place
2309 Ponce de Leon
West Palm Beach, FL 33407
(407) 832-6185

Georgia

Georgia Council on Child Abuse
Athens, GA
(404) 548-7794
(800) 532-3208 (in Atlanta)

Georgia Network Against Domestic
  Violence
250 Georgia Avenue, S.E.
Atlanta, GA 30312
(404) 524-3847

Grady Hospital Rape Crisis
  Center
80 Butler Street, S.E.
Atlanta, GA 30335
(404) 588-4861

Mothers Against Raping Children
920 Curlew Street
Atlanta, GA 30327
(404) 843-8884

Parents of Murdered Children
1809 Wilkinson Circle
Augusta, GA 30904
(404) 738-6183

Rape Crisis/Sexual Assault
  Services
1350 Walton Way
Augusta, GA 30910-3599
(404) 722-9022

Columbus Alliance for Battered
  Women, Inc.
P.O. Box 5804
Columbus, GA 31906
(404) 324-3850

Columbus Rape Crisis, Inc.
1314 Munro Avenue
Columbus, GA 31906
(404) 323-5010

Missing Children Info Center
Georgia Bureau of Information
P.O. Box 370808
Decatur, GA 30037
(404) 244-2554

Victim Assistance Services
Macon-Bibb County
P.O. Box 56, Mercer University
Macon, GA 31207
(912) 745-9293

Rape Crisis Center of
  the Coastal Empire
P.O. Box 8492
Savannah, GA 31412
(912) 354-6742

SAFE Shelter
P.O. Box 22487
Savannah, GA 31403
(912) 232-2342

Hawaii

Shelter for Abused Spouses
  and Children
200 North Vineyard Boulevard
Honolulu, HI 96817
(808) 521-2377

Hawaii Criminal Justice
  Commission
222 South Vineyard Street
Honolulu, HI 96813
(808) 538-6714

Hawaii State Committee on Family
  Violence
1154 Fort Street Mall
Honolulu, HI 96813
(808) 538-7216

Parents United
Daughters United
Adults Molested as Children
Child and Family Service
200 North Vineyard
Honolulu, HI 96817
(808) 521-2377

Sexual Abuse Treatment Center
1415 Kalakaua Avenue
Honolulu, HI 96826
(808) 947-8337

Parents of Murdered Children
46-217 Lilipuna Road
Kaneohe, HI 96744
(808) 235-4222

Idaho

Idaho Network for Children
P.O. Box 6032
Boise, ID 83707
(208) 333-4780

Idaho Network to Stop
  Violence Against Women
4355 Emerald
Boise, ID 83706
(208) 334-6800

Parents of Murdered Children
11911 Ustick Road
Boise, ID 83704
(208) 323-1552

Reachout Ministries
P.O. Box 4415
Boise, ID 83711
(208) 376-5000

VANGUARD
(Victim Assistance Network)
1421 North 21st Street
Boise, ID 83701
(208) 345-9094

Nez Perce Victim Advocate
  Project
P.O. Box 365
Lapwai, ID 83540
(208) 843-2718

Pocatello YWCA
Women's Advocates
454 North Garfield
Pocatello, ID 83204
(208) 232-0742

Volunteers Against Violence
P.O. Box 2444
Twin Falls, ID 83303
(208) 733-5054

Illinois

Child Sexual Abuse Treatment
  & Training Center of Illinois
345 Manor Court
Bollingbrook, IL 60439
(312) 739-0491

Parents of Murdered Children
2025 State Street
Calumet City, IL 60409
(708) 862-9811

American Professional Society
  on the Abuse of Children
c/o University of Chicago
969 East 60th Street
Chicago, IL 60637
(312) 702-9419

Center for Sibling Loss
1700 West Irving Park
Chicago, IL 60613
(312) 883-0268

Chicago Abused Women Coalition
Greenhouse Shelter
P.O. Box 476608
Chicago, IL 60647
(312) 278-4110

Crime Victim Support Groups
Ravenswood Hospital
4545 North Damen Avenue
Chicago, IL 60625
(312) 769-6200

Horizons
(Gay/Lesbian Resource)
3225 North Sheffield
Chicago, IL 60657
(312) 472-6469

MADD State Office
180 North LaSalle, #2107
Chicago, IL 60601
(312) 782-6266

National Committee for the
  Prevention of Child Abuse
332 South Michigan Avenue
Chicago, IL 60604-4357
(312) 663-3520

Society for Traumatic Stress
  Studies
435 North Michigan Avenue, #1717
Chicago, IL 60611
(312) 644-0828

VOICES—Victims of Incest
   Can Emerge Survivors
P.O. Box 148309
Chicago, IL 60614
(312) 327-1500

Woman Abuse Action Project
4520 North Beacon
Chicago, IL 60640
(312) 561-3500

Volunteers of America
8787 State Street
East St. Louis, IL 62203
(618) 398-7764

Self-Help Center
(Statewide Services)
Evanston, IL
(800) 322-MASH

Crisis Line of Will County
P.O. Box 2354
Joliet, IL 60434
(815) 744-5280

RID—Illinois State
2661 35th Street
Moline, IL 61265
(309) 764-9774

The Compassionate Friends
National Office
P.O. Box 3696
Oak Brook, IL 60522
(703) 990-0010

Tri-County Womenstrength
P.O. Box 3172
Peoria, IL 61614
(309) 691-0551

Parents United
Institute for Human Resources
P.O. Box 768
Pontiac, IL 61764
(815) 844-6109

Quad Counties Counseling Center
530 Park Avenue East
Princeton, IL 61356
(815) 875-4458

National Association for
   Family Based Service
P.O. Box 005
Riverdale, IL 62327

Rockford Sexual Assault
   Counseling, Inc.
202 West State Street, #51
Rockford, IL 61101
(815) 229-6470

Alliance of American Insurers
1501 Woodfield Road
Schaumberg, IL 60195-4980
(312) 490-8514

Illinois Coalition Against
   Domestic Violence
937 South 4th Street
Springfield, IL 62703
(217) 789-2830

Illinois Coalition Against Sexual
   Assault
123 South 7th Street
Springfield, IL 62701
(217) 753-4117

I-Search (Illinois State Enforcement
   Agencies to Recover Children)
Illinois State Police
200 Armory Building
Springfield, IL 62706
(217) 782-6429
(800) 843-5763 (in Illinois)

A Woman's Fund, Inc./Rape Crisis
   Services
505 West Green
Urbana, IL 61801
(217) 384-4462

Indiana

Parents United
Central Mental Health, Inc.
645 South Rogers
Bloomington, IN 47401
(812) 339-1691

RID Coordinator
28467 C.R. 20
Elkhart, IN 46517
(219) 295-8133

YWCA Battered Women's Shelter
118 Vine Street
Evansville, IN 47708
(812) 422-1191

Rape Awareness Program
303 East Washington Boulevard
Fort Wayne, IN 46802
(219) 424-7977

Gary Mental Health Center
1100 West 6th Avenue
Gary, IN 46402
(219) 885-4264

Adult & Child Mental Health
    Center
8110 Madison Avenue
Indianapolis, IN 46227
(317) 882-5122

MADD State Office
4475 Allisonville Road
Indianapolis, IN 46205
(317) 546-9711

Parents of Murdered Children
State Coordinator
P.O. Box 17095
Indianapolis, IN 46227
(317) 684-6711

Women in Crisis Program
YWCA of Lafayette
605 North 6th Street
Lafayette, IN 47901
(317) 742-0075

Sex Offense Services
403 East Madison Street
South Bend, IN 46617
(219) 234-0061

Bethany House/Catholic Charities
1402 Locust Street
Terre Haute, IN 47807
(812) 232-4978

National VORP Resource Center
PACT Institute of Justice
254 South Morgan Boulevard
Valparaiso, IN 46383
(219) 462-1127

Protect the Innocent
Rural Route 1, Box 232
Waveland, IN 47989
(317) 435-2170

Iowa

Parents of Murdered Children
512-½ 3rd Avenue, SW
Cedar Rapids, IA 52404
(319) 364-6078

Children's Square USA
Christian Home Association
Council Bluffs, IA 51502
(712) 325-1662

Quad City Domestic Violence/
    Sexual Assault Counseling
    Program
P.O. Box 190
Davenport, IA 52805
(319) 323-1852

Coalition Against Domestic
    Violence
Lucas Building
Des Moines, IA 50319
(515) 281-7284

Des Moines Chapter of SLAM
2934 Dean Avenue
Des Moines, IA 50317
(515) 262-4446

Family Violence Center
1101 Walnut Street
Des Moines, IA 50309
(515) 243-6147 crisis
(800) 942-0333 (in Iowa)

Iowa Coalition Against Sexual
  Abuse
Lucas State Office Building
Des Moines, IA 50319
(515) 242-5096

RID
2908 Patricia Drive
Des Moines, IA 50322
(515) 276-5828

YWCA—Battered Women Program
35 North Booth
Dubuque, IA 52001
(319) 556-3371

Domestic Violence Project
P.O. Box 733
Iowa City, IA 52244
(319) 351-1042

Iowa Organization for
  Victim Assistance
1918 Waterfront Drive
Iowa City, IA 52244
(319) 351-5500

National Resource Center
  on Family-Based Services
N240 Oakdale Boulevard
Iowa City, IA 52244
(319) 335-2200

Council on Sexual Assault &
  Domestic Assault
P.O. Box 1565
Sioux City, IA 51102
(712) 258-7233

Rape/Sexual Assault & Abuse
  Intervention
2530 University Avenue
Waterloo, IA 50701
(319) 233-8484

Kansas

Child Abuse Hotline
(800) 392-3738 (in Kansas)

Crime Hotline
Kansas Bureau of Investigation
(800) KS-CRIME (in Kansas)

Elderly Abuse and Neglect Hotline
(800) 392-0210 (in Kansas)

Community Service Center, Inc.
2048 North 5th Street
Kansas City, KS 66101
(913) 371-3148

Kansas Committee for Prevention
  of Child Abuse
112 West 6th Street, #305
Kansas City, KS 66603

Kansas Coalition Against Sexual
  & Domestic Violence
Box 633
Lawrence, KS 66044
(913) 841-6887

Victim Offender Reconciliation
  Program
726 North Main
Newton, KS 67114
(316) 283-2038

The Lost Child Network
P.O. Box 6442
Shawnee Mission, KS 66206
(800) 843-5678 (in Kansas)

MADD State Office
3601 S.W. 29th, #244
Topeka, KS 66614
(913) 271-7525

AVIS—Adolescent Victims of
  Incest & Survivors
1035 Parklawn
Wichita, KS 67218
(316) 686-3388

Kansans for Effective
   Criminal Justice
1315 North Armour
Wichita, KS 67216
(316) 682-6606

Kansas Organization of Sexual
   Assault Centers
1801 East 10th Street
Wichita, KS 67214
(316) 263-0185

Parents of Murdered Children
State Coordinator
460 Pamela
Wichita, KS 67212
(316) 722-2907

YWCA Women's Crisis Center
P.O. Box 1740
Wichita, KS 67201
(316) 263-2313

Kentucky

Kentucky Crime Victims' Hotline
(800) 372-2551
(800) 752-6200 child abuse

Pathways, Inc.
(Sexual Assault Resource)
201 22nd Street
Ashland, KY 41101
(606) 329-8588

Parents of Murdered Children
2401 Carlisle Avenue
Fort Mitchell, KY 41017
(606) 331-1807

Kentucky Domestic Violence
   Association
316 Wilkinson Boulevard
Frankfort, KY 40602
(502) 875-4132

MADD State Office
P.O. Box 274
Harrodsburg, KY 40330
(606) 734-0090

Crime Victims for Equal Rights
3193 Pepperhill Drive
Lexington, KY 40502
(606) 231-2217

YWCA Spouse Abuse Center
P.O. Box 12526
Lexington, KY 40583
(606) 252-5521

Citizens & Victims for
   Justice Reform
816 Starks Building
Louisville, KY 40202
(502) 589-3371

Exploited Children's
   Help Organization (ECHO)
720 West Jefferson Street
Louisville, KY 40202
(502) 585-3246

Family & Children's Agency, Inc.
P.O. Box 3784
Louisville, KY 40201
(502) 583-1741

Parents United, Inc.
2305 Taylorsville Road
Louisville, KY 40205
(502) 473-1844

SAME—Surviving a Murder
   Effectively
1930 Bishop Lane
Louisville, KY 40218
(502) 458-0260

Childwatch, Inc.
2625 Washingotn St.
Paducah, KY 42001
(502) 443-1440

Christian Appalachian Project
Bethany House/Family Abuse
   Shelter
P.O. Box 864
Somerset, KY 42501
(606) 679-1553

Louisiana

Louisiana Council on Child
  Abuse
333 Laurel Street
Baton Rouge, LA 70801
(504) 346-0222
(800) 348-KIDS (In Louisiana)

MADD State Office
P.O. Box 66770
Baton Rouge, LA 70896
(504) 383-3000

Parents of Murdered Children
P.O. Box 338
Clinton, LA 70722
(504) 683-5316

Victim Witness Assistance Bureau
1020 Ryan Street
Lake Charles, LA 70601
(318) 437-3400

YWCA—Rape Crisis Center
1515 Jackson Street
Monroe, LA 71202
(318) 323-1543

Methodist Home of New Orleans
(Child Abuse Resource)
P.O. Box 15109
New Orleans, LA 70130
(504) 895-7709

Metropolitan Battered Women's
  Program
P.O. Box 10775
New Orleans, LA 70181
(504) 889-6636

YWCA Rape Crisis Program
601 South Jefferson Davis Parkway
New Orleans, LA 70119
(504) 488-2693

YWCA Family Violence Program
Children's Program
710 Travis Street
Shreveport, LA 71101
(318) 222-2117

Maine

Abused Women's Advocacy Project
P.O. Box 713
Auburn, ME 04212
(207) 795-4020

Family Violence Project
59 Court Street
Augusta, ME 04332-0304
(207) 623-8637

Looking Up
(Incest Resource)
P.O. Box K
Augusta, ME 04332
(207) 626-3402

Maine Coalition on Rape
P.O. Box 5326
Augusta, ME 04330
(207) 772-3459

Parents of Murdered Children
245 Main Street
Cumberland, ME 04021
(207) 829-4296

YWCA Intervention Program
130 East Avenue
Lewiston, ME 04240-5525
(207) 795-4054

Parents United
Community Counseling Center
P.O. Box 4016
Portland, ME 04101
(207) 774-5727

Rape Crisis Assistance, Inc.
P.O. Box 924
Waterville, ME 04901
(207) 872-0601
(800) 525-4441

Maryland

Families of Murdered Loved Ones
3800 Hebron Terrace
Abington, MD 21009
(410) 679-1316

Maryland Network Against
Domestic Violence
YWCA Women's Center
167 Duke of Gloucester Street
Annapolis, MD 21401
(410) 268-4393

MADD State Office
14 Hudson Street
Annapolis, MD 21401
(410) 841-6633

Maryland Victim Assistance
Network
P.O. Box 333
Annapolis, MD 21401
(410) 269-7816

People Against Child Abuse
125 Cathedral Street
Annapolis, MD 21401
(410) 269-7816
(800) 422-3055 (in Maryland)

Family and Children's Services
of Central Maryland
7131 Liberty Road
Baltimore, MD 21217
(410) 281-1334

Parents of Murdered Children
4001 Old Court Road, #316
Baltimore, MD 21208
(410) 486-6028

Sexual Assault/Domestic
Violence Center, Inc.
6229 North Charles Street
Baltimore, MD 21212
(410) 377-8111

Survivors of Incest Anonymous
P.O. Box 21817
Baltimore, MD 21222
(410) 282-3400

Montgomery County Crisis Center
4910 Auburn Avenue
Bethesda, MD 20814
(301) 656-9161

National Sudden Infant Death
Syndrome Foundation
10500 Little Putuxent Parkway
Columbia, MD 21044
(800) 221-SIDS

CASA/New Directions for Women
116 West Baltimore Street
Hagerstown, MD 21740
(301) 739-4990

American Correctional Association
8025 Laurel Lakes Court
Laurel, MD 20707
(410) 206-5100

Missing & Exploited
Children's Association
P.O. Box 608
Lutherville, MD 21093
(301) 667-0718

People Against Telephone
Terrorism and Harassment
18159 Village Mart Drive
Olney, MD 20832
(800) 783-5959

National Victims Resource
Center
P.O. Box 6000
Rockville, MD 20850
(301) 251-5550
(800) 627-6872

PACA—People Against Child Abuse
P.O. Box 1742
Rockville, MD 20850
(301) 468-6238
(800) 422-3055

Concerns of Police Survivors, Inc.
9423-A Marlboro Pike
Upper Marlboro, MD 20772
(301) 599-0445

Stephanie Roper Committee
14804 Pratt Street
Upper Marlboro, MD 20772
(301) 952-0063

The Chesapeake Institute
11141 Georgia Avenue
Wheaton, MD 20902
(301) 949-5000

Massachusetts

First Call for Help
Jones Library
43 Amity Street
Amherst, MA 01002
(413) 256-0121
(800) 282-7779

Resolve, Inc. (Child Loss)
5 Water Street
Arlington, MA 02174
(617) 643-2424

Children's Hospital
(Child Abuse Resource)
300 Longwood Avenue
Boston, MA 02115
(617) 735-7979

Massachusetts Office for
   Victim Assistance
30 Winter Street
Boston, MA 02108
(617) 727-5200

Parents of Murdered Children
35 Jersey Avenue
Braintree, MA 02184
(617) 848-2179

The Women's Center
46 Pleasant Street
Cambridge, MA 02139
(617) 354-8807

MADD State Office
1661 Worcester Road, #205
Framingham, MA 01701
(508) 875-3736

Alternative House
(Domestic Violence Resource)
P.O. Box 2096
Lowell, MA 01851
(508) 458-0274

Victims for Victims
7 Butternut Avenue
Peabody, MA 01960-3288
(508) 535-9647

ARCH—Abuse & Rape Crisis
   Hotline
P.O. Box 80632
Springfield, MA 01138
(413) 733-1588

National Institute for the
   Prevention of Elder Abuse
Medical Center of Central
   Massachusetts
119 Belmont Street
Worcester, MA 01605
(508) 793-6166

New England KIDS
(Missing Children Resource)
516 Grafton Street
Worcester, MA 01604
(800) 392-6090 (in Massachusetts)

Massachusetts Society for the
   Prevention of Cruelty to Children
286 Lincoln Street
Worcester, MA 01605
(508) 753-2967

Worcester Rape Crisis Program
1016 Main Street
Worcester, MA 01603
(508) 791-9546

Michigan

Domestic Violence Project/
   SAFE House
P.O. Box 7052
Ann Arbor, MI 48107
(313) 973-0242

Battle Creek Organization
   Against Domestic Violence
P.O. Box 199
Battle Creek, MI 49016
(616) 965-6086

Parents United
Lutheran Child & Family Service
6019 West Side Saginaw Road
Bay City, MI 48707
(517) 686-7650

Children's Aid Society
7700 2nd Avenue
Detroit, MI 48202
(313) 875-0020

Interim House—YWCA
P.O. Box 904
Detroit, MI 48221
(313) 861-5300

SOSAD
453 Martin Luther King Jr.
   Boulevard
Detroit, MI 48201
(313) 833-3030

Team for Justice
(Sexual Assault Resource)
1035 St. Antoine
Detroit, MI 48226
(313) 965-3242

Help Me, Inc.
(Adult Survivors of Incest)
P.O. Box 480
East Detroit, MI 48021
(313) 521-4097

Harbor
(Domestic Violence Resource)
398 Park Lane
East Lansing, MI 48823
(517) 337-2527
(800) 292-3925 (in Michigan)

Runaway Assistance Program
(Missing Children Resource)
398 Park Lane
East Lansing, MI 48823
(517) 337-1611

SAFE House of Flint YWCA
310 East 3rd Street
Flint, MI 48502
(313) 238-7621

Cornerstone Community Mental
   Health Services
240 Cherry Street, S.E.
Grand Rapids, MI 49503
(616) 774-3909

RID
565 Forest Hills, S.E.
Grand Rapids, MI 49506
(616) 949-5557

YWCA Counseling Center
25 Sheldon Avenue, S.E.
Grand Rapids, MI 49503
(616) 459-4652

Parents of Murdered Children
5340 Milford Road
Highland, MI 48356
(313) 887-3446

Michigan Coalition Against
   Domestic Violence
P.O. Box 7032
Huntington Woods, MI 48070
(313) 547-8888
(800) 333-7233

National Child Safety Council
4065 Page Avenue
Jackson, MI 49204
(517) 764-6070

Council Against Domestic Assault
P.O. Box 14149
Lansing, MI 48901
(517) 372-5572

Sexual Assault Information Network
P.O. Box 20112
Lansing, MI 48901
(517) 371-7140

MADD State Office
910 Eastlawn
Midland, MI 48642
(517) 631-6233

Midland Chapter of SLAM
2525 Sturgeon Road
Midland, MI 48640
(517) 832-3556

HAVEN (Domestic Violence
  & Sexual Assault Resource)
92 Whittemore Street
Pontiac, MI 48058
(313) 334-1284

Minnesota

Victims Crisis Center
300 8th Avenue, N.W.
Austin, MN 55912
(507) 437-6680

Northwoods Coalition
  for Battered Women
P.O. Box 563
Bemidji, MN 56601
(218) 751-6346

Aid to Victims of Sexual Assault
424 West Superior Street
Duluth, MN 55802
(218) 726-4751

Domestic Abuse Intervention
  Project
206 West 4th Street
Duluth, MN 55806
(218) 722-2781

Southwestern Mental Health
  Center Sexual Assault Program
2 Round Wind Road
Luverne, MN 56156
(507) 283-9511
(800) 642-1525

Black, Indian, Hispanic and
  Asian Women in Action
122 West Franklin Avenue
Minneapolis, MN 55404
(612) 870-1193

Minnesota Citizens Council on
  Crime & Justice
822 South 3rd Street
Minneapolis, MN 55415
(612) 340-5432

Domestic Abuse Project
(Violent Partner Program)
204 West Franklin Avenue
Minneapolis, MN 55404
(612) 874-7063

Minnesota Association for
  Crime Victims
822 South 3rd Street
Minneapolis, MN 55415
(218) 726-2323

Pornography Resource Center
734 East Lake Street
Minneapolis, MN 55407
(612) 822-1476

Rape & Sexual Abuse Center
2431 Hennepin Avenue
Minneapolis, MN 55405
(612) 825-2409

Minnesota Migrant Council
  Services for the Abused
35 Wilson Avenue, N.E.
St. Cloud, MN 56302
(612) 253-7010

MADD State Office
450 North Syndicate Street
St. Paul, MN 55104
(612) 649-0370

Minnesota Association for Crime
  Victims
P.O. Box 19626
St. Paul, MN 55109

Minnesota Office of Crime
  Victims Ombudsman
1821 University Avenue
St. Paul, MN 55104
(612) 642-0397

Parents of Murdered Children
1251 Edgcumbe Road
St. Paul, MN 55105
(612) 698-2526

Mississippi

Gulf Coast Women's Center
P.O. Box 333
Biloxi, MS 39533
(601) 436-3809

Mississippi Coalition Against
  Domestic Violence
P.O. Box 333
Biloxi, MS 39533
(601) 436-3809

Children's Defense Fund
P.O. Box 1684
Jackson, MS 39205
(601) 355-7495

MADD State Office
1923 Dunbarton Drive
Jackson, MS 39216
(601) 981-5660

Mississippi Gay Alliance
236½ West Capitol Street
Jackson, MS 39204
(601) 353-7611

Rape Crisis Center
P.O. Box 2248
Jackson, MS 39225
(601) 355-5520

RID of Mississippi
Voices for Victims, Inc.
2624-B Southerland Drive
Jackson, MS 39216
(601) 982-8239

Parents of Murdered Children
840 Marion Drive, Apt. C-1
McComb, MS 39648
(601) 684-4599

Domestic Violence Project
P.O. Box 286
Oxford, MS 38655
(601) 234-5085

SAFER (Survivors Against Felons'
  Early Release)
Route 3, Box 842
Sumrall, MS 39482

Missouri

MADD State Office
1021 Southwest Boulevard
Jefferson City, MO 65109
(314) 636-2460

Missouri Coalition Against
  Domestic Violence
311 East McCarty
Jefferson City, MO 65101
(314) 634-4161

VICTIMS TOO
610 Main
Joplin, MO 64801
(417) 781-3581

The Children's Place
2 East 59th Street
Kansas City, MO 64113
(816) 363-1898

Justice Campaign of America
3110 East 55th Street
Kansas City, MO 64130
(816) 333-2979

Metropolitan Organization to
  Counter Sexual Assault
3515 Broadway
Kansas City, MO 64111
(816) 931-4527

NEWS House for Battered Women
P.O. Box 4509
Kansas City, MO 64124
(816) 241-0311

Family Center
P.O. Box 1011-SSS
Springfield, MO 65805
(417) 865-0373

Family Guidance Center
(Assault Victim Resource)
910 Edmond Street
St. Joseph, MO 64501
(816) 364-1502

Aid for Victims of Crime
4050 Lindell Boulevard
St. Louis, MO 63108
(314) 652-3623

AMEND (Child Death Resource)
4324 Berrywick Terrace
St. Louis, MO 63128
(314) 487-7528

Family & Children Services
9109 Watson Road
St. Louis, MO 63126
(314) 968-2870

Women's Self-Help Center
2838 Olive
St. Louis, MO 63103
(314) 531-9100

Parents Anonymous
(Domestic Violence Resource)
925 South Central
St. Louis, MO 63105
(314) 534-9438

Parents of Murdered Children
8139 Cornell Court
St. Louis, MO 63130-3639
(314) 863-4939

Salvation Army
(Domestic Violence Resource)
3744 Lindell Boulevard
St. Louis, MO 63108
(314) 534-1250

Victim Service Council
7900 Carondelet Avenue
St. Louis, MO 63105
(314) 889-3075

Montana

Parents of Murdered Children
2915 Rockrim Lane
Billings, MT 59102
(406) 256-5326

Salvation Army Gateway House
P.O. Box 1903
Billings, MT 59103
(406) 245-4659

Bozeman Area Battered Women's
  Network
P.O. Box 752
Bozeman, MT 59715
(406) 586-0263

Safe Space
Christian Community Center
1131 West Copper
Butte, MT 59703
(406) 782-2111

Great Falls Chapter of SLAM
2820 3rd Avenue North
Great Falls, MT 59401
(406) 453-6378

Rape Action Line
113 6th Street North
Great Falls, MT 59401
(406) 727-7273

Friendship Center of Helena
1503 Gallatin
Helena, MT 59601
(406) 442-6800

Jeannette Rankin House
1130 West Broadway
Missoula, MT 59802
(406) 543-6691

Nebraska

Friendship House
P.O. Box 95125
Lincoln, NE 68509
(402) 474-4709

Nebraska Coalition for Victims
of Crime
Lincoln Police Department
233 South 10th Street
Lincoln, NE 68508
(402) 471-7181

Nebraska Crime Commission
Box 94946
301 Centennial Mall South
Lincoln, NE 68509
(402) 471-2194

Murder, Assault, Rape & Robbery
Victim Assistance Program
5008 Dodge Street, #300
Omaha, NE 68104
(402) 553-6945

Nebraska Task Force on Domestic
Violence and Sexual Assault
YWCA
222 South 29th Street
Omaha, NE 68131
(402) 345-6555

Parents of Murdered Children
P.O. Box 11506
Omaha, NE 68111
(402) 455-6332

Parents United
1313 Farnam on the Mall
Omaha, NE 68102
(402) 444-6839

Nevada

Parents of Murdered Children
Families of Murder Victims
410 Rutile Way
Henderson, NV 89015
(702) 564-5919

Citizens Committee on
Victim Rights
3441 West Sahara
Las Vegas, NV 89102
(702) 368-1533

Community Action Against Rape
749 Veterans Memorial Drive
Las Vegas, NV 89101
(702) 368-1533

GFWC—Nevada Federation
of Women's Clubs and Child
Abuse Coalition
1501 Birch Street
Las Vegas, NV 89102
(702) 382-5863

Nevada Crime Prevention
Association
400 East Stewart Avenue
Las Vegas, NV 89101
(702) 386-3501

Nevada Network Against
Domestic Violence
P.O. Box 6540
Reno, NV 89513
(702) 882-6209

Victims Training Projects
National Council of Juvenile and
Family Court Judges
P.O. Box 8987
Reno, NV 89507
(702) 784-4836

New Hampshire

New Hampshire Coalition Against
  Domestic and Sexual Violence
P.O. Box 353
Concord, NH 03301
(603) 224-8893

Treatment Center for
  Traumatic Stress
P.O. Box 82
Concord, NH 03302
(603) 596-2222
(800) 202-2222 (in New Hampshire)

Victim/Witness Assistance
State House Annex
Concord, NH 03301
(603) 271-3671

Child & Family Services of New
  Hampshire
99 Hanover Street
Manchester, NH 03101
(603) 668-1920

Women's Crisis Service of the
  Manchester YWCA
72 Concord Street
Manchester, NH 03101
(603) 625-5785

Rape and Assault Support
  Services
P.O. Box 217
Nashua, NH 03061
(603) 883-5521 ext. 2208

Parents of Murdered Children
79 Elm Street, Box 172
Penacook, NH 03303
(603) 753-4966

New Mexico

Albuquerque MADD
2920 Carlisle, N.E.
Albuquerque, NM 87110
(505) 243-5210

Albuquerque Rape Crisis Center
1025 Hermosa, S.E.
Albuquerque, NM 87108
(505) 266-7711

Concerns of Police Survivors
1208 Arizona, N.E.
Albuquerque, NM 87110
(505) 266-1063

Court Update
(Court Monitors & Other
  Programs)
820 Valverde, S.E.
Albuquerque, NM 87108
(505) 255-0288

New Mexico Coalition of Sexual
  Assault Programs
4253 Montgomery, N.E.
Albuquerque, NM 87109
(505) 883-8020

New Mexico Victim Assistance
  Organization
P.O. Box 25322
Albuquerque, NM 87125
(505) 843-0815

Incest Survivors Resource
  Network
P.O. Box 7375
Las Cruces, NM 88006
(505) 525-4818

New Mexico Coalition Against
  Domestic Violence
P.O. Box 2463
Las Cruces, NM 88004
(505) 526-2819

Southwest Counseling Center
(Sexual Assault Resource)
1480 North Main Street
Las Cruces, NM 88001
(505) 526-3371

Family Resource Center
(Child Abuse Resource)
Pera Building, Room 515
Santa Fe, NM 87503
(505) 827-4112

New Jersey

Concerns of Police Survivors
RD 2, Box 63BB
Belvidere, NJ 07823
(201) 453-2024

Parents of Murdered Children
52 Brower Drive
Brick, NJ 08723
(201) 477-4827

Volunteers of America
418 Cooper Street
Camden, NJ 08103
(609) 964-5100

Collingswood Chapter of SLAM
P.O. Box 346
Collingswood, NJ 08108
(609) 858-7800

Justice for Murder Victims
31 Brookdale Road
Cranford, NJ 07016
(201) 276-0811

Women's Referral Central
(Sexual Assault Resource)
7 State Street
Glassboro, NJ 08625
(609) 881-7045
(800) 322-8092 crisis (in New
   Jersey)

Voices for Victims
4 Laurie Terrace
Hackettstown, NJ 07840
(201) 850-9600

MADD State Office
100 Mercer Street
Hightstown, NJ 08520
(609) 448-0990

Sexual Assault Victims
   Assistance
114 Clifton Place
Jersey City, NJ 07304
(201) 915-1234

YWCA of Jersey City
Battered Women's Project
270 Fairmont Avenue
Jersey City, NJ 07306
(201) 333-5700

Coalition of Crime Victim
   Rights Organizations of
   New Jersey
95 Doasa Avenue
Livingston, NJ 07936
(201) 992-0660

New Jersey Council on
   Crime Victims
P.O. Box 303
Mount Freedom, NJ 07970
(201) 684-0266

Essex Family Violence Project
755 South Orange Avenue
Newark, NJ 07106
(201) 484-1704

SIDS
(Infant Death Resource)
16 Cresant Drive
Parsippany, NJ 07054
(201) 263-6730

Justice for Murder Victims
1170 Terrill Road
Scotch Plains, NJ 07076
(201) 322-8824

Commission on Missing Persons
Building 12A, CN-119
Trenton, NJ 08625
(609) 588-3742

Compassionate Friends
P.O. Box 9416
Trenton, NJ 08650
(609) 587-5717

New Jersey Coalition for
  Battered Women
2620 White Horse
Hamilton Square Road
Trenton, NJ 08618
(609) 584-8107

State Rape Care Program
New Jersey Department of Health
Trenton, NJ 08635
(609) 984-1311

New York

Compassionate Friends
83 Brookline Avenue
Albany, NY 12203
(518) 872-2222

Comprehensive Crime Victim
  Assistance
12 State Street
Albany, NY 12207
(518) 447-5500

MADD State Office
90 State Street, #1538
Albany, NY 12207
(518) 463-6233

State Federation on Child
  Abuse and Neglect
134 South Swan Street
Albany, NY 12210
(518) 445-1273
(800) 342-PIRC

State Head Injury Association
194 Washington Avenue
Albany, NY 12210
(518) 434-3037
(800) 228-8201

Victim Assistance Administrator
Division of Criminal Justice Services
Executive Park Tower
Albany, NY 12203
(518) 457-6113

American Children Held Hostage
30 Stepney Lane
Brentwood, NY 11717
(516) 231-6240

Bronx Women Against Rape
3101 Kingsbridge Terrace
Bronx, NY 10463
(212) 884-0700

Center for the Elimination of
  Violence in the Family
P.O. Box 279
Brooklyn, NY 11220
(718) 439-4612

Crime Victims' Counseling
  Services
G.P.O. Box 023003
Brooklyn, NY 11292
(718) 875-5862

Crime Victims Program
Congress of Italian American
  Organizations
5901 New Utrecht Avenue
Brooklyn, NY 11219
(718) 871-9149

Elder Abuse Training and
  Resource Center
203 Park Place
Brooklyn, NY 11238
(718) 230-5158

National Congress of Neighborhood
  Women
249 Manhattan Avenue
Brooklyn, NY 11211
(718) 388-6666

Erie Citizens Committee on Rape,
  Sexual Assault & Sexual Abuse
95 Franklin Street
Buffalo, NY 14202
(716) 846-7879

Parents of Murdered Children
938 Parkside
Buffalo, NY 14216
(716) 832-6923

The Salvation Army
(Domestic Violence Resource)
960 Main Street
Buffalo, NY 14202
(716) 883-9800

Adelphi Resource Center for
Crime Victim/Advocates
Adelphi University School
of Social Work
P.O. Box 703
Garden City, NY 11530
(516) 228-7407

Victims Information Bureau
515 Route 111
Hauppauge, NY 11788
(516) 360-3730

Incest Survivors Resource
Network International
P.O. Box 911
Hicksville, NY 11802
(516) 935-3031

Child Find of America, Inc.
7 Innis Avenue
New Paltz, NY 12501
(914) 255-1848
(800) I-AM-LOST

Anti-Defamation League
of B'nai B'rith
823 United Nations Plaza
New York, NY 10017
(212) 490-2525

Children's Rights Project
American Civil Liberties Union
132 West 43rd Street
New York, NY 10036
(212) 944-9800

Crime Victims Assistance Program
386 Park Avenue South
New York, NY 10016
(212) 582-7575

Institute for Youth Advocacy
(Missing Children Resource)
Covenant House
460 West 41st Street
New York, NY 10036
(212) 613-0349

Jewish Board of Family
& Children's Services
235 Park Avenue South
New York, NY 10003
(212) 460-0900

Lambda Legal Defense Fund
666 Broadway
New York, NY 10012-2317
(212) 995-8585

National Center on Women and
Family Law
799 Broadway
New York, NY 10003
(212) 674-8200

New York City Gay/Lesbian
Anti-Violence Project
208 West 13th Street
New York, NY 10011
(212) 807-6761

New York Society for the Prevention
of Cruelty to Children
161 William Street
New York, NY 10038
(212) 233-5500

New York Women Against Rape
666 Broadway, Suite 610
New York, NY 10012
(212) 477-0819

Parents of Murdered Children of
    New York State, Inc.
26 West 84th Street
New York, NY 10024
(212) 873-3361

Steps to End Family Violence
104 East 107th Street, 4th Floor
New York, NY 10029
(212) 867-0367

Support for Orthodox Victims of
    Rape & Incest
54 Nagle Avenue
New York, NY 10040
(212) 304-0951

Victim Services Agency
2 Lafayette Street
New York, NY 10007
(212) 577-7700
(Offices in all boroughs)

Adam Walsh Center
249 Highland Center
Rochester, NY 14620
(716) 461-1000

Alternatives for Battered Women
50 Chestnut Street
Rochester, NY 14624
(716) 232-7353

Center for Dispute Settlement
VORP
87 North Clinton Avenue
Rochester, NY 14614

RID New York State
11 Cardinal Drive
Rochester, NY 14624
(716) 247-1498

Rape Crisis Service of Planned
    Parenthood
414 Union Street
Schenectady, NY 12305
(518) 374-5236

RID-USA, Inc.
1013 Nott Street
P.O. Box 520
Schenectady, NY 12301
(518) 372-0034

Rape Crisis Center of Syracuse
423 West Onondaga Street
Syracuse, NY 13202
(315) 422-7273

YWCA
(Domestic Violence Resource)
960 Salt Springs Road
Syracuse, NY 13224
(315) 445-1418

YWCA Rape Crisis Services
1000 Cornelia Street
Utica, NY 13501
(315) 732-2159

New York Coalition Against
    Domestic Violence
5 Neher Street
Woodstock, NY 12498
(914) 679-5231

My Sister's Place
(Domestic Violence Resource)
P.O. Box 1245
Yonkers, NY 10702
(914) 969-5800

North Carolina

North Carolina Crisis Assistance
    Ministries
500 Spratt Street
Charlotte, NC 28222
(704) 371-3035

Victim Assistance Program
United Family Services
825 East 4th Street
Charlotte, NC 28202
(704) 336-2190

North Carolina Coalition Against
  Domestic Violence
P.O. Box 877
Concord, NC 28026

Durham YWCA Rape Crisis Center
809 Proctor Street
Durham, NC 27707
(919) 688-4396

Orange/Durham Coalition for
  Battered Women
P.O. Box 51848
Durham, NC 27717
(919) 489-1955

Reach Out Center for
  Missing Children
1003 Stadium Drive
Durham, NC 27704
(919) 471-3112

People Assisting Victims
P.O. Box 53892
Fayetteville, NC 28305
(919) 323-4573

Parents of Murdered Children
595 Concord Road
Fletcher, NC 28732
(704) 687-0109

Family Services
(Sexual Assault Resource)
410 Gatewood Avenue
High Point, NC 27262
(919) 889-6161

Sandhills Center
(Sexual Assault Resource)
P.O. Box 639
Pinehurst, NC 28374
(919) 295-6853

Interact
(Domestic Violence Resource)
(Sexual Assault Resource)
(Child Abuse Resource)
P.O. Drawer 11096
Raleigh, NC 27604
(919) 755-6453

MADD State Office
4915 Waters Edge Drive, #120
Raleigh, NC 27606
(919) 851-6233

North Carolina Council on
  Status of Women
526 North Wilmington Street
Raleigh, NC 27611
(919) 733-2455

Victim Advocacy Program
P.O. Box 590
Raleigh, NC 27602
(919) 890-3180

Victim Witness Coordination
  Program
P.O. Box 31
Raleigh, NC 27602
(919) 733-6317

Family Services
P.O. Box 604
Winston-Salem, NC 27102
(919) 724-3979

North Dakota

North Dakota Council on Abused
  Women's Services
418 East Rosser Avenue
Bismarck, ND 58501
(701) 255-6240
(800) 472-2911 (in North Dakota)

North Dakota State MADD
250 Redstone Drive
Bismarck, ND 58501
(701) 255-1571

Parents of Murdered Children
318 Hannifin Street
Bismarck, ND 58501
(701) 223-5417

Rape & Abuse Crisis Center
1221 North 8th
Fargo, ND 58102
(701) 293-7273

North Dakota Crime Victim
  Program
P.O. Box 1599
Jamestown, ND 58401
(701) 224-4151

Women's Action Program
405 3rd Avenue S.E.
Minot, ND 58701
(701) 852-2258

Ohio

Child Sexual Abuse Program
Children's Hospital Medical
  Center of Akron
281 Locust Street
Akron, OH 44308
(216) 379-8254

YWCA Rape Crisis Center
146 South High Street
Akron, OH 44308
(216) 253-6131
(800) 433-7273

American Red Cross/Rape Crisis
618 2nd Street, N.W.
Canton, OH 44703
(216) 453-0146

Parents of Murdered Children
14840 Hillbrook Drive
Chagrin Falls, OH 44022
(216) 247-4565

ADVOISE—Adolescent Victims of
  Indecent Sexual Encounters
8075 Reading Road
Cincinnati, OH 45237
(513) 821-2209

Parents of Murdered Children
National Headquarters
100 East 8th Street
Cincinnati, OH 45202
(513) 721-5683

Talbert House Victim Service
  Center
308 Reading Road
Cincinnati, OH 45202
(513) 241-4484

Cleveland Rape Crisis Center
3101 Euclid Avenue
Cleveland, OH 44115
(216) 391-3914

Resources for Women
  Consulting Services
P.O. Box 18427
Cleveland, OH 44118
(216) 932-1570

St. Clair Superior Coalition
Victim Advocacy Project
6408 St. Clair Avenue
Cleveland, OH 44103
(216) 881-0644

ACTION for Battered Women
P.O. Box 15673
Columbus, OH 43216
(614) 221-1255

MADD State Office
471 East Broad Street, #1310
Columbus, OH 43216
(614) 461-6233

National Assault Prevention
  Project
P.O. Box 02084
Columbus, OH 43229
(614) 291-2540

Parents United/Grace House
(Sexual Abuse Resource Center)
301 Forest Avenue
Dayton, OH 45405
(513) 449-1555

Parents United
Center for Children & Youth
356 3rd Street
Elyria, OH 44035
(216) 322-6700

Association for Death Education
and Counseling
2211 Arthur Avenue
Lakewood, OH 44107

Crossroads Crisis Center
P.O. Box 643
Lima, OH 45802
(419) 228-6692

Parents United
Richland County Stop, Inc.
220 Home Avenue
Mansfield, OH 44903
(419) 756-8444

Southern Ohio Task Force on
Domestic Violence
P.O. Box 754
Portsmouth, OH 45662
(614) 354-2001

Assistance for Victims Center
520 Madison Building
Toledo, OH 43604
(419) 241-1212

National Exchange Club Foundation
for the Prevention of Child Abuse
3050 Central Avenue
Toledo, OH 43606
(419) 535-3232

Toledo Chapter of SLAM
3554 Hazelhurst
Toledo, OH 43612
(419) 478-7030

Battered Person's Crisis Center
25 West Rayen Avenue
Youngstown, OH 44503
(216) 744-5374

Oklahoma

Southeastern Oklahoma Services
for Battered Women
P.O. Box 185
Antlers, OK 74523
(405) 298-5575
(800) 522-7233 (in Oklahoma)

Justice for Crime Victims, Inc.
Route 1, Box 321
Cookson, OK 74427
(918) 457-4106

Norman Shelter for Battered
Women
P.O. Box 5089
Norman, OK 73070
(405) 364-9424

Survivors of Homicide
Support Group
1604 Wilburn Drive
Oklahoma City, OK 73127
(405) 789-3674

YWCA Crisis Intervention Service
2460 N.W. 39th Street
Oklahoma City, OK 73105
(405) 947-4506

Call RAPE, Inc.
2121 South Columbia
Tulsa, OK 74114
(918) 744-7362

Domestic Violence
Intervention Services
1331 East 15th Street
Tulsa, OK 74120
(918) 585-3143

MADD State Office
5525 East 51st Street, #120
Tulsa, OK 74135
(918) 622-6233

Parents of Murdered Children
3107 South Columbia Circle
Tulsa, OK 75105
(918) 743-4451

Vanished Children's Alliance
5716 East 24th Place
Tulsa, OK 74117
(918) 622-7640

Oregon

COBRA—Central Oregon
  Battering & Rape Alliance
P.O. Box 1086
Bend, OR 97709
(503) 382-9227

Rape Crisis Network
P.O. Box 3589
Eugene, OR 97403
(503) 485-3254
(800) 888-7273

Parents United
P.O. Box 189
Grants Pass, OR 97526
(503) 474-3120

Wednesday's Child
121 Iowa Street
Klamath Falls, OR 97601
(503) 884-6175

Citizens for Justice
Crime Victims United
P.O. Box 19480
Portland, OR 97219
(503) 246-5368

MADD State Office
4035 N.E. Sandy Boulevard, #210
Portland, OR 97212
(503) 284-7399

Oregon Coalition Against
  Domestic & Sexual Violence
2336 S.E. Belmont
Portland, OR 97214
(503) 239-4486

Parents of Murdered Children
4059 North Overlook Terrace
Portland, OR 97227
(503) 284-7228

Portland Women's Crisis Line
P.O. Box 42610
Portland, OR 97242
(503) 232-9751

Battered Persons' Advocacy
  Project
P.O. Box 1942
Roseburg, OR 97470
(503) 673-7867

Domestic Violence Program
Children's Services Division
198 Commercial Street, S.E.
Salem, OR 97310
(503) 378-4325

Pennsylvania

Children's Rights of Pennsylvania
(Missing Children Resource)
509 North 7th Street
Allentown, PA 18105
(215) 437-2971

Crime Victims Council of Lehigh
  Valley
P.O. Box 1445
Allentown, PA 18105
(215) 437-6610

Toughlove
P.O. Box 1069
Doylestown, PA 18901
(215) 348-7090

Erie County Rape Crisis Center
313 Wallace Street
Erie, PA 16507
(814) 870-7087

Parents of Murdered Children
125 West 18th Street
Erie, PA 16501
(800) 352-7273 (in Pennsylvania)

Security on Campus, Inc.
618 Shoemaker Road
Gulph Mills, PA 19406
(215) 768-9330

MADD State Office
4800 Jonestown Road
Harrisburg, PA 17109
(717) 657-3911

Pennsylvania Coalition Against
Rape
2200 North 3rd Street
Harrisburg, PA 17110
(717) 232-6445
(800) 692-7745 (in Pennsylvania)

Victim Assistance Administrator
415 Executive House
Harrisburg, PA 17108
(717) 787-8559

Action Alliance Elderly Victim
Assistance Program
1211 Chestnut Street
Philadelphia, PA 19107
(215) 564-1666

Crime Victim Services
Episcopal Community Services
174 West Allegheny Avenue
Philadelphia, PA 19140
(215) 425-5252

Domestic Violence Project
1340 Frankford Avenue
Philadelphia, PA 19125
(215) 426-8610

Families of Murder Victims
1421 Arch Street, 7th Floor
Philadelphia, PA 19102
(215) 686-8078

National Clearinghouse for
the Defense of Battered Women
125 South 9th Street
Philadelphia, PA 19107
(215) 351-0010

Support Center for Child Advocates
1315 Walnut Street, #1508
Philadelphia, PA 19107
(215) 735-0210

Victims of Professionals
3584 Kyle Road
Philadelphia, PA 19154
(215) 281-1565

Center for Victims of Violent
Crimes
1520 Pennsylvania Avenue
Pittsburgh, PA 15222
(412) 392-8582

Friends of Child Find
P.O. Box 10682
Pittsburgh, PA 15235
(412) 244-0729

Pittsburgh Action Against Rape
3712 Forbes Avenue
Pittsburgh, PA 15213
(412) 682-0219

Society for Advocacy of Victims'
Rights
Office of the Coroner
542 4th Avenue
Pittsburgh, PA 15219
(412) 355-0990

Women's Center Shelter of Greater
Pittsburgh
P.O. Box 9024
Pittsburgh, PA 15224
(412) 687-8017

Center for Victims/People Against
Rape
230 North 5th Street
Reading, PA 19601
(215) 372-RAPE

Women's Resource Center
P.O. Box 975
Scranton, PA 18501
(717) 346-4671

Centre County Women's Resource
Center
140 West Nittany Avenue
State College, PA 16801
(814) 238-7066

Women's Shelter, YWCA
42 West Maiden Street
Washington, PA 15301
(412) 223-9190

Crime Victims Center of Chester
County
236 West Market Street
West Chester, PA 19382
(215) 692-1926

National Association of Town Watch,
Inc.
7 Wynnewood Road
Wynnewood, PA 19096
(215) 649-7055

Rhode Island

Rhode Island Council
on Domestic Violence
324 Broad Street
Central Falls, RI 02863
(401) 723-3051

Rhode Island Rape Crisis Center
1660 Broad Street
Cranston, RI 02905
(401) 941-2401

Parents United
The Sexual Abuse Project
Emma Pendleton Bradley Hospital
East Providence, RI 02915
(401) 434-3400

RID Rhode Island
42 Almy Street
Newport, RI 02840
(401) 846-1099

Society for Young Victims
(Missing Children Resource)
54 Broadway
Newport, RI 02840
(401) 847-5083

Justice Assistance
169 Weybosset Street
Providence, RI 02903
(401) 272-1330

Rhode Island Family Court
(Child Abuse Resource)
1 Dorrance Plaza
Providence, RI 02903
(401) 277-3334

Women's Liberation Union of
Rhode Island
Committee on Criminal Sex
Offenses
316 Nelson Street
Providence, RI 02908
(401) 861-5511

South Carolina

Crisis Ministries Hotline
P.O. Box 1925
Anderson, SC 29622
(803) 226-0297

Child Abuse Prevention Association
P.O. Box 531
Beaufort, SC 29901
(803) 524-4350

Citizens Opposed to Domestic
Abuse
P.O. Box 1775
Beaufort, SC 29901
(803) 525-1009
(800) 868-2632

Citizens Against Violent Crimes
7515 Northside Drive
Charleston, SC 29418
(803) 553-6497

Crime Victims Research
& Treatment Center
Medical University of South
Carolina
171 Ashley Avenue
Charleston, SC 29425
(803) 792-2945

Juvenile Restitution Program
4356 Headquarters Road
Charleston, SC 29405
(803) 744-3381

People Against Rape
701 East Bay Street
Charleston, SC 29403
(803) 577-9471

Adam Walsh Child Resource Center
1632 Hampton Street
Columbia, SC 29201
(803) 254-ADAM

Child Abuse and Neglect
   Training Project
College of Social Work, USC
Columbia, SC 29208
(803) 777-5291

Citizens Advocating Decency and
   Revival of Ethics
(Sexual Assault/Pornography
   Resource)
1900 Broad River Road
Columbia, SC 29210
(803) 798-5299

Citizens Against Violent Crime
P.O. Box 5985
Columbia, SC 29250
(803) 252-CAVE

Council on Child Abuse &
   Neglect
1800 Main Street
Columbia, SC 29201
(803) 733-5430

Help Line
P.O. Box 6336
Columbia, SC 29260
(803) 799-6329

MADD State Office
800 Dutch Square Boulevard, #105
Columbia, SC 29210
(803) 731-0506

Missing Person Information Center
State Law Enforcement Division
P.O. Box 21398
Columbia, SC 29221
(803) 737-9000
(800) 322-4453

Parents of Murdered Children
3029 Lindenwood Drive
Columbia, SC 29204
(803) 799-6820

South Carolina Coalition Against
   Domestic Violence and Sexual
   Assault
P.O. Box 7776
Columbia, SC 29202
(803) 669-4694

Churches Assisting People
800 3rd Avenue
Conway, SC 29526
(803) 248-5534

Help-Line
P.O. Box 1086
Greenville, SC 29602
(803) 242-0955

Justice for Sexually Abused
   Children
30 Palmetto Estates
Greenville, SC 29611
(803) 294-1569

Family Care Counsel
P.O. Box 2413
Spartanburg, SC 29304
(803) 573-HELP

South Dakota

Women Escaping a
   Violent Environment
903 Crook Street
Custer, SD 57730
(605) 673-3622

People Against Violence
P.O. Box 903
Martin, SD 57551
(605) 685-6829

Victim Assistance Administrator
Department of Commerce and
    Regulation
910 East Sioux
Pierre, SD 57501
(605) 773-3177

MADD
1811 9th Street
Rapid City, SD 57701
(605) 343-5066
(800) 543-6233

Women Against Violence
P.O. Box 3042
Rapid City, SD 57709
(605) 341-3292

Citizens Against Rape and Domestic
    Violence
P.O. Box 867
Sioux Falls, SD 57101
(605) 339-4357

Sioux Falls YWCA
(Domestic Violence Resource)
100 West 11th Street
Sioux Falls, SD 57102
(605) 336-3660

Vermillion Coalition Against
    Domestic Violence
P.O. Box 144
Vermillion, SD 57069
(605) 624-5311

Tennessee

MADD State Office
783 Old Hickory Boulevard, #357W
Brentwood, TN 37027
(615) 370-5947

Family & Children's Services
323 High Street
Chattanooga, TN 37403
(615) 755-2800

YWCA of Knoxville
420 West Clinch Avenue
Knoxville, TN 39902
(615) 523-6126

Parents of Murdered Children
1119 Greenfield Drive
Maryville, TN 37801
(615) 982-9103

Commission on Missing and
    Exploited Children
P.O. Box 310
Memphis, TN 38101
(901) 528-2005

Rape Crisis Program
2600 Poplar
Memphis, TN 38104
(901) 528-2162

Exchange Club Center for
    Prevention of Child Abuse
900 Inverness Hill
Nashville, TN 37204
(615) 297-8922

PEACE—Project to End Abuse
    Through Counseling & Education
211 Union Street, #626
Nashville, TN 37201
(615) 255-0721

Tennessee Coalition Against
    Sexual Assault
P.O. Box 120831
Nashville, TN 37210
(615) 259-9055

YWCA Shelter & Domestic
    Violence Program
1608 Woodmont Boulevard
Nashville, TN 37215
(615) 297-8833

Texas

Texas Crime Victim Clearinghouse
P.O. Box 12428
Austin, TX 78711
(512) 463-1886

MADD State Office
2525 Wallingwood, #700
Austin, TX 78746
(512) 328-6233

Parents Anonymous of Texas
4301 Russell Drive
Austin, TX 78704
(512) 440-8666

People Against Violent Crime
P.O. Box 15960
Austin, TX 78761
(512) 837-PAVC

Texas Coalition for Prevention
  of Child Abuse
P.O. Box 49648
Austin, TX 78765
(512) 320-5633

Texas Council on Family Violence
3415 Greystone
Austin, TX 78731
(512) 794-1133

Sexual Assault & Crime Victim
  Services
921 Ayers
Corpus Christi, TX 78415
(512) 887-9818
(800) 284-9818

Dallas County Rape Crisis and
  Child Sexual Abuse Center
P.O. Box 35728
Dallas, TX 75235
(214) 521-1020

Dallas Gay Alliance Hotline
Box 190712
Dallas, TX 75235
(214) 528-4233

Episcopal-Presbyterian
  Women's Shelter, Inc.
P.O. Box 4538
Dallas, TX 75208
(214) 942-2998

Incest Recovery Association
6200 North Central Expressway
Dallas, TX 72506
(214) 349-6173

MADD National Office
P.O. Box 541688
Dallas, TX 75359
(800) GET-MADD

Family Service of El Paso
2930 North Stanton
El Paso, TX 79902
(915) 533-2491

National Victim Center
307 West 7th Street
Fort Worth, TX 76102
(817) 877-3355

Women's Haven of Tarrant County
P.O. Box 1456
Fort Worth, TX 76101
(817) 535-6462

Family Outreach Centers of
  America
(Child Services Resource)
11612 Memorial Drive
Houston, TX 77024
(713) 974-4825

Mothers Without Custody
National Headquarters
P.O. Box 56762
Houston, TX 77256-6762
(718) 840-1622

Parents of Murdered Children
1105 Berthea
Houston, TX 77006
(713) 522-0945

Parents United
4625 Lillian
Houston, TX 77007
(713) 861-4849

Salvation Army Women's
  and Children's Residence
1603 McGowen
Houston, TX 77004
(713) 222-8253

Mujeres Unidas/Women Together
  Foundation, Inc.
420 North 21st
McAllen, TX 78501
(512) 630-4878

Midland Rape Crisis Center
P.O. Box 10081
Midland, TX 79702
(915) 682-7278

Alamo Area Rape Crisis Center
P.O. Box 27802
San Antonio, TX 78227
(512) 674-4900

Family Outreach Centers
  of America
950 Donaldson
San Antonio, TX 78228
(512) 732-1278

Family Violence Research
  and Treatment Program
2900 University Boulevard
Tyler, TX 75701
(214) 566-7060

First Step, Inc.
P.O. Box 773
Wichita Falls, TX 76307
(817) 767-3330

Utah

Citizens Against Physical
  & Sexual Abuse
P.O. Box 3617
Logan, UT 84321
(801) 752-4493

Salt Lake Chapter of SLAM
6039 South 530 West
Murray, UT 84107
(801) 262-4093

Parents United
3595 Washington Boulevard
Ogden, UT 84403
(801) 394-7548

Center for Women and Children
  in Crisis
P.O. Box 1075
Provo, UT 84603
(801) 374-9351

Parents of Murdered Children
P.O. Box 17166
Salt Lake City, UT 84117
(801) 278-6943

Salt Lake Rape Crisis Center
2085 South 1300 East
Salt Lake City, UT 84105
(801) 531-7273

Utah Domestic Violence Council
150 West North Temple
Salt Lake City, UT 84103
(801) 355-2846

Victims United
P.O. Box 26422
Salt Lake City, UT 84126
(801) 583-0385

Vermont

Project Against Violent Encounters
P.O. Box 227
Bennington, VT 05201
(802) 442-2370

Women Helping Battered Women
P.O. Box 1535
Burlington, VT 05402
(802) 658-3131

Women's Rape Crisis Center
P.O. Box 92
Burlington, VT 05402
(802) 863-1236

Parents Anonymous of Vermont
P.O. Box 829
Montpelier, VT 05602
(802) 229-5724

National Coalition for
   Children's Justice
(Missing Children Resource)
4345 Shelburne Road
Shelburne, VT 05482
(802) 985-8458

Vermont Coalition for Victim
   Services
620 Hinesburg Road
South Burlington, VT 05403
(802) 864-4513

Parents of Murdered Children
689 Breezy Hill
Springfield, VT 05156
(802) 885-4932

Parents Assistance Line
103 South Main Street
Waterbury, VT 05676
(802) 241-2249
(800) PARENTS (in Vermont)

Virginia

Fairfax Victim Assistance Network
8119 Holland Road
Alexandria, VA 22306
(703) 360-6910

Mothers of Children Who Are
   Victims of Incest
Mount Vernon YWCA
8009 Fort Hunt Road
Alexandria, VA 22308
(703) 765-2385

National District Attorneys
   Association
1033 North Fairfax Street
Alexandria, VA 22314
(703) 549-4253

National Sheriffs' Association
1450 Duke Street
Alexandria, VA 22314
(703) 836-7827

National Center for Missing
   and Exploited Children
2101 Wilson Boulevard
Arlington, VA 22201
(703) 235-3900

National Hospice Organization
1901 North Moore Street
Arlington, VA 22201
(703) 243-5900

Campus Violence Intervention
10041 Marshall Pond Road
Burke, VA 22015
(703) 250-2594

Parents of Murdered Children
P.O. Box 141
Clear Brook, VA 22642
(703) 667-4953

Virginia State MADD
10560 Main Street
Fairfax, VA 22030
(703) 591-9612
(800) 533-MADD (in Virginia)

Peninsula Council on
   Battered Women
P.O. Box 561
Hampton, VA 23669
(804) 722-2261

First Step, Inc.
P.O. Box 621
Harrisonburg, VA 22801
(703) 434-0295

Virginians Aligned Against
   Sexual Assault
P.O. Box 409
Ivy, VA 22945
(804) 979-9002

Sudden Infant Death Syndrome
8201 Greenboro Drive
McLean, VA 22102
(703) 821-8955

Contact Peninsula
(Sexual Assault Resource)
6901 Huntington Avenue
Newport News, VA 23607
(804) 244-0594

Family Services of Tidewater
222 19th Street West
Norfolk, VA 23517
(804) 622-7017

Tidewater Chapter of SLAM
1305 Calla Avenue
Norfolk, VA 23503
(804) 587-5059

Pastoral Counseling and
   Consultation Centers of Greater
   Washington
P.O. Box 39
Oakton, VA 22124
(703) 281-1870

MADD State Office
P.O. Box 14839
Richmond, VA 23221
(804) 288-3081

Women's Advocacy Program/YWCA
6 North 5th Street
Richmond, VA 23219
(804) 643-6761

Parents United
Child Abuse Prevention Council
325 Campbell Avenue
Roanoke, VA 24016
(703) 344-3579

Alternatives for Abused Adults
P.O. Box 1414
Staunton, VA 24401
(703) 886-6800

White Collar Crime 101
8300 Boone Boulevard
Vienna, VA 22182
(703) 848-9248

Justice for Victims of Crime
2212 Laurel Cove Drive
Virginia Beach, VA 23454
(804) 481-7708

Washington

Victim/Witness Notification
   Program
(statewide)
(800) 322-2201

STOP ABUSE
P.O. Box 2086
Everett, WA 98203
(206) 25-ABUSE

Washington Coalition of Sexual
   Assault Programs
110 East 5th
Olympia, WA 98501
(206) 754-7583

Washington Shelter Network
110 5th Avenue, S.E.
Olympia, WA 98501
(206) 753-4621
(800) 562-6025 (in Washington)

Alternatives to Fear
2811 East Madison
Seattle, WA 98112
(206) 328-5347

Asian Counseling and Referral
   Service
1032 South Jackson Street
Seattle, WA 98104
(206) 447-3606

Council for Prevention of Child
   Abuse & Neglect
1305 4th Avenue
Seattle, WA 98101
(206) 343-2590

The Dorian Group
(Gay/Lesbian Resource)
340 15th Avenue
Seattle, WA 98112
(206) 322-1501

Families & Friends of Missing
    Persons & Violent Crime Victims
(Statewide Services)
P.O. Box 27529
Seattle, WA 98125
(206) 362-1081

Seattle Rape Relief
1825 South Jackson
Seattle, WA 98144
(206) 325-5531 (V/TTY)

Washington Association of County
    Child Abuse Councils
P.O. Box 9602
Seattle, WA 98109
(206) 624-4307

Washington Victim Witness Services
P.O. Box 17437
Seattle, WA 98117
(206) 322-2926

Recovery: Aid to Victims of Sexual
    and Domestic Abuse
P.O. Box 1132
Shelton, WA 98584
(206) 426-5878
(800) 562-6025 (in Washington)

Rape Crisis Network
Lutheran Social Services of
    Washington
7 South Howard
Spokane, WA 99204-0323
(509) 327-7761

YWCA Alternatives to
    Domestic Violence
West 829 Broadway
Spokane, WA 99201
(509) 327-9534

Parents of Murdered Children
7413-D 142nd Avenue East
Sumner, WA 98390
(206) 863-5380

Evergreen Human Services
(Domestic Violence Resource)
Box 8004
Tacoma, WA 98408
(206) 474-2294
(800) 562-6025 crisis (in
    Washington)

Tennis Shoe Brigade of Washington
P.O. Box 12157
Tacoma, WA 98412
(206) 535-4940

YWCA Women's Support Shelter
405 Broadway
Tacoma, WA 98402
(206) 272-4181

West Virginia

Women's Resource Center
P.O. Box 1476
Beckley, WV 25802
(304) 255-2559

Family Services of Kanawha Valley
922 Quarrier Street
Charleston, WV 25301
(304) 340-3676

Parents of Murdered Children
1207 7th Avenue
Charleston, WV 25302
(304) 342-5237

HOPE, Inc.
P.O. Box 626
Fairmont, WV 26555
(304) 367-1100

MADD State Office
P.O. Box 2102
Huntington, WV 25721
(304) 523-6277

Contact of Huntington
P.O. Box 2963
Huntington, WV 25729
(304) 523-3447

West Virginia Rape Information
   Center
P.O. Box 1083
Martinsburg, WV 25401
(304) 263-8522

Rape & Domestic Violence
   Information Center
P.O. Box 4228
Morgantown, WV 26505
(304) 292-5100

Domestic Violence Coalition of
   Parkersburg
P.O. Box 695
Parkersburg, WV 26101
(304) 428-3707

YWCA—Abuse Shelter for Women
1100 Chapline Street
Wheeling, WV 26003
(304) 232-0511

Wisconsin

Sexual Assault Crisis Center
Fox Cities, Inc.
P.O. Box 344
Appleton, WI 54912
(414) 733-8119

RID-USA Advisory Board
1030 Oak Ridge Drive
Eau Clair, WI 54701
(715) 834-3313

Association for the Prevention
   of Family Violence
P.O. Box 1007
Elkhorn, WI 53121
(414) 723-4653

Family Violence Center, Inc.
P.O. Box 13536
Green Bay, WI 54307
(414) 498-8282

Men Stopping Rape
306 North Brooks Street
Madison, WI 53715
(608) 257-4444

Parents of Murdered Children
5113 South Hill Drive
Madison, WI 53705
(608) 238-6086

Wisconsin Coalition Against
   Women Abuse
1051 Williamson Street
Madison, WI 53703
(608) 255-0539

Wisconsin Committee for the
   Prevention of Child Abuse and
   Neglect
1045 East Dayton Street
Madison, WI 53703
(608) 253-3374

Wisconsin Crime Victims' Council
P.O. Box 7951
Madison, WI 53707
(608) 266-7877

Crime Prevention Program for
   Senior Citizens
1927 North 4th Street
Milwaukee, WI 53212
(414) 226-8629

Milwaukee Task Force on
   Sexual Assault & Domestic
   Violence
200 East Wells Street
Milwaukee, WI 53202
(414) 278-2997

National Funeral Directors
   Association
11121 West Oklahoma Avenue
Milwaukee, WI 53227
(414) 541-2500

Women's Crisis Line, Inc.
Good Samaritan Medical Center
2000 West Kilborne Avenue
Milwaukee, WI 53233
(414) 344-8800

Rape Crisis/Domestic Abuse
  Services
201 Ceape
Oshkosh, WI 54901
(414) 426-1460

Women's Resource Center
P.O. Box 1764
Racine, WI 53401
(414) 633-7777

Center Against Sexual and
  Domestic Violence
2231 Catlin Avenue
Superior, WI 54880
(715) 392-3136

Rape & Incest Victim Advocacy
The Human Resource Center
39 North 25th Street East
Superior, WI 54880
(715) 394-8129

Wyoming
Self Help
341 East E Street
Casper, WY 82601
(307) 235-2814

Safehouse/Sexual Assault
  Services, Inc.
P.O. Box 1621
Cheyenne, WY 82003
(307) 634-8655

Crisis Intervention Services
P.O. Box 1324
Cody, Wy 82414
(307) 587-3545

Parents of Murdered Children
Box 603
Gillette, WY 82716
(307) 686-7372

Wyoming Coalition on Family
  Violence & Sexual Assault
416 South 25th Street
Laramie, WY 82070
(307) 745-7776

MADD
452 Road 8 North, Route 1
Powell Way, WY 82435
(307) 754-9230

Office on Family Violence
  and Sexual Assault
P.O. Box 1127
Riverton, WY 82501
(307) 856-0942
(800) 442-0980 (in Wyoming)

DIRECTORY D

Reference Books on Victims' Rights

American Association of Retired Persons. *Issues Affecting Crime Victims*. Washington: AARP, 1989.

Austern, David. *The Crime Victims Handbook*. New York: Penguin USA, 1987.

Bard, Morton, and Sangrey, Dawn. *The Crime Victim's Book*. New York: Brunner/Mazel, 2d Edition, 1986.

Boland, Mary L. *Sexual Assault: A Court Advocate's Guide*. Springfield, Ill.: Illinois Coalition Against Sexual Assault, 1988.

Braswell, Linda. *Quest for Respect*. Ventura, Calif.: Pathfinder Publishing, 1989.

Carrington, Frank, and Edmunds, Christine N. *Legal Remedies for Crime Victims Against Perpetrators*. Arlington, Va.: National Victim Center, 1992.

Carrington, Frank, and Rapp, James A. *Victims' Rights: Law and Litigation*. New York: Matthew Bender, 1989.

Caulfield, Barbara A., and Horowitz, Robert M. *Child Abuse and the Law*. Chicago: National Committee for Prevention of Child Abuse, 2d Edition, 1987.

Crisp, Jayne, *et al. Surviving Violent Crime*. Greenville, S.C.: Victim Witness Assistance Program of Greenville, South Carolina, 1987.

Delaplane, David W. *Victim Assistance Manual for Clergy and Congregations*. Sacramento: The Spiritual Dimension in Victims Services, 1990.

Finn, Peter, and Colson, Sarah. *Civil Protection Orders*. Washington: National Institute of Justice, 1990.

Finn, Peter, and Lee, Beverly N.W. *Serving Crime Victims and Witnesses*. Washington: National Institute of Justice, 1987.

Friedman, Joel, Boumil, Marcia Mobilia, and Taylor, Barbara Ewert. *Sexual Harassment*. Deerfield Beach, Fla.: Health Communications, Inc., 1992.

Goolkasian, Gail A. *Confronting Domestic Violence: A Guide for Criminal Justice Agencies*. Washington: National Institute of Justice, 1986.

Howell, Jay C., *et al. Selected State Legislation / A Guide for Effective State Laws to Protect Children*. Arlington, Va.: National Center for Missing & Exploited Children, 1989.

Kushner, Harold S. *When Bad Things Happen to Good People*. New York: Avon Books, 1981.

Kusic, Jane Y. *White-Collar Crime 101*. Vienna, Va.: White-Collar Crime 101, 1989.

Lipman, Ira A. *How to Protect Yourself From Crime*. Chicago: Contemporary Books, 1989.

Lord, Janice Harris. *No Time for Goodbyes*. Ventura, Calif.: Pathfinder Publishing, 1990.

Madara, Edward J., and Meese, Abigail. *The Self-Help Sourcebook / Finding and Forming Mutual Aid Self-Help Groups*. Denville, N.J.: St. Clares–Riverside Medical Center, 1988.

Minick, Lynn Jett. *The Victim Goes to Court / A Victim's Guide*. Fayetteville, N.C.: People Assisting Victims of North Carolina, 1990.

Moore, James T. *Florida Juvenile Handbook*. Tallahassee: Florida Department of Law Enforcement, 1989.

Roberts, Albert R., Editor. *Helping Crime Victims / Research, Policy, and Practice*. Newbury Park, Calif.: Sage, 1990.

Romano, Linda J., and Ayres, Marilyn B. *Child Sexual Assault: Confronting the Crisis*. Alexandria, Va.: National Sheriffs' Association, 1989.

Simons, Janet M., Finlay, Belva, and Yang, Alice. *The Adolescent & Young Adult Fact Book*. Washington: Children's Defense Fund, 1991.

Smith, Barbara E., Davis, Robert C., and Hillenbrand, Susan W. *Improving Enforcement of Court Ordered Restitution*. Chicago: American Bar Association, 1989.

Smith, Michael Clay, and Smith, Margaret D. *Wide Awake / A Guide to Safe Campus Living in the 90s*. Princeton: Peterson's Guides, 1990.

Stark, James, and Goldstein, Howard W. *The Rights of Crime Victims*. New York: Bantam Books, 1985.

Villmoare, Edwin, and Benvenuti, Jeanne. *California Victims of Crime Handbook*. Sacramento: McGeorge School of Law, 1988.

Whitcomb, Debra, Shapiro, Elizabeth R., and Stellwagen, Lindsey D. *When the Victim Is a Child*. Washington: National Institute of Justice, 1985.

Wolf, Rosalie S., and Pillemer, Karl A. *Helping Elderly Victims / The Reality of Elder Abuse*. New York: Columbia University Press, 1989.

Women in Dialogue. *Everywoman's Handbook on Compensation for Rape & Other Crimes in Pennsylvania*. Philadelphia: Women in Dialogue, 1992.

Yant, Martin. *Presumed Guilty / When Innocent People Are Wrongly Convicted*. Buffalo: Prometheus Books, 1991.

Index